STUDIES IN MANUSCRIPT ILLUMINATION

NUMBER 7

STUDIES IN MANUSCRIPT ILLUMINATION

KURT WEITZMANN, *GENERAL EDITOR*

1. AN EARLY MANUSCRIPT OF
THE AESOP FABLES OF AVIANUS AND RELATED MANUSCRIPTS
BY ADOLPH GOLDSCHMIDT

2. ILLUSTRATIONS IN ROLL AND CODEX
A STUDY OF THE ORIGIN AND METHOD OF TEXT ILLUSTRATION
BY KURT WEITZMANN

3. THE JOSHUA ROLL
A WORK OF THE MACEDONIAN RENAISSANCE
BY KURT WEITZMANN

4. GREEK MYTHOLOGY IN BYZANTINE ART
BY KURT WEITZMANN

5. THE ILLUSTRATION OF
THE HEAVENLY LADDER OF JOHN CLIMACUS
BY JOHN RUPERT MARTIN

6. THE ILLUSTRATIONS OF
THE LITURGICAL HOMILIES OF GREGORY NAZIANZENUS
BY GEORGE GALAVARIS

7. THE ILLUSTRATED BIBLES FROM TOURS
BY HERBERT L. KESSLER

———————

PUBLISHED FOR THE

DEPARTMENT OF ART AND ARCHAEOLOGY

PRINCETON UNIVERSITY

THE
ILLUSTRATED BIBLES
FROM TOURS

BY HERBERT L. KESSLER

PRINCETON UNIVERSITY PRESS
PRINCETON, NEW JERSEY

Copyright © 1977 by Princeton University Press

Published by Princeton University Press, Princeton, New Jersey
In the United Kingdom, Princeton University Press, Guildford, Surrey

Library of Congress Cataloging in Publication Data will
be found on the last printed page of this book

This book has been composed in
Linotype Times Roman

Printed in the United States of America
by Princeton University Press, Princeton, New Jersey

LIBRARY OF CONGRESS CATALOGING IN PUBLICATION DATA

Kessler, Herbert L.   1941–
  The illustrated Bibles from Tours.

  (Studies in manuscript illumination; no. 7)
  Based on the author's thesis, Princeton, 1965.
  Includes bibliographical references and index.
  1. Bible—Pictures, illustrations, etc.   2. Illumination of books
and manuscripts, Carlovingian—France—Tours.   3. Illumination of
books and manuscripts—France—Tours.   I. Title.   II. Series.
ND3355.K47   745.6'7   76–45902
ISBN 0–691–03923–2

IN MEMORY OF

MY MOTHER

CONTENTS

LIST OF ILLUSTRATIONS

Source of photograph, if different from possessor of the object, is provided in parentheses.

xi

PREFACE

I BEGAN this investigation of Carolingian Bible illustration in a seminar on medieval manuscript illumination conducted by Professor Kurt Weitzmann during the spring of 1962; and I submitted a version of it, limited to the Genesis, Exodus, Majestas, and Apocalypse frontispieces, as my doctoral dissertation to Princeton University in 1965. Since then, many friends and colleagues have reviewed my arguments and conclusions about the ninth-century frontispiece Bibles. Hugo Buchthal, Otto Demus, Robert Deshman, Ernst Kitzinger, Carl Nordenfalk, John Plummer, Michael Taylor and the late Jean Porcher, Paul Underwood, and Carl Kraeling all read my dissertation and made valuable criticisms of it. I have benefited from the comments of these scholars and have considered their criticisms carefully while preparing this book.

I have been able to complete my study only because of the generosity of many institutions and foundations. From the very beginning of my work, I have depended on the Index of Christian Art and the magnificent Marquand Library at Princeton; and I am especially grateful to Miss Frederica Oldach, the librarian of Marquand, for her intelligent and gracious assistance. A grant from the Woodrow Wilson Fellowship Foundation permitted me to travel abroad to study the manuscripts while I was working on my dissertation. A term as a Junior Fellow at Dumbarton Oaks Center for Byzantine Studies in Washington and a summer fellowship from the National Endowment for the Humanities enabled me to explore several problems tangential to the Carolingian Bibles. The Division of the Humanities and the College of the University of Chicago provided continuous support for my research and granted two extended periods of release from my teaching duties so that I could complete this book. In 1970, I was a Herodotus Fellow at the Institute for Advanced Study in Princeton and during 1972–73, I was a John Simon Guggenheim Fellow in New York. While working in New York, I made extensive use of the Pierpont Morgan Library and the facilities of Columbia University. My gratitude to the staffs and faculties of these organizations is deep. Lynda Hunsucker helped me in myriad ways, always with intelligence and good humor.

Kurt Weitzmann made essential contributions to every phase of my investigation. He directed me to the topic of ninth-century Bible illustration in the first place, and he provided the methodological principles I have followed in trying to solve the many problems involved in that subject. With characteristic generosity, he opened to me the facilities for manuscript study he has constructed at Princeton; and he liberally shared with me both his time and his knowledge. He patiently edited several drafts of my dissertation and read everything derived from it, including this book, before it went to press. His knowledge, resources, and labor have greatly improved this study; because he always has encouraged me to maintain an independent position, however, he is not responsible for any errors found in it.

My wife, Johanna Zacharias, also made numerous fundamental contributions to this undertaking. Her example and criticisms gave clarity to the writing; her love and encouragement sustained the author.

Herbert L. Kessler
The Johns Hopkins University

ABBREVIATIONS

Each chapter of this book is basically independent of the others and contains, in its footnotes, full bibliographic references. There is no general bibliography. The books cited throughout the volume are abbreviated as follows.

Bibel von Moutier-Grandval.	J. Duft *et al., Die Bibel von Moutier-Grandval* (Bern, 1971).
Charlemagne.	*Charlemagne* (catalogue of an exhibition. Aachen, 1965).
CLA.	E. A. Lowe, *Codices latini antiquiores* (Oxford, 1934ff.).
Gaehde, "Bible Manuscript."	J. Gaehde, "The Painters of the Carolingian Bible Manuscript of San Paolo fuori le mura in Rome," (Unpublished Ph.D. dissertation. New York University, 1963).
Gaehde, "Turonian Sources."	J. Gaehde, "The Turonian Sources of the San Paolo Bible," *Frühmittelalterliche Studien*, V (1971), 359ff.
Goldschmidt, *Elfenbeinskulpturen.*	A. Goldschmidt, *Die Elfenbeinskulpturen* (Berlin, 1914ff.).
Karl der Grosse.	*Karl der Grosse: Lebenswerk und Nachleben* (ed. W. Braunfels. Düsseldorf, 1966f.).
Kessler, "Sources and Construction."	H. Kessler, "The Sources and the Construction of the Genesis, Exodus, Majestas, and Apocalypse Frontispiece Illustrations in the Ninth-Century Turonian Bibles," (Unpublished Ph.D. dissertation. Princeton University, 1965).
Köhler, *Kar. Min.*	W. Köhler, *Die karolingischen Miniaturen* (Berlin, 1933ff.).
MGH	*Monumenta Germaniae historica.*
PG.	J. P. Migne, ed., *Patrologia graeca* (Paris, 1857ff.).
PL.	J. P. Migne, ed., *Patrologia latina* (Paris, 1844ff.).
Weitzmann, *Roll and Codex.*	K. Weitzmann, *Illustrations in Roll and Codex* (2nd ed. Princeton, 1970).
Weitzmann, "Selection of Texts."	K. Weitzmann, "The Selection of Texts for Cyclic Illustration in Byzantine Manuscripts," *Byzantine Books and Bookmen* (Washington, D.C., 1975).
Weitzmann, *Studies.*	K. Weitzmann, *Studies in Classical and Byzantine Manuscript Illumination* (ed. H. Kessler, Chicago, 1971).

Bible passages are quoted from the *New English Bible* (Oxford and Cambridge, 1970). Latin texts are cited in the original language; Greek passages are translated.

THE ILLUSTRATED BIBLES
FROM TOURS

I. THE ILLUSTRATED BIBLES
FROM TOURS

SINGLE volume Bibles known as pandects had been compiled long before the manuscripts that constitute the subject of this study were produced at Tours toward the middle of the ninth century.[1] Information about these early Bibles is scarce and almost entirely indirect. The most famous example from the West[2] is the sixth-century *Codex grandior* of Cassiodorus which was described by its editor, "in codice grandiore littera clariore conscripto . . . in quo septuaginta interpretum translatio veteris testamenti libri . . . cui subjuncti sunt novi testamenti. . . ."[3] Cassiodorus' pandect served as the model for three similar volumes produced under Abbot Ceolfrid (689–716) in the monastery of Wearmouth/Jarrow; and one of those copies, the Codex Amiatinus in Florence (Biblioteca Medicea-Laurenziana, Cod. Am. 1)[4] is the only early Latin pandect that survives intact. The existence of others, however, can be deduced.[5] Remains of a seventh-century Spanish pandect survive in Leon (Cathedral, Cod. 15);[6] and a north Italian Bible seems to have served as the model for the ninth-century St. Germain Bible in Paris (Bibliothèque Nationale, Cod. lat. 11553).[7] Before the ninth century, however, one-volume Bibles were exceptional. Normally, the Bible was circulated in smaller units.

Charlemagne provided the major impetus for the first extended production of full Bibles.[8] Several pandects were created during his reign, the result of the same intellectual activities that had led to the revisions of text and script. Of the various undertakings to produce full Bibles, the most important for this study was the one begun by Alcuin in the monastery of St. Martin at Tours.[9] Alcuin had retired to Tours in 796 and before his death in 804 he had supervised the production of at least six pandects.[10] Judging from the earliest surviving Touronian Bibles, in particular, the manuscript of c. 801–804 in St. Gall (Stiftsbibliothek, Cod. 75),[11] Alcuin's pandects were inferior in writing and orthography to other Carolingian editions. At Tours, the full Bible

[1] Cf. R. Loewe, "The Medieval History of the Latin Vulgate," in *The Cambridge History of the Bible*, II (Cambridge, 1969), pp. 102ff. and B. Fischer, "Bibelausgaben des frühen Mittelalters," in *Settimane di Studio del Centro Italiano di Studi sull'alto Medioevo* (Spoleto, 1963), 519ff.

[2] Full Bibles in Greek from a much earlier date exist. The Codex Sinaiticus (London, British Library, Cod. Add. 43725) is the most famous example.

[3] *PL*, LXX, col. 1125; Fischer, *op. cit.*, pp. 557ff. and *idem*, "Codex Amiatinus und Cassiodor," *Biblische Zeitschrift*, N.F. VI (1962), 57ff.

[4] *Ibid.*, pp. 65ff. and T. J. Brown, "The Origin of the Latin Text," *Codex Lindisfarnensis* (Olten, 1960), pp. 51ff.

[5] A smaller pandect is also described by Cas-

siodorus, cf. Fischer, "Bibelausgaben," p. 558.

[6] *Ibid.*, pp. 561ff.; *CLA*, XI, no. 1636.

[7] Fischer, "Bibelausgaben," pp. 576ff.

[8] *Ibid.*, pp. 586ff. B. Fischer, "Bibeltext und Bibelreform unter Karl dem Grossen," *Karl der Grosse*, II, 156ff. and *idem*, "Die Alkuin-Bibeln," in *Bibel von Moutier-Grandval*, pp. 49ff.

[9] Fischer, "Bibelausgaben," pp. 591ff.; "Bibeltext," pp. 160ff.; *Die Alkuin-Bibel* (Freiburg, 1957); and "Alkuin-Bibeln," pp. 49ff.

[10] F. Ganshof, "La revision de la Bible par Alcuin," *Bibliothèque d'humanisme et renaissance*, IX (1947), 7ff. Also Fischer, *Alkuin-Bibel*, pp. 5ff.; "Bibelausgaben," pp. 591ff.; "Bibeltext," p. 159; and "Alkuin-Bibeln," pp. 50ff.

[11] Köhler, *Kar. Min.*, I₁, 40ff., 84ff., *et passim*; Fischer, *Alkuin-Bibel*, pp. 71ff.

was perfected only under Alcuin's successors. The script was refined under Fridigus (807–34) and the ornament was developed under Adalhard (834–43) and Vivian (844–51). As Bonifatius Fischer has demonstrated,[12] it was not until c. 830 that the Touronian atelier matched the level of the Theodulf Bibles produced a generation before.

The monks at Tours retained a special interest in the production of one-volume Bibles long after the deaths of Alcuin and Charlemagne. Fourteen examples are still known and the widespread influence of Touronian pandects after c. 835 can be traced.[13] These Bibles from Tours are remarkably consistent in contents and format.[14] They seem to mark the first time that pandects were produced as standard items in a scriptorium.

Considering the rarity of pre-Carolingian pandects, it seems unlikely that the Bible was often illustrated as a single unit before the ninth century. The surviving manuscripts support this conclusion. Of the numerous illustrated manuscripts from the Early Christian period, only two are full Bibles: the Codex Amiatinus and the sixth or seventh century Syriac Bible in Paris (Bibliothèque Nationale, Cod. Syr. 341).[15] The Paris Bible has lost many of its illustrations. From those that remain, however, it is evident that the volume was decorated with single depictions at the head of individual biblical books. A few of these were narrative scenes. Most, however, were simple author portraits. The illustration of the Codex Amiatinus, which may reflect the decoration of Cassiodorus' *Codex grandior*,[16] is even more limited. It comprises a portrait of the scribe Ezra (fol. v^r), a picture of the tabernacle (fols. 3^r–4^r), and a *Majestas Domini* (fol. 796^v, Fig. 71). The earliest illustrated Byzantine Bible is the tenth-century codex in the Vatican (Cod. Regina gr. 1),[17] one book of a three-volume edition.

Unlike the full Bible, individuals books of the Old and New Testaments were extensively illustrated from an early time.[18] The Cotton Genesis in London (British Library, Cod. Cotton Otho B. VI)[19] and the Vienna Genesis (Nationalbibliothek, Cod. Theol. gr. 31)[20] are the best known examples of early biblical illustration; but others can also be cited, among them, the Itala Fragments (Kings), and the Rossano, Rabbula, and Augustine Gospels. In addition to narrative illustrations, early biblical manuscripts were often provided with author portraits. Full-page miniatures of the evangelists

[12] *Ibid.*, p. 8.

[13] Fischer, "Alkuin-Bibeln," pp. 95ff.

[14] Fischer, "Alkuin-Bibeln," pp. 61ff.

[15] J. Leroy, *Les manuscrits syriaques à peintures* (Paris, 1964), pp. 208ff.

[16] Fischer, "Amiatinus," pp. 68ff.

[17] *Miniature della Bibbia cod. Vat. Regina Gr. 1 e del Salterio cod. Vat. Palat. Gr. 381* (Milan, 1905); K. Weitzmann, *Die byzantinische Buchmalerei des IX. und X. Jahrhunderts* (Berlin, 1935), pp. 40ff.; and "The Illustration of the Septuagint," *Studies*, pp. 49ff.; C. Mango, "The Date of Cod. Vat. Reg. gr. 1 and the Macedonian Renaissance," *Acta ad archaeologiam et artium petinentia*, IV (1969), 121ff.

[18] *Ibid.*, pp. 45ff. and Weitzmann, "Selection of Texts," pp. 71f.

[19] K. Weitzmann, "Observations on the Cotton Genesis Recension," *Late Classical and Mediaeval Studies in Honor of Albert Mathias Friend, Jr.* (Princeton, 1955), pp. 112ff.

[20] H. Gerstinger, *Die Wiener Genesis* (Vienna, 1931).

were especially popular.[21] During the later Middle Ages, the procedures for illustrating the Bible changed little. Single books or small compendiums such as the Pentateuch, the Octateuch, Kings, or the Gospels were the basic biblical units throughout the period. In Byzantium, full Bibles were seldom illustrated, the Regina Bible being a unique example. In the West, decorated pandects were more common; but compared to other types of illustrated manuscripts, they were still rare.

THE TOURONIAN MANUSCRIPTS

The first extended production of illustrated pandects seems to have accompanied the publication activities at ninth-century Tours. Three manuscripts from this production still survive and at least three others are known indirectly. This is not surprising, for once they had revised the text and perfected the script and ornament of their pandects, it was natural for the Carolingian monks to illustrate their manuscripts. Sources for certain of these illustrations may have been available in the diverse exemplars assembled by Alcuin and his successors for their philological work.[22] Other pictorial material could have been gathered elsewhere in the realm.

Abbot Adalhard may have sponsored the first illustrated Bible; the earliest extant examples date from his abbacy. These are the Moutier-Grandval Bible in London (British Library, Cod. Add. Ms. 10546)[23] and the so-called "Alcuin Bible" in Bamberg (Staatsbibliothek, Msc. Bibl. 1).[24] Apparently the Grandval Bible predates the Bamberg volume by several years, but the latter manuscript contains the more basic system of illustration. In the Bamberg Bible, a sequence of scenes from the Book of Genesis (fol. 7ᵛ, Fig. 2) serves as the frontispiece to the Old Testament and a *Majestas Domini* (fol. 339ᵛ, Fig. 47) precedes the New Testament. The Grandval Bible contains four miniatures: Genesis (fol. 5ᵛ, Fig. 1) and *Majestas* pages (fol. 352ᵛ, Fig. 48) and illustrations to Exodus (fol. 25ᵛ, Fig. 87) and to the Book of Revelation (fol. 449ᵛ, Fig. 107).

The system of illustration was expanded further under Abbott Vivian. In the Vivian Bible, also known as the First Bible of Charles the Bald (Paris, Bibliothèque Nationale, Cod. lat. 1),[25] in addition to Genesis (fol. 10ᵛ, Fig. 3) *Majestas* (fol. 329ᵛ, Fig. 49), Exodus (fol. 27ᵛ, Fig. 88), and Apocalypse pages (fol. 415ᵛ, Fig. 108), there are

[21] A. M. Friend, Jr., "Portraits of the Evangelists in Greek and Latin Manuscripts," *Art Studies*, v (1927), 115ff. and vii (1929), 3ff.

[22] Cf. Fischer, "Bibel-text," pp. 171ff. and "Alkuin-Bibeln," pp. 85ff.

[23] A complete description, analysis, and history of the Grandval Bible is available in the facsimile, *Die Bibel von Moutier-Grandval* (Bern, 1972). On the basis of script and ornament, the contributors to the facsimile commentary have dated the Grandval Bible to the transitional period be-

tween the abbacies of Fridigus and Adalhard.

[24] To account for the differences between the Bamberg Bible and the main group of Touronian manuscripts, Köhler proposed that the former was written and decorated, not at St. Martin's, but at the minor monastery of Marmoutier (*Kar. Min.*, I₁, 209ff.). Köhler's proposal and his date of the manuscript to the abbacy of Adalhard have been accepted by subsequent commentators. Cf. Fischer, *Alkuin-Bibel*, p. 14 and "Alkuin-Bibeln," p. 63.

[25] Köhler, *Kar. Min.*, I₁, 238ff.

frontispieces portraying Jerome Preparing the Vulgate (fol. 3ʳ, Fig. 130), David Composing the Psalms (fol. 215ʳ, Fig. 140), and the Conversion of St. Paul (fol. 386ʳ, Fig. 173), as well as a dedication portrait (fol. 423ʳ, Fig. 196). The Vivian Bible, which must date between 845 and 851 and which was probably produced c. 845–46,[26] represents the high point and culmination of Bible illustration at Tours.

Carl Nordenfalk has adduced important evidence of the existence of other illustrated pandects from Tours. In 1936, he introduced thirty-four fragments of a Touronian codex which, he concluded, must be the remains of a manuscript akin to the Vivian Bible.[27] During the Middle Ages, this manuscript was preserved at St. Maximin in Trier. Additional fragments of the Trier codex have been discovered since Nordenfalk first presented this theory[28] and these leave little doubt that another great Touronian pandect did exist. They raise the question, however, of whether that manuscript was as closely related to the Vivian Bible as Nordenfalk had supposed. Mütherich's analysis of the ornament and text of the fragments shows them to be closer to Köhler's Marmoutier group.[29] If Mütherich is right, then Nordenfalk's arguments that, like the Vivian Bible, the Trier manuscript was decorated with seven or eight frontispieces, are questionable. Furthermore, a work from Marmoutier would not account for the Touronian influences detectable in Ottonian art from the region of Trier.[30]

Mütherich has pointed out that at least two other illustrated Bibles from Tours may have been available near Trier during the eleventh century. The Vivian Bible itself seems to have been a possession of the Cathedral of Metz just to the south of Trier;[31] and a "Bibliothecam cum imaginibus et maioribus characteribus" which had been a gift of Lothar, was preserved in the Benedictine Abbey at nearby Prüm.[32] That the Prüm Bible was illustrated in a manner similar to the Grandval and Vivian manuscripts is suggested by a twelfth-century fresco at the Abbey church of Münstereifel (Fig. 110). Münstereifel was a priory of Prüm. The fresco on the triumphal arch of the church clearly was copied from a Touronian Apocalypse frontispiece.[33] It is apparent, therefore, that one illustrated Touronian pandect (and possibly two)—in addition to the Vivian Bible—was available in the area around Trier during the early Middle Ages.

Nordenfalk's hypothesis that yet another lost Touronian Bible had served as the

[26] *Ibid.*, pp. 339f.; P. Lauer, "Iconographie Carolingienne, Vivian et Charlemagne," *Mélanges en hommage à la Mémoire de Fr. Martroye* (Paris, 1940), pp. 191ff.; and below, Chapter IX.

[27] "Beiträge zur Geschichte der Turonischen Buchmalerei," *Acta Archaeologica*, VII (1936), 281ff.

[28] Cf. F. Mütherich, "Die touronische Bibel von St. Maximin in Trier," *Kunsthistorische Forschungen. Otto Pächt zu seinem 70. Geburtstag* (Salzburg, 1973), pp. 44ff. and Fischer, "Alkuin-Bibeln," p. 63.

[29] *Op. cit.*, pp. 49f.

[30] Nordenfalk, "Beiträge," pp. 284ff. and H. Schnitzler, "Südwestdeutsche Kunst um das Jahr 1000 und die Schule von Tours," *Trierer Zeit-schrift*, XIV (1939), 154ff.

[31] K. Hoffmann, however, has proposed that the Vivian Bible was in St. Denis until at least the thirteenth century, cf. "Sugers 'Anagogisches Fenster' in St. Denis," *Wallraf-Richartz Jahrbuch*, XXX (1968), 64.

[32] Mütherich, *op. cit.*, p. 49 and *idem, Mittelalterliche Schatzverzeichnisse* (Munich, 1967), p. 80. The inventory is dated 1003.

[33] R. Schmitz-Ehmke, "Programm der Apsis Malerei in der Ehemaligen Stiftskirche St. Chryzanthus und Daria in Münstereifel," *Beiträge zur Rheinischen Kunstgeschichte und Denkmalpflege. Festschrift R. Wesenberg* (Düsseldorf, 1970), pp. 103ff. and below Chapter v.

model for certain miniatures of the Bible of San Paolo fuori le Mura in Rome[34] is especially important for the study of Touronian illumination.[35] The San Paolo Bible was not made at Tours. As Nordenfalk noted, however, seven of its twenty-four frontispieces (fols. 3[v], 8[v], 31[v], 170[v], 259[v], 310[v] and 334[v], Figs. 4, 50, 89, 131, 141, 174, 197), are so like their counterparts in the Vivian Bible that there can be no doubt they were based on a Touronian model. Nordenfalk supposed that this source was neither the Vivian Bible nor the Trier manuscript but rather another Bible, produced at Tours shortly before 846.[36] Recent studies by Joachim Gaehde have generally borne out Nordenfalk's hypothesis.[37] Gaehde's detailed analysis of the San Paolo manuscript demonstrates convincingly that a lost Touronian Bible, very similar to the

[34] There is no agreement about the date and place of origin of the San Paolo Bible. Janitschek had assigned the San Paolo Bible to his "Corbie School" (K. Menzel *et al.*, *Die Trierer Ada-Handschrift* [Leipzig, 1889], pp. 96ff.). Subsequent scholars have tended to view the San Paolo Bible as a somewhat exceptional member of the "Corbie group," nevertheless, they have tied its localization to that late Carolingian school. There is no question that the San Paolo Bible is related to the last School of Charles the Bald. The sites for that school have been narrowed to two: St. Denis and Reims. A. M. Friend, Jr., who first proposed St. Denis as the home of the "Corbie School" based his conclusions principally on theological and historical arguments. He pointed out that from 867, Charles the Bald, the patron of several of the "Corbie" manuscripts, had been lay abbot of the monastery of St. Denis and that prayers and inscriptions in certain of the volumes of the group also point to St. Denis. He attempted to show that the writings of the Pseudo-Dionysius, which were especially valued at St. Denis, had exerted an influence on the iconography of the "Corbie" illustrations. Cf. "Carolingian Art in the Abbey of St. Denis," *Art Studies*, I (1923), 67ff. and "Two Manuscripts of the School of St. Denis," *Speculum*, I (1926), 59ff. In his publication of the Codex Aureus of St. Emmeram (*Der Codex aureus der bayerischen Staatsbibliothek in München* [Munich, 1921–26], vol. VI, 118ff.), G. Leidinger questioned most of Friend's conclusions. Leidinger's arguments were expanded by H. Schade in "Studien zu der karolingischen Bilderbibel aus St. Paul vor den Mauern in Rom," *Wallraf-Richartz Jahrbuch*, XXI (1959), pp. 9ff. Schade subscribed to the theory that the San Paolo Bible was produced in Reims. As early as 1902, G. Swarzenski had noted the relationship of the San Paolo Bible and certain early Reims manuscripts ("Die karolingische Malerei und Plastik in Reims," *Jahrbuch der königlich Preussischen Kunstsammlungen*, XXIII [1902], 81ff.) and the Reims origin

has been gaining acceptance in recent years. The Reims attribution is based on style and palaeography. Reims has been advocated by A. Boeckler ("Zwei St. Galler Fragmente," *Festschrift für Hans Jantzen.* [Berlin, 1951], pp. 39f.), C. Nordenfalk (*Early Medieval Painting* [New York, 1957], pp. 151f.), Schade (*op. cit.*), and Köhler (*Buchmalerei das frühen Mittelalters* [Munich, 1972], pp. 145f.). Gaehde has proposed that the San Paolo Bible was produced in an atelier "predominantly staffed by scribes and artists trained at Reims" ("The Bible of San Paolo fuori le mura in Rome," *Gesta*, V [1966], 9ff. also "Turonian Sources," p. 359). The problem of attributing the San Paolo Bible is complicated by the fact that it stands apart from the group of manuscripts, the "Corbie School," to which it is most closely related. It is hoped that the forthcoming facsimile edition of the San Paolo manuscript will adduce new material bearing on the issue. The date of the Bible depends on the identification of the king and his consort on the dedication miniature (fol. 334[v], Fig. 197). Since 1955, there has been general agreement with Ernst Kantorowicz that the king is Charles the Bald ("The Carolingian King in the Bible of San Paolo fuori le mura," *Late Classical and Mediaeval Studies in Honor of Albert Mathias Friend, Jr.* [Princeton, 1955], p. 287ff.). Whether the manuscript should be dated between 870 and 875 as Kantorowicz proposed or whether it should be assigned to 866–870 as Gaehde has argued ("The Bible of San Paolo") depends on the identification of Charles' consort and on the relationship of the San Paolo Bible to the Codex Aureus of St. Emmeram. This problem is discussed below, Chapter IX. A thorough survey of the art-historical literature on the San Paolo Bible is available in Gaehde, "Bible Manuscript," II, 16ff.

[35] Nordenfalk, "Beiträge," pp. 295ff.

[36] It could not have been the Prüm Bible which had been given to the monastery by Lothar.

[37] See especially, "Turonian Sources."

Vivian manuscript, was copied in certain of the San Paolo miniatures. These "Touronian" pages, though a step removed from the prototypes, are important, independent reflections of the sources employed at Tours to construct the Bible illustrations. They must, therefore, be incorporated into any study of the Touronian Bibles.[38] Throughout this study, the San Paolo frontispieces will be treated as copies of a lost Bible from Tours.

In 1971, Nordenfalk postulated the existence of still another illustrated Bible from Tours.[39] He detected the influence of this pandect in the text of the Bible of Bishop Bernward (Hildesheim, Cathedral, Cod. 61) and in the depictions of the life of Adam and Eve on the bronze door of St. Michael's at Hildesheim (Fig. 5).[40] Actual fragments of this Bible may be preserved in Wolfenbüttel (Niedersächsisches Staatsarchiv, 12 Slg. 14) and Braunschweig (Stadtarchiv, Umschlag zu Bod. Rep. Abl. VII).[41] Nordenfalk proposed that the model used at Hildesheim dated from the reign of Abbot Fridigus. Therefore, it must have been one of the earliest illustrated Bibles. Apparently, it was also the simplest. There is evidence of only one frontispiece, a miniature depicting the life of Adam and Eve, presumably at the head of the Old Testament.

The fragments and later reflections add significantly to an understanding of the Touronian Bible illustration because they establish that the production of illustrated pandects at Tours was not limited to the three extant manuscripts. They suggest the existence of at least four other Bibles. One from the abbacy of Fridigus was known at Hildesheim during the eleventh century. It served there as the source of the text of Bernward's Bible and the model of the Genesis scenes on the door of St. Michael's. A Bible, given by Lothar to the monastery at Prüm and recorded in an eleventh-century inventory, may have been the source of the Münstereifel fresco. Fragments of a third Bible which, during the Middle Ages had been kept at St. Maximin at Trier, survive; but the nature of the decoration of that manuscript remains unknown. Seven frontispieces in the San Paolo Bible were based on a fourth Touronian pandect. Wherever it is relevant, the information provided by these fragments and copies will be incorporated into this study.

THE PICTORIAL SOURCES

Ever since the second part of *Die Schule von Tours* appeared in 1933, discussion of the Touronian Bibles has been dominated by Köhler's carefully reasoned theory of the pictorial sources.[42] From his analysis of the Grandval and Vivian Bible frontispieces, Köhler had concluded that the illustrations in these two manuscripts were

---

[38] Köhler (*Kar. Min.*, I₂, 110) recognized that the San Paolo Bible depended on the Touronian tradition, but he ignored this later manuscript in his iconographic study. See also Köhler, *Buchmalerei*, p. 170.

[39] "Noch eine turonische Bilderbibel," *Festschrift Bernhard Bischoff* (Stuttgart, 1971), pp.

153ff.

[40] The relationship of the Hildesheim Genesis cycle to the Touronian Bibles had long been noted. Cf. *ibid.*, n. 3 and below, Chapter II.

[41] *Ibid.*, p. 162.

[42] *Kar. Min.*, I₂, 109ff.

independent reflections of the same pre-Carolingian model; and through a detailed analysis of the style and subject matter of the Touronian copies, he attempted to reconstruct and date that model. Köhler advanced the theory that the primary source of the Touronian Bible frontispieces was a great pandect produced in Italy during the fifth century and illustrated with four frontispieces. He contended that in most details, as in overall format, the Grandval Bible is a faithful replica of this model. The Vivian manuscript, according to Köhler, is a less accurate reflection of the same source. In it, the core illustrations have been modified and the number of frontispieces has been increased with borrowings from other sources. Köhler concluded that the fifth-century Bible used at Tours had been created to express a specific theological program. He proposed that the Genesis picture was intended to present the events that necessitated God's intervention, the Exodus miniature depicted the institution of the Old Testament covenant, and the two New Testament frontispieces represented the resolution and fulfillment of the Old Testament. According to Köhler, the four pictures were a unified cycle which, he believed, had been devised to express the philosophical ideas of St. Augustine and Pope Leo the Great. It was Köhler's contention, in fact, that the Bible model known at Tours had been created as a propaganda device in Pope Leo's battle against the Manichaeans.[43]

Köhler's theory of the "Leo Bible" has been generally accepted. Among the early reviewers, Roger Hinks and Carl Nordenfalk embraced its essential postulates although both suggested certain modifications. Hinks, for example, doubted that the *Majestas* composition could have been a fifth-century invention.[44] Nordenfalk, on the other hand, questioned whether the "Leo Bible" was limited to the Genesis, Exodus, *Majestas*, and Apocalypse frontispieces and suggested that the fifth-century model may have contained Jerome, Psalms, and St. Paul frontispieces as well.[45] He noted the similarity in format of the Genesis, Jerome, and St. Paul pages and of the *Majestas* and Psalms frontispieces; and he emphasized the unity of all seven sets of verses in the Vivian Bible. Nordenfalk also introduced into the discussion the San Paolo manuscript which tends to support his hypothesis of a model illustrated with seven frontispieces. Even though his suggested modification of Köhler's theory raises serious questions about the theological program of the presumed model, Nordenfalk accepted the basic premise that the source of the Touronian illustrations was a Bible produced for Pope Leo the Great.[46]

Subsequent commentators have, in general, simply reiterated Köhler's theory; and the existence of a fifth-century model behind the Grandval and Vivian Bibles has become an axiom of medieval manuscript studies. C. R. Dodwell's recent summary is typical.

> One thing is clear: however profound may be the symbolism, it (the Grandval Bible) is an anachronism in the Carolingian historic situation. Its message is quite appropriate to the fifth century, but has no relevance to the ninth. It seems as

[43] *Ibid.*, pp. 193ff.
[44] *Carolingian Art* (London, 1935), p. 113.
[45] "Beiträge," pp. 295ff.
[46] *Ibid.*, p. 297.

though the Carolingian artists have taken over a fifth-century Italian source quite uncritically. . . . The Carolingians must have had an illustrated Bible of Leo the Great before them and, despite an occasional solecism, their paintings are almost exact copies of the fifth-century originals. They are "facsimiles" like the "classical" illustrations we have referred to earlier.[47]

In a Ph.D. dissertation submitted to the Department of Art and Archaeology of Princeton University in 1965, the author began a critical re-examination of Köhler's hypothesis.[48] A report of one aspect of that review was published subsequently[49] and the results of the thesis investigation have been incorporated into this book.

A. A. Schmid also reached conclusions at variance with Köhler's. In the 1972 facsimile edition of the Grandval Bible,[50] Schmid argued that the models of certain of the "Leo Bible" pages could not have originated before the late fifth century and he attributed greater originality to the ninth-century illuminators than had Köhler. Schmid's study, however, is limited to the four frontispieces of the Grandval Bible; and consequently, a study of all the Touronian Bible illustrations is still needed.

A NEW STUDY

A re-examination of Köhler's findings must not be based exclusively on a study of the two manuscripts from St. Martin's; it must incorporate the evidence of the Bamberg Bible and the copies of lost Touronian manuscripts as well. Köhler had ignored the Bamberg volume because "im strengen Sinne" it contains only one Bible illustration.[51] He also did not consider the "Touronian" pages of the San Paolo Bible. These omissions, which resulted from Köhler's organization of his corpus according to stylistic groups or "schools," seriously detract from his iconographic analysis. Although the Bamberg and San Paolo Bibles were produced outside St. Martin's, their illustrations were derived independently from the same models used for the Grandval and Vivian manuscripts. The frontispieces in these manuscripts have great significance, therefore, in any attempt to reconstruct and evaluate the pictorial sources. Reflections of lost Touronian Bibles—at Hildesheim and Münstereifel—need also to be considered in the new study.

Köhler used the verses that accompany the illustrations in the Grandval and Vivian Bibles to determine which details most faithfully copy the model.[52] He assumed that these same *tituli* had been used as the textual basis of the frontispieces in the hypothetical "Leo Bible." The date and origin of the *tituli* have always been disputed.

[47] *Painting in Europe: 800–1200* (Harmondsworth, 1971), p. 36.

[48] "The Sources and the Construction of the Genesis, Exodus, Majestas, and Apocalypse Frontispiece Illustrations in the Ninth-Century Touronian Bibles."

[49] "Hic homo formatur: The Genesis Frontispieces of the Carolingian Bibles," *Art Bulletin*, LIII (1971), 143ff.

[50] *Bibel von Moutier-Grandval*, p. 184f.

[51] *Kar. Min.*, I₂, 110.

[52] *Ibid.*, I₂, 109ff.

L. Traube first thought that they were Carolingian and included them in the third volume of *Poetae latini aevi Carolini*.[53] At a later date, however, Traube changed his mind and concluded that the verses were from a "viel ältere italienische Bibel."[54] Supported in his opinion by Karl Strecker, Köhler agreed that they were not of ninth-century origin; but he divided the verses into two groups: (1) the *tituli* common to the Grandval and Vivian Bibles and (2) those unique to the Vivian manuscript.[55] According to Köhler, Strecker had dated the first of these two groups to the sixth century. Nordenfalk returned to Traube's view that all the *tituli* in the Vivian Bible originated at the same time, but he concluded that the art-historical evidence precludes a date so late as the sixth century.[56] Finally, Schmid has returned to the position that the verses were composed during the ninth century.[57]

There is every reason to suppose that the *tituli* were written to elucidate the illustrations they accompany. Therefore, if it can be shown that the frontispieces of the Grandval and Vivian Bibles were constructed during the ninth-century, it will follow that the verses, too, are Carolingian. Whatever their origins, however, it is certain that the Latin captions did not serve as the textual basis of the illustrations. Many elements of the depictions are not specifically referred to in the *tituli*; and it can be shown that in numerous details, the Touronian representations conform, not to the verses, but to pre-existent pictorial traditions.

The verses accompanying the pictures in the Bamberg and San Paolo Bibles were certainly Carolingian inventions.[58]

Advances since 1933 in the understanding of Early Christian, Byzantine, and Carolingian art, perhaps more than any other factor, make a review of Köhler's findings necessary. The expanded knowledge of the Cotton Genesis family bears on Köhler's conclusions about the Genesis pages; a new understanding of various cycles of Acts illustrations affects his evaluation of the Epistles frontispieces; and additional information about *Majestas Domini* compositions, about Apocalypse illustrations, and about medieval Psalters contributes fundamentally to an analysis of the other Touronian depictions.

The work of Kurt Weitzmann is especially consequential. In numerous books and articles, Weitzmann has outlined anew the history of early medieval Bible illustration[59] and many of his observations have direct bearing on the Bibles from Tours. His studies of the Cotton Genesis family, of Acts illustration, and of Psalters have been fully utilized in the following chapters and the methods he has developed for the study

---

[53] *MGH. Poetae latini*, III, 248.

[54] "Palaeographische Anzeigen," *Neues Archiv der Gesellschaft für ältere Deutsche Geschichtskunde*, 1902, pp. 264ff. It was reprinted in *Vorlesungen und Abhandlungen von Ludwig Traube* (Munich, 1920), pp. 244ff.

[55] *Kar. Min.*, I₂, 109.

[56] "Beiträge," p. 297.

[57] *Bibel von Moutier-Grandval*, p. 184.

[58] Cf. Gaehde, "Bible Manuscript," II, 132ff.

[59] Especially, *Roll and Codex*, "The Illustration of the Septuagint," *Studies*, pp. 45ff. and "Selection of Texts."

of medieval text illustration have been employed throughout. Carl Nordenfalk's contributions to the history of Touronian art, Schmid's investigation of the Grandval manuscript, and Joachim Gaehde's analyses of the San Paolo Bible have also added substantially to this reassessment of Köhler's study.

Each chapter of this book is devoted to one of the frontispiece themes. Each is essentially independent of the others and, therefore, the ordering of the chapters is not very significant. The order follows the frequency of the appearance of each theme in the ninth-century manuscripts. Genesis and *Majestas* frontispieces are found in all four Carolingian Bibles; Exodus and Apocalypse pages occur in three; and Jerome, Psalter, Epistles, and Dedication depictions appear in only two. To a certain extent, this arrangement seems also to conform to the development of biblical illustration at Tours, a subject which is the principal topic of the concluding chapter of this book.

II. HIC HOMO FORMATUR

FULL-PAGE miniatures illustrating the life of Adam and Eve serve as Old Testament frontispieces in all four ninth-century Bibles (Figs. 1–4).[1] These frontispieces are alike in overall format and in most details. Sequences of scenes, beginning with the Creation of Adam, are arranged along three or four horizontal registers and are elucidated by Latin *tituli*. A beardless man is the Creator in all four cycles; in the scenes of Expulsion, angels evict the sinful couple; and Eve is represented holding her child in the four depictions of Labor following the Expulsion. These and numerous other elements connect the Carolingian Genesis pages to each other, but it cannot be shown that any one of the frontispieces is a copy of another. The number of scenes depicted on each, the selection of episodes, and the manner of representing each phase vary from manuscript to manuscript. Their derivation from the same model best explains the similarities evident in these pages. An independence toward the model or the intrusion of other sources accounts for the differences.

In his study of two of these Genesis frontispieces, Köhler concluded that the Grandval page is, in general, a faithful replica of one page in his hypothetical "Leo Bible" and that the Vivian frontispiece is a freer copy of this model and also contains elements borrowed from other sources.[2] Köhler also argued that the fifth-century frontispiece, which had served as the model, had been composed from a narrative cycle akin to the Cotton Genesis, a fifth- or sixth-century Greek manuscript (London, British Library, Cod. Cotton Otho B. VI) that is known primarily through the thirteenth-century copy of it among the mosaics of San Marco in Venice.[3] Köhler ignored the other reflections of this model in the Bamberg and San Paolo Bibles, and instead of utilizing the Cotton Genesis material to evaluate the authenticity of the Touronian depictions, he relied on the Latin captions that accompany them. Since the publication of *Die Schule von Tours*, knowledge of the Cotton Genesis has been enhanced considerably.[4] Most significant has been the introduction of the Millstatt Genesis (Klagenfurt, Museum Rudolfinum, Cod. VI, 19)[5] into the pictorial family.[6] The illustrations of this twelfth-

[1] Grandval Bible, fol. 5ᵛ; Bamberg Bible, fol. 7ᵛ; Vivian Bible, fol. 10ᵛ; and San Paolo Bible, fol. 8ᵛ. Cf. Köhler, *Kar. Min.*, I₂, 118ff.; Gaehde, "Bible Manuscript," I, 137ff. and "Turonian Sources," pp. 365ff.; and Schmid, *Bibel von Moutier-Grandval*, pp. 165ff. A preliminary report by the author has been published, "*Hic homo formatur*: The Genesis Frontispieces of the Carolingian Bibles," *Art Bulletin*, LIII (1971), 143ff.

[2] *Kar. Min.*, I₂, 128f.

[3] *Kar. Min.*, I₂, 119ff. For the Cotton Genesis, see J. J. Tikkanen, *Die Genesismosaiken in Venedig* (Acta Societatis Scientiarum Fennicae, vol. XVII, Helsinki, 1889) and K. Weitzmann, "Observations on the Cotton Genesis Fragments," *Late Classical and Mediaeval Studies in Honor of*

Albert Mathias Friend, Jr. (Princeton, 1955), pp. 122ff.

[4] Weitzmann, "Observations"; *idem*, "The Illustrations of the Septuagint," *Studies*, pp. 45ff.; H. Kessler, "An Eleventh-Century Ivory Plaque from South Italy and the Cassinese Revival," *Jahrbuch der Berliner Museen*, VIII (1966), 67ff.; and S. Tsuji, "Un essai d'identification des sujets des miniatures fragmentaires de la Genèse de Cotton," *Bijutsushi*, XVII (1967), 35ff.

[5] *Millstätter Genesis und Physiologus Handschrift* (Graz, 1967).

[6] Weitzmann, *Roll and Codex*, p. 140 and "Observations," pp. 121ff.; R. B. Green, "The Adam and Eve Cycle in the Hortus Deliciarum," *Late Classical and Mediaeval Studies in Honor of Albert*

century German poem, which were copied from a biblical manuscript closely related to the Cotton manuscript, are important independent witnesses of the Early Christian cycle.

A review of Köhler's conclusions based on all four Carolingian frontispieces and on the expanded Cotton Genesis material is required. Such a review must also take into account the sequence of Genesis scenes that adorn the left valve of the bronze doors of St. Michael's at Hildesheim (Fig. 5).[7] The close connection of the Hildesheim cycle to the Touronian frontispieces has been recognized for some time.[8] Nordenfalk's recent demonstration that the Hildesheim cycle was probably copied from an illustrated Bible from Tours, earlier than any of the extant manuscripts,[9] gives Bernward's reliefs special significance for this study.

THE INDIVIDUAL SCENES

The five Genesis sequences begin with scenes of the Creation of Adam. In the Grandval Bible, the Creator is shown bending over the rigidly outstretched body of Adam and grasping his head and left shoulder. Two orant angels watch the event at the right. Köhler identified the Grandval scene as the physical forming of man[10] which is indicated by the *titulus* and which is described in Gen., II, 7, "The Lord God formed man from the dust of the ground. . . ." Weitzmann, on the other hand, concluded that the scene illustrated the subsequent moment of creation, the Enlivenment, when "[the Lord] breathed into his nostrils the breath of life."[11] Weitzmann's conclusion is sup-

Mathias Friend, Jr. (Princeton, 1955), pp. 340ff. Apparently unaware of Weitzmann's observations, H. Menhardt published an extensive study in which he attempted to show that the illustrations of the Millstatt Genesis were derived from a Middle Byzantine Octateuch ("Die Bilder der Millstätter Genesis und ihre Verwandten," *Beiträge zur ältern Europäischen Kulturgeschichte. Festschrift für Rudolf Egger* [Klagenfurt, 1954], 248ff.). Menhardt's arguments have been refuted by H. Voss, *Studien zur illustrierten Millstätter Genesis* (Munich, 1962). In rejecting Menhardt's conclusions, Voss gave additional support to Weitzmann's theory that the Millstatt Genesis, while showing certain other influences, is fundamentally a part of the Cotton Genesis family. In his two articles, "Zu den Bildern der altdeutschen Genesis," *Zeitschrift für Deutsche Philologie*, LXXV (1956), 23ff. and LXXXVIII (1964), 99ff., E. P. Pickering did not deal with the question of pictorial origins.

[7] R. Wesenberg, *Bernwardinische Plastik* (Berlin, 1955), pp. 65ff.

[8] Cf. F. Debelius, *Die Bernwardstür zu Hildes-* heim (Strassburg, 1907); A. Goldschmidt, *Die deutschen Bronzetüren des frühen Mittelalters* (Marburg, 1926); H. Jantzen, *Ottonische Kunst* (Munich, 1947); H. Schnitzler, "Südwestdeutsche Kunst um das Jahr 1000 und die Schule von Tours," *Trierer Zeitschrift*, XIV (1939), 180ff.; F. Tschan, *Saint Bernward of Hildesheim* (Notre Dame, 1951); Wesenberg, *loc. cit.* Diverging somewhat from the general opinion, H. von Einem proposed that the Hildesheim door merged the cycle of the supposed "Leo Bible" with elements from the frescoes of San Paolo fuori le mura ("Zur Hildesheimer Bronzetür," *Jahrbuch der Preussischen Kunstsammlungen* [LIX] 1938, 3ff.).

[9] "Noch eine turonische Bilderbibel," *Festschrift Bernhard Bischoff* (Stuttgart, 1971), pp. 153ff.

[10] *Kar. Min.*, I₂, 119f.

[11] Weitzmann, *Roll and Codex*, 176f.; and "Septuagint," pp. 69ff. In the new edition of *Roll and Codex* (Princeton, 1971), p. 257, Weitzmann again took up the question in response to the re-interpretation by H. Schade, "Das Paradies und die Imago Dei," *Probleme der Kunstwissen-*

ported by the mosaics of San Marco and by analogies that exist between the Grandval composition and depictions of Prometheus on late-antique sarcophagi. The physical forming, as represented in San Marco (Fig. 6) and presumably in the Cotton Genesis, shows the Creator molding the arm of the still featureless Adam. This scene actually illustrates the account of the Creation in Gen., I, 27. Although the Creator does hold Adam's shoulder in the Grandval scene, his basic activity is very different from that in the mosaic. He bends over to breathe life into the face of the fully formed but inanimate man.

The Creation of Adam in the Millstatt Genesis (fol. 3ʳ, Fig. 7) corresponds to the Grandval composition. As he is throughout the twelfth-century cycle, the Creator is portrayed as Christ; he is bearded and stands erect. As in the Grandval Bible, however, he holds the head of the stiffly outstretched man while an angel looks on.

A different composition was used to illustrate the creation of Adam in the Bamberg Bible. Adam sits upright on the ground and reaches out toward the Creator who approaches him from the right. A distant ancestor of Michelangelo's Sistine Creation scene, the Bamberg depiction is probably to be identified as the Animation of Adam described in Gen., II, 7, "Thus man became a living Creature." Adam is formed but is not yet fully capable of movement. A similar composition is found among the fifth-century frescoes in San Paolo fuori le mura in Rome (Fig. 8)[12] and was popular in later Italian cycles.[13]

A third type of Creation is found in the Vivian Bible. Adam stands before the Creator who extends his right arm toward the man. The orant angel behind the two men recalls the Grandval scene but otherwise, the two depictions are distinctly different from one another. By analogy with the San Marco mosaics (Fig. 9), where the Creator literally gives Adam a soul in the form of a classical Psyche, the Vivian scene can be positively identified as the Animation of Adam. The Animation in the Millstatt Genesis (fol. 6ʳ, Fig. 10) is even closer to the Vivian scene. The psyche is not depicted and an orant angel observes the event.

The inclusion in the Millstatt Genesis of two creation scenes, one representing the Enlivenment and the other the Animation, suggests that the model known at Tours during the ninth century also illustrated the Creation of Adam in more than one phase. The Touronian illuminators simply made different selections from this source. The

schaft, II (1966), 79ff. Weitzmann's conclusion that the Creator is not lifting Adam by the head finds support in the details of the Millstatt scene.

[12] Cf. S. Waetzoldt, Die Kopien des 17. Jahrhunderts nach Mosaiken und Wandmalereien in Rom (Vienna, 1964), pp. 56ff. The San Paolo frescoes had been restored prior to their destruction in 1823. Fortunately, they had been recorded during the seventeenth-century (Vatican, Cod. Barb. lat. 4406) but it is not clear which details

in the copies belong to the Early Christian cycle and which were added during the thirteenth-century repainting. The Creator's globe in the Genesis sequences seems to be a later addition, cf. Kessler, "Eleventh Century," pp. 90ff.

[13] These include an eleventh-century ivory plaque in Berlin (cf. Kessler, "Eleventh Century") and the mosaics in the cathedral of Monreale (cf. O. Demus, The Mosaics of Norman Sicily [London, 1948], pls. 93–96).

15

Grandval master chose the Enlivement and the artist of the Vivian Bible copied the Animation. One need not conclude with Köhler that they consulted two sources.[14] It is possible that the Bamberg illuminator derived his Creation of Adam from a second model. Because of the similarity of the Bamberg Creator and Adam figures to those in the other Touronian illustrations, however, it is likelier, that he fashioned the scene from the same source, creating a new composition that is intermediary between the horizontal Enlivement and the vertical Animation.

While one Touronian artist copied the Enlivement, another copied the Animation, and yet another merged the two, a fourth illuminator retained both scenes. In the San Paolo Bible, Adam is first shown on the ground, his arms cleaving to his sides as the Creator bends over him and touches his shoulder and upper arm. In its basic elements, the composition conforms to the scenes of the Enlivement in the Grandval and Millstatt manuscripts, although the position of the Creator's hands may have been taken from the Forming. The Creator has simply been moved to the right, apparently to save space. The second episode in the San Paolo Bible closely parallels the Animation scenes in the Vivian Bible and the Millstatt Genesis. Adam, his arm slightly bent, faces the creator who gestures toward him. Because the composition is reversed, it resembles San Marco more closely than do the other manuscripts. The San Paolo Bible confirms that the Enlivement and Animation were both illustrated in the Genesis model used at Tours; and it makes it easy to imagine how the Bamberg artist could have constructed his new composition from such a model by combining Adam from one scene and the Creator from the other.

The basic action of the first scene on the Hildesheim door is closer to the San Paolo Bible than to the other Carolingian manuscripts.[15] The Creator, holding Adam's shoulder and upper arm, bends down to breathe life into the man. The praying angel, however, ties the Ottonian relief to the Grandval and Vivian manuscripts and to the Millstatt Genesis. It is an important indication that the door was not based on any of the known Carolingian Bibles but was derived from the same ultimate model, presumably through a lost Touronian intermediary.

The curious figure at the right of the Hildesheim panel may be a vestige of the second scene of creation.[16] His slightly raised arm recalls Adam's gesture in the San Paolo Bible Animation scene. He may also illustrate another moment in the Genesis narrative, namely Adam in the Garden of Eden, "The Lord God planted a garden in Eden away to the east, and there he put the man whom he had formed" (Gen., II, 8). In San Marco, the Animation of Adam is followed by a depiction of the Creator leading Adam into Paradise. In the Millstatt Genesis (Fol. 8r, Fig. 11), it is followed by a

[14] Köhler, *Kar. Min.*, I₂, 119ff. Köhler recognized that the duplication of angels in the Grandval Bible indicates the existence of two creation scenes in the model but he dismissed this idea as being contradictory to the other evidence.

[15] Cf. Wesenberg, *op. cit.*, p. 71, n. 170.

[16] *Ibid.*, pp. 70f.

16

miniature showing Adam alone surveying the paradisical garden.[17] The Hildesheim figure could have been derived from a similar representation.

The Creation of Eve is illustrated in similar fashion in the four Bibles. The depictions follow Gen., II, 21, "And the Lord God put the man into a trance, and while he slept, he took one of his ribs and closed the flesh over the place." The Creator bends over Adam and draws a rib from his side. In the Grandval and Vivian Bibles, the action reads from left to right; in the Bamberg and San Paolo Bibles, it goes from right to left. But this is a minor variation. The fact that in all four manuscripts the Creator draws only the rib and not the fully formed Eve from Adam's side connects the Touronian compositions to one another and distinguishes them from most other medieval representations of the event including the fresco in San Paolo f.l.m. (Fig. 12).[18]

Similar representations appear in San Marco (Fig. 13) and in the Millstatt Genesis (fol. 9ᵛ, Fig. 14). The parallels with the San Paolo Bible are especially striking because Adam is shown resting his head on his right arm and the Creator draws the rib from his left side. Reminiscences of Adam's original pose are found in the Bamberg Bible and also in the Grandval manuscript where Adam's head is to the right and his arm is bent and brought to his face. Of the four Carolingian depictions, however, the one in the San Paolo Bible is certainly the most accurate replica of the prototype.[19]

The San Paolo Bible also illustrates the Shaping of Eve, "The Lord God then built the rib, which he had taken out of the man, into a woman" (Gen., II, 22). The Creator is shown bending over Eve and touching her shoulder. The composition parallels the Enlivement of Adam directly above it; but the Shaping of Eve was not necessarily devised of elements copied from the first register.[20] The Shaping of Eve is required by the narrative and is illustrated as a separate scene at San Marco (Fig. 13). San Marco shows Eve, as well as the Creator standing; as in the San Paolo Bible, however, the Creator touches Eve's shoulder. Whereas the Carolingian illuminator may have been influenced by the scene of the Forming of Adam, the basic source of his Shaping of Eve apparently was an independent composition similar to the scene in San Marco.

The Introduction of Adam and Eve, the subsequent depiction in all four manuscripts and on the Hildesheim door, is described in Gen., II, 22–23, "He brought her to man, and the man said: 'Now this, at last—bone of my bones, flesh from my flesh—this shall be called woman, for from man was this taken.'" The five compositions are virtually identical to one another. The Creator, standing behind Eve, rests his hand on her shoulder. Adam approaches from the right, his arm raised in the gesture of naming.

[17] Green, op. cit., p. 343.

[18] In San Paolo f.l.m., the woman actually emerges from behind Adam. The full figure of Eve may be a later addition.

[19] H. Schade, "Hinweise zur frühmittelalterlichen Ikonographie," Das Münster, XI (1958), 375ff., sought to explain Adam's open eyes in the San Paolo Bible as a reflection of an Augustinian interpretation. Judging from the three other Carolingian Bibles and from San Marco and the Millstatt Genesis, Adam's eyes were not open in the archetype. It seems that this is a stylistic rather than a theological element because in the San Paolo scene of the Creation of Adam, Adam's eyes are also open.

[20] Gaehde, "Turonian Sources," p. 366.

The Introduction is not illustrated in the Millstatt Genesis. The scene in San Marco (Fig. 15), however, is virtually identical to the Carolingian compositions. Remains of the scene can also still be discerned on a fragment of the Cotton Genesis (Fig. 16). In this case, it appears that the Vivian Bible is closest to the pictorial model.

Three distinct versions of the Temptation and Fall appear in the four manuscripts. The Grandval Bible represents Eve twice. First she is shown taking fruit from the mouth of a serpent entwined around a tree, and then she is depicted eating the fruit while simultaneously offering a piece of it to Adam who also eats of the forbidden food. The Grandval representation is virtually identical to the scene in San Marco (Fig. 18). The serpent is missing in the mosaic, but it appears in the previous scene, the Temptation (Fig. 17). The three episodes, in San Marco, the Temptation, Taking the Fruit, and Eating the Fruit, were based on Gen., III, 1–6:

> The serpent was more crafty than any wild creature that the Lord God had made. He said to the woman, "Is it true that God has forbidden you to eat from any tree in the garden?" The woman answered the serpent, "We may eat the fruit of any tree in the garden, except for the tree in the middle of the garden; God has forbidden us either to eat or to touch the fruit of that; if we do, we shall die." The serpent said, "Of course you will not die. God knows that as soon as you eat it, your eyes will be opened and you will be like gods knowing both good and evil." When the woman saw that the fruit of the tree was good to eat, and that it was pleasing to the eye and tempting to contemplate, she took some and ate it. She also gave the husband some and he ate it.

It is quite possible that in the model, the two scenes of Temptation and Eating the Fruit were already merged into a single composition as they are in the Grandval Bible and the Millstatt Genesis (fol. 10ʳ, Fig. 19).

In the Bamberg and Vivian Bibles, the three scenes of Temptation, Taking the Fruit, and Eating, have been merged into one. As in the Grandval Bible and Millstatt Genesis, Eve is shown facing the tree and removing a piece of fruit from the mouth of a serpent coiled around its trunk. At the same time, with her left arm awkwardly extended behind her she passes fruit to Adam. In the Vivian Bible, Adam is already eating the fruit. There is no reason to assume, as Köhler had, that the illuminators consulted a second source for the Paris (or Bamberg) compositions.[21] The individual figures, as well as the trees and serpents, have close counterparts in the Grandval Bible and at San Marco. To save space, the artists simply did not repeat the figure of Eve but attempted to combine the first figure with elements of the second scene.

The fusion was more felicitous at Hildesheim. Eve turns from the serpent and tree toward Adam who reaches for the fruit. The composition is reversed but it was clearly based on a scene of Temptation and Fall similar to those in the Bamberg and Vivian frontispieces.

[21] *Kar. Min.*, I₂, 122ff.

18

The depiction of the Fall is very different in the San Paolo Bible. Adam stands to the left of the tree and eats the fruit while he covers his nakedness with a great leaf. Eve stands at the right and she too covers her nudity while extending a piece of the fruit to Adam. At the right, the Creator calls to the sinning couple. The figure of the Lord is not well integrated into the composition, and Gaehde[22] has pointed out that the San Paolo scene must merge depictions of the Temptation and Fall with the Hiding of Nakedness and Calling reported in Gen., III, 7–10:

> Then the eyes of both of them were opened and they discovered that they were naked; so they stitched fig-leaves together and made themselves loincloths. The man and his wife heard the sound of the Lord God walking in the garden at the time of the evening breeze and hid from the Lord God among the trees of the garden. But the Lord God called to the man and said to him, "Where are you?" He replied, "I heard the sound as you were walking in the garden, and I was afraid because I was naked, and I hid myself."

These events are depicted as six separate scenes at San Marco (Figs. 17, 18, 20, 21, and 22); and it is not difficult to imagine how the San Paolo illuminator could have constructed a new composition from elements in his model. The core of the depiction is not very different from the San Marco Eating scene. The tree has been placed between Adam and Eve and leaves have been added, perhaps from the Covering. The poses of Adam and Eve in the San Marco Temptation are especially close to those in the San Paolo Bible. To organize his new representation, the San Paolo master may also have consulted a symmetrical composition of the Fall of Man similar to those that are common in Early Christian art.[23] The San Paolo frescoes (Fig. 23) offer a good example of this early type of representation. A similar composition also appears in the Millstatt Genesis (fol. 11ʳ, Fig. 24). As Rosalie Green has noted, the Millstatt depiction is a conflation of several moments and includes elements of Adam and Eve Hiding their Nakedness.[24] Its similarity to the San Paolo scene, therefore, is not due to a direct relationship. It resulted from similar rearrangements of the same models.

The Creator who reproves Adam and Eve in the San Paolo scene is a borrowing from still another illustration in the prototype. A nearly identical figure is included in the scene of Reproval in the Vivian Bible;[25] but in the earlier manuscript the Creator is better integrated into the action. The Vivian frontispiece shows Adam and Eve huddled together in fear of the Lord who strides toward them with his arm raised. The scene illustrates the Hiding recounted in Gen., III, 8. Köhler believed that the Vivian composition had been copied from a manuscript related to the Vienna Genesis.[26] Similarities with the Hiding scene of the Vienna Genesis (Nationalbibliothek, Cod. gr. theol. 31, page 1, Fig. 25) do exist, but these are only superficial. The figure types, the

---

[22] "Bible Manuscript," I, pp. 146ff. and "Turonian Sources," p. 368.

[23] "Bible Manuscript," I, p. 147, and "Turonian Sources," pp. 368f.

[24] *Op. cit.*, p. 345.

[25] Cf. Gaehde, "Turonian Sources," p. 369.

[26] *Kar. Min.*, I, 125.

degree of overlapping, and even the gestures are different. Furthermore, a scene of Hiding must have been available in the basic model. The angry Lord from it was copied in the San Paolo Bible, and the crouching figures of Adam and Eve appear as a separate scene in the Bamberg manuscript.

The depictions of the Reproval in San Marco (Fig. 21) and in the Millstatt Genesis (fol. 12^r, Fig. 26) agree essentially with one another. The Creator stands at the left and points to the sinful couple; Adam and Eve try to run from him. The fresco in San Paolo f.l.m. (Fig. 27) is similar.[27] The striding Lord is not unlike the Carolingian representations, but the relationship of the Touronian Hiding scenes to the other depictions is otherwise not evident.

In the Grandval Bible, the Reproval of Adam and Eve is represented by a different composition. The Creator, standing behind the tree of wisdom, reprimands Adam and Eve. The sinners cover their nakedness and seek to transfer blame away from themselves. Adam points to the woman; Eve points to the serpent. The Bamberg Bible and Hildesheim door contain similar, though more animated, compositions which evidently illustrate the Denial of Blame described in Gen., III, 11–13:

> God answered, "Who told you that you were naked? Have you eaten from the tree which I forbade you?" The man said, "The woman you gave me for a companion, she gave me fruit from the tree and I ate it." Then the Lord God said to the woman, "What is this that you have done?" The woman said, "The serpent tricked me, and I ate."

That the Denial of Blame would have been depicted in the same model as the Hiding scenes is established by the Bamberg Bible. The scenes represent different phases of the narrative and both are also included in San Paolo f.l.m. (Fig. 28) and in San Marco (Fig. 22). Although the Italian murals show the Lord enthroned, his gestures and those of Adam and Eve closely parallel those in the Grandval and Bamberg Bibles and on the Hildesheim door.

Two types of Expulsion scenes also occur in the manuscripts and on the Hildesheim relief. In the Bamberg and Grandval Bibles, an angel rests his hand on Adam's shoulder and escorts the couple from Eden. Adam and Eve are clothed in long tunics and gaze longingly back. In the Vivian and San Paolo Bibles and at Hildesheim, the couple is nude[28] and Eve raises her hand to her face in an expression of despair. In the San Paolo Bible, the gentle angel has been replaced by a vigorous young man who brandishes a sword.

Both Expulsion scenes may have been derived from one model. The Vienna Genesis (page 2)[29] and the Octateuchs[30] represent the Expulsion twice. In accord with Gen.,

[27] The globe is a common element in the San Paolo frescoes. Eve's garment seems to be a later addition or copyist's mistake. In San Marco, the Creator is frequently enthroned. This may be a modification of the original.

[28] The togas are certainly an addition in the Vivian Bible.

[29] W. von Hartel and F. Wickhoff, *Die Wiener Genesis* (Vienna, 1895), pl. 11.

[30] Cf. D. C. Hesseling, *Miniatures de l'octateuque grec de Smyrne* (Leiden, 1909), pl. 23.

20

III, 24–25, they depict Adam and Eve before the gates and again outside Eden, "So the Lord God drove him out of the garden to till the ground from which he was taken. He cast him out and to the east of the garden of Eden he stationed the cherubim and a sword whirling and flashing to guard the way of the tree of life." In the Greek manuscripts, the angel appears only after the couple has left Paradise. Eve's upraised hand is a motif common to all the examples. The Hildesheim door suggests that the Vivian-San Paolo composition should be identified as the Expulsion before the Gates. The backward glances of Adam and Eve in the Bamberg-Grandval scenes indicates that the couple has already left Eden.

In San Marco (Fig. 29) and in the Millstatt Genesis (fol. 14ᵛ, Fig. 30), the Creator personally expels Adam and Eve. Eve's complicated pose in the latter is so like that on the Hildesheim panel, however, that it is difficult to deny a relationship between the representations. The costumes and Eve's look backward seem to relate the San Marco representation to the Grandval and Bamberg Expulsions. The San Paolo fresco (Fig. 31) depicts the angel rather than the Lord as evicter. It therefore resembles the Vivian-San Paolo-Hildesheim composition even though the gate is behind the couple.

The uniformity of the depictions strongly indicates that both the Grandval-Bamberg Expulsion and the Vivian-San Paolo-Hildesheim composition were in the basic model. It is possible that originally one of the depictions represented the Reproval rather than the Expulsion. Clear similarities exist between the San Marco and Millstatt Reproval scenes (cf. Figs. 21 and 26) and the compositions in the Vivian and San Paolo Bibles and on Bernward's door.[31] It is likelier, however, that in the model the Expulsion was represented twice—before the gates and outside Eden. The angel, which has no counterpart in San Marco or in the Millstatt Genesis, was certainly also a feature of the model.[32] The sword-brandishing man who evicts Adam and Eve in the San Paolo Bible, must depend on a source different from the one that served as the model for the Grandval, Bamberg, and Vivian Bibles. He is identified in the *titulus* as "flammeus et gladius" and he must have been taken from a representation of the "sword whirling and flashing" similar to the one depicted on folio 16ᵛ of the Millstatt Genesis (Fig. 32). The Millstatt figure is less dramatic than the man in the San Paolo Bible, but as in the ninth-century Bible, he is a nimble youth who clutches his garment in one hand and swings his sword with the other. The substitution of swords for scepters in the Bamberg Bible and at Hildesheim may also be due to the influence of this figure.

The Carolingian Expulsion compositions were apparently derived from three distinct scenes in the model: Expulsion before the Gates, Expulsion outside Eden, and the Sword Whirling and Flashing. Some similarities with the ninth-century illustrations exist in San Marco, San Paolo f.l.m., and the Millstatt Genesis. Except for the Sword

[31] Removed from the text, the two Millstatt scenes would both appear to be Expulsions. Such is the case, for example, on the Berlin ivory. Cf. Kessler, "Eleventh Century," pp. 89ff.

[32] A wingless angel accompanies the Lord in the Millstatt scene. An angel expels Adam and Eve in the Salerno antependium which could have derived either from the Cotton Genesis or Octateuch traditions. Cf. Weitzmann, "Observations." pp. 122f.: Kessler, "Eleventh-Century," p. 90 and R. Bergman, "The Salerno Ivories" (unpublished Ph.D. dissertation, Princeton, 1972), pp. 25f.

scene, however, the relationship of the Bible frontispieces to the wall paintings and German paraphrase is not clear.

> As punishment for their sins, the Lord imposed labor on Adam and Eve. And to the woman he said "I will increase your Labor and your groaning, and in labor you shall bear children. You shall be eager for your husband and he shall be your master." And to the man he said, ". . . With labor you shall win your food from the ground all the days of your life." (Gen., III, 16–17)

In all four manuscripts and on the Hildesheim door, Adam is shown cultivating the earth with a mattock while Eve nurses a child.[33] Although his clothing, like Eve's, varies to conform with that of the Expulsion, Adam is virtually the same in all examples. Eve and the child differ from manuscript to manuscript only in insignificant details. The Grandval and San Paolo Bibles and the Hildesheim door show Eve nursing the child; in the Vivian Bible, the child sits upright in her lap and she gestures toward Adam. Adam and Eve are placed at opposite corners of the Bamberg frontispiece and Eve and the child are shown in profile. The five representations are certainly variations on the same model. This model must have included the bower which is represented in the Grandval and San Paolo manuscripts and on the Ottonian door. A vestige of it is found also in the Vivian Bible. The angel who addresses Adam on the Hildesheim door has no counterpart in the Touronian Bibles. He may be an eleventh-century addition.

Adam tilling the soil with a mattock is represented in San Marco (Fig. 29). The mosaic, however, shows Eve holding a spindle and distaff rather than the child. These weaving implements, like Eve's throne, are Marian elements that must have been interpolated into the Genesis cycle.[34] The model reflected in the Bibles certainly showed Eve with a child. Unfortunately, the Millstatt Genesis does not portray the Labor, but the scene is depicted in San Paolo f.l.m. (Fig. 33) where, alongside the toiling man, Eve is shown holding a child. Consequently, there is every reason to suppose that an Early Christian model represented Eve as in the Touronian Bibles. In the Ashburnham Pentateuch (Paris, Bibliothèque Nationale, Cod. nouv. acq. lat. 2334, fol. 6ʳ, Fig. 34),[35] Eve not only holds a child but is seated in a bower. Because there is evidence that the Ashburnham Pentateuch was at Tours during the ninth century,[36] it is tempting to see in this motif the direct influence of the Paris manuscript. It is unlikely, however, that the Touronian illuminators consulted the Ashburnham Pentateuch for this scene. In the latter manuscript, Eve sits on a bench within a shelter constructed of two posts

---

[33] No evidence supports F. Leitschuh's identification of this child as Seth (*Geschichte der karolingischen Malerei* [Berlin, 1894], pp. 101f.).

[34] Without referring to Mary, the Syrian commentary on Genesis notes that God "instructed the woman (Eve) in the art of weaving" (*The Early Syrian Fathers on Genesis*, ed. A. Levene [London, 1951], p. 79. I owe this reference to Mr. Michael Levin).

[35] O. van Gebhardt, *The Miniatures of the Ashburnham Pentateuch* (London, 1883), p. 3.

[36] B. Narkiss, "Towards a Further Study of the Ashburnham Pentateuch (Pentateuque de Tours)," *Cahiers Archéologiques*, XIX (1969), 45ff.

and a flat roof. In the Bibles, she sits on the ground beneath a bower made of a garland and forked poles. Furthermore, in the Ashburnham Pentateuch, Adam uses a plow pulled by an ox team to cultivate the fields. Eve nursing her child in a bower has a textual basis.[37] Independent derivation from this text, rather than direct influence, probably accounts for the agreement of the Ashburnham Pentateuch and Touronian images.

Unique scenes are illustrated in the Grandval and Bamberg manuscripts and on the Hildesheim door. The Naming of the Animals, for example, appears only in the Bamberg Bible. Adam stands at the left and points toward a herd of animals. The Creator stands at the right and he, too, extends his arm toward the beasts, among which a deer, camel, elephant, lion, duck, pig, and serpent can be identified. The scene illustrates Gen., II, 19–20, "He brought (the animals) to the man to see what he would call them, and whatever the man called each living creature, that was its name. Thus, the man gave names to all cattle, to the birds of heaven, and to every wild animal." The illustration of these verses at San Marco (Fig. 35) is not unlike the Bamberg composition except that the Creator is enthroned behind Adam. (The enthroned Creator, repeated throughout the San Marco mosaics, was interpolated into the archetypal cycle.) The Millstatt Genesis (fol. 9r, Fig. 36) is closer; as in the ninth-century Bible, Adam and the Lord both raise their arms toward the pyramidal group of animals standing between them.

God's Admonition to Adam and Eve concerning the tree of wisdom is illustrated only in the Grandval Bible. Adam and Eve stand respectfully at the right of the tree as the Creator warns them not to eat of its fruit. The episode is described in Gen., II, 16, "He told the man, 'You may eat from every tree in the garden of Eden, but not from the tree of the knowledge of good and evil; for on the day you eat from it, you will certainly die.' " According to the biblical account, only Adam was warned about the tree. Eve was not yet created (cf. Gen., II, 22–23). Eve's anachronistic presence at the Admonition may account for the absence of the scene in the other Bibles. The Admonition is also lacking in San Marco, in San Paolo f.l.m., and in the Millstatt Genesis. It is illustrated, however, in the Hortus Deliciarum (Strasbourg, Bibliothèque de la Ville, fol. 17r, Fig. 37), a manuscript whose Genesis cycle is closely connected to the Millstatt Genesis.[38] Adam and Eve stand before the Lord who grasps Adam's wrist and warns the couple not to eat from the tree.

On the Hildesheim door, in the Bamberg manuscript, and possibly in the Grandval Bible as well, the Genesis cycle extends beyond the life of Adam and Eve and includes episodes from the story of Cain and Abel. At Hildesheim, three events are represented. First, Cain and Abel are shown presenting their offerings to the Lord, "The day came

[37] See below, p. 30.
[38] Cf. Green, op. cit., p. 344. It also appears in the fourteenth-century manuscript of the Homilies of Gregory Nazianzenus in Paris (Bibliothèque Nationale, Cod. gr. 543, fol. 116v). According to

G. Galavaris (The Illustrations of the Liturgical Homilies of Gregory Nazianzenus [Princeton, 1969], pp. 118ff.), the Adam and Eve cycle in this manuscript was derived from the same archetype as the Cotton Genesis.

when Cain brought some of the produce of the soil as a gift to the Lord; and Abel brought some of the first-born of his flock, the fat portions of them. The Lord received Abel and his gift with favor; but Cain and his gift he did not receive" (Gen., IV, 3–5). At the left, Abel offers a kid to God who is symbolized by a hand; and at the right, Cain tenders a sheaf of grain. Except for the Hand of God, the representation in San Marco (Fig. 38) is quite different from the Hildesheim composition. Abel bears the offering on his shoulders and Cain approaches with a cornucopia. The San Paolo frescoes (Fig. 39) and the Millstatt Genesis (fol. 19ʳ, Fig. 40) are closer to the relief. The Hand of God has been omitted in both; and both include an altar, but the gestures and offerings recall those in the Hildesheim depiction.

In the lowest panel of Bernward's door, the Slaughter of Abel is represented. Cain bludgeons Abel and his victim falls dead to the ground. The use of a club as the murder weapon is significant. The Bible does not specify the instrument, "While they were there, Cain attacked his brother Abel and murdered him" (Gen., IV, 8). San Marco (Fig. 41) also shows Cain attacking his brother with a club. Cain's violent pivot in the mosaic, however, is not paralleled in the relief. The San Paolo fresco (Fig. 42) is more like the Hildesheim composition. Abel falls on one knee as at San Marco but Cain simply rushes toward him wielding his club over his head. The Millstatt Genesis (fol. 19ᵛ, Fig. 43) is closer still to the Hildesheim relief. Cain bends to attack Abel who tumbles forward onto his hands. In the manuscript, Cain's club actually finds its mark, but the two compositions are otherwise alike.

The Slaughter of Abel may also be depicted in the Grandval Bible.[39] Beneath the right tip of the garland that forms Eve's bower is a tiny sketch (Fig. 44). Two figures are delineated within a lightened square. One stands at the left and extends his arm toward the figure at the right who seems to be trying to balance himself as he falls backward. The figures may be no more than illuminator's scribbles. They are, however, part of the ninth-century painting; and, on the basis of similarities with San Marco and San Paolo f.l.m., they can perhaps be identified as the Slaughter of Abel.

The condemnation of Cain recounted in Gen., IV, 9–11 terminates the Old Testament cycle of the Hildesheim door:

> Then the Lord said to Cain, "Where is your brother Abel?" Cain answered, "I do not know. Am I my brother's keeper?" The Lord said, "What have you done? Hark! Your brother's blood that has been shed is crying out to me from the ground. Now you are accursed, and banished from the ground."

God, symbolized by a hand emerging from the cloud, rebukes Cain who still holds the murder weapon.

In San Marco (Fig. 45), the composition is reversed, but Cain clutches his cloak and raises his right arm toward the Hand of God. The representation of the Condem-

---

[39] H. Kessler, "An Unnoticed Scene in the Grandval Bible," *Cahiers Archéologiques*, XVIII (1967), 113ff.

nation in San Paolo f.l.m. (Fig. 42) is basically the same as that on the door except, in the fresco, a flying figure of the Lord was added at a later date to replace the hand and arc.

That the Bamberg artist also had access to a creation cycle that included illustrations of the Cain and Abel story is proven by the picture at the center of the fourth register. The picture represents Cain bending over the wrapped corpse of his brother and attempting to dig his brother's grave. The Burial of Abel is not described in the Bible and is not depicted elsewhere. Reasons for believing that the Bamberg scene was derived from the same model as the other illustrations, however, will be presented below.

THE MODEL OF THE GENESIS FRONTISPIECES

Sixteen or perhaps seventeen episodes from the second, third, and fourth chapters of Genesis are depicted in the Touronian Bibles. These are:

Enlivement of Adam (perhaps combined with Forming) Gen., II, 7.
  G, SP, H (MG)[40]

Animation of Adam.[41] Gen., II, 7.
  V, SP (SM, MG, SPF)

Admonition. Gen., II, 16–17.
  G (HD)

Naming the Animals. Gen., II, 19.
  B (SM, MG)

Drawing Adam's Rib. Gen., II, 21.
  G, B, V, SP (SM, SPF)

Shaping Eve. Gen., II, 21.
  SP (SM)

Introduction of Eve to Adam. Gen., II, 21–23.
  G, B, V, SP, H (SM)

Picking the Fruit (combined with Temptation). Gen., II, 1–6.
  G, B, V, SP (SM, MG)

Fall. Gen., II, 6.
  G, B, V, SP, H (SM, MG, SPF)

Hiding (Reproval). Gen., III, 8–9.
  B, V, SP (SM, MG, SPF)

Denial of Blame. Gen., III, 10–13.
  G, B, H (SM, SPF)

Expulsion I. Gen., III, 23.
  V, SP, H

Expulsion II. Gen., III, 24.
  G, B (SPF)

Whirling Sword. Gen., III, 24.
  SP (MG)

Labor. Gen., III, 16–17.
  G, B, V, SP, H (SM, SPF)

Slaughter of Abel. Gen., IV, 8.
  G?, H (SM, MG, SPF)

Burial of Abel.
  B

The differences in the rendering of the episodes in the several manuscripts is not great and it is fairly easy to reconstruct the narrative model behind the Carolingian scenes.

---

[40] G = Grandval Bible; B = Bamberg Bible; V = Vivian Bible; SP = San Paolo Bible; H = Hildesheim door; SM = San Marco Mosaics; MG = Millstatt Genesis; and SPF = San Paolo frescoes.

[41] The Enlivement and Animation may have been merged in the Bamberg Bible.

As Köhler had shown, the Touronian Genesis illustrations are closely related to the mosaics of San Marco. Not only are the scenes of Animation, Drawing of Adam's Rib, Introduction, Picking, Fall, and Denial of Blame in the Grandval and Vivian Bibles virtually identical to those in the mosaic cycle, so are the Bamberg Naming of Animals and the San Paolo Shaping of Eve. Only the Expulsion scenes differ from the Cotton Genesis-San Marco depictions.

In certain aspects, the illustrations of the Millstatt Genesis are even closer to the Carolingian miniatures. The miniatures of the German paraphrase correspond well to the Enlivement and Animation of Adam, the Naming of Animals, Drawing Adam's Rib, Picking the Fruit, Fall, Reproval, and Whirling Sword. Furthermore, significant details such as the praying angels at Adam's Creation, which are not in San Marco, are included in the Millstatt Genesis.

The close connection with the Millstatt Genesis is not surprising because the pictures of this twelfth-century German manuscript can be shown to belong to the family of the Cotton Genesis.[42] In other words, both the San Marco mosaics and the Klagenfurt manuscript depended ultimately on the same model, although each is only a limited selection from the extensive archetype.

The frescoes in San Paolo f.l.m. may also reflect the same cycle. Although they are known only through seventeenth-century copies of frescoes that were already restored during the thirteenth century,[43] the paintings resemble the San Marco and Millstatt cycles in such details as the anthropomorphic Creator and especially in the scenes of Denial of Blame and Slaughter of Abel.

The San Marco mosaics, the Millstatt Genesis, and the San Paolo frescoes are independent and reduced selections from the archetypal cycle. The Cotton Genesis, which may itself have been an abridged cycle, contained approximately 330 miniatures of which about one-third were copied in the mosaics.[44] Ninety scenes are included in the Millstatt Genesis and only twenty-eight in San Paolo f.l.m. An idea of the original cycle can be approximated only through a tabulation of the several reflections, but even that is not sufficient. Certain scenes of the archetype were not chosen by any of the copyists. These include the monotonous genealogical miniatures which are known to have existed in the Cotton manuscript.[45] They also include the Admonition, a scene so important for the narrative that one would have assumed that it had been depicted in the archetype even if it had not been copied in the Hortus Deliciarum, another offshoot of the Cotton Genesis family.

The model of the Carolingian Bibles must have been a very dense reflection of the same cycle. The sequence of miniatures followed the Genesis text almost verse by verse. It is no wonder that the Touronian illuminators abridged the model to create their frontispieces. The source used at Tours could have been neither the Cotton Genesis itself nor the source of the Millstatt Genesis. In the Cotton and Klagenfurt manu-

[42] See note 6, above.

[43] See note 12, above.

[44] Cf. Weitzmann, "Observations," p. 117.

[45] Weitzmann, "Septuagint," pp. 45ff.

scripts the Creator is identified as Christ by his cross nimbus. This Christological feature is absent from all the ninth-century manuscripts and therefore seems not to have been in the model. It is not possible to ascertain the relationship of the model to the San Paolo frescoes because of the state of preservation of the paintings. The model of the Touronian Bibles must have been an extensive reflection of the Cotton Genesis archetype but was not clearly related to any of the other known copies.

The Genesis door at Hildesheim was based on the same ultimate model. The scenes of Enlivement, Introduction, Fall, Denial of Blame, Expulsion, Labor, and Slaughter of Abel are dependent on the Cotton Genesis tradition as are the illustrations of Adam in Eden (Gen., II, 15), the Offerings of Cain and Abel (Gen., IV, 3–4), and the Condemnation of Cain (Gen., IV, 9–11). The question arises: was the Hildesheim cycle based on an independent reflection of the archetype, on the model of the ninth-century Genesis pictures, or on a Touronian intermediary, presumably a lost Touronian Bible frontispiece?

At Hildesheim as in the Millstatt Genesis, Christ is bearded and wears a cross nimbus. This suggests that the Bernwardian cycle may have been derived from the archetype independently of the Carolingian Bibles. The beard and nimbus are also features of Christ on the right valve of the Hildesheim door, however, and it is possible that those features were derived from the New Testament illustrations.[46] Certain elements of the Hildesheim Genesis cycle tie it to the Touronian Bibles so closely that there can be little doubt that they were based on the same ultimate model. These include the angel-expeller and Eve's bower in the scene of labor. The Hildesheim depictions of the Enlivement and the Fall suggest that the relief cycle depended, not on the source, but on a Touronian frontispiece. The Enlivement is an adjusted composition paralleled in the San Paolo Bible and the scene of the Fall represents a merger of several of the original episodes similar to that in the Bamberg and Vivian Bibles. Together with Nordenfalk's demonstration that a Touronian Bible was known in Hildesheim during the eleventh century, these details are strong evidence that the Hildesheim Genesis cycle was copied from a lost ninth-century frontispiece. If it was, then the model used at Tours must have included the three episodes found only at Hildesheim as well as the sixteen or seventeen subjects depicted in the extant Bibles.

It is extremely unlikely that the nineteen or more episodes which can be restored to the model of the Touronian Bibles could have been illustrated on a single page. There would not have been sufficient space. What is more, the ninth-century frontispieces do not exhibit the consistency of arrangement or the distinct patterns of scene linkage that one would expect to discover had they been derived from a frontispiece model.

A manuscript with individual illustrations interspersed through its text is the type of model most consistent with the evidence. Two principal members of the Genesis family, the Cotton manuscript and the Millstatt paraphrase have such a format; and

---

[46] Wesenberg, *op. cit.*, pp. 77ff.

some sense of the separate scenes is still preserved in the neat columns of the Grandval page. Presumably each Touronian artist made an independent selection from this model to construct his frontispiece. Occasionally, as in the Drawing of the Rib and the Introduction, all the artists copied the same illustration. In other instances, such as the Creation of Adam, they chose different moments in the narrative sequence. The Grandval and Hildesheim masters selected the Enlivenment; the Vivian illuminator copied the Animation; and the San Paolo artist repeated both. Unique scenes appear in all the frontispieces. These resulted either from an unrepeated selection from the prototype or from the merger of individual scenes. In no case, however, did the Carolingian artists refer to a second Genesis model.

THE TEXTUAL SOURCES

The model of the Touronian frontispieces illustrated the Genesis text in an extremely literal manner. Virtually every verse of the second, third, and fourth chapters was represented by one and sometimes by several scenes. There can be no doubt, therefore, that the archetype was an illustrated Genesis.

Certain elements depicted in the miniatures were not, however, derived from the biblical text. These are: (1) an angel in prayer at the Creation of Adam;[47] (2) Eve's anachronistic presence at the Admonition; (3) the tree of knowledge represented as a fig tree; (4) the tempter as a serpent bearing a comb and beard; (5) an angel rather than the Lord God as the expeller; (6) Eve sitting in a bower after the expulsion; (7) Cain's use of a bludgeon to kill Abel, and (8) the Burial of Abel.

Like the Touronian Bibles, San Marco, San Paolo f.l.m., and the Millstatt Genesis represent the tempter as a serpent coiled around the tree. In the Grandval and Vivian Bibles and, hence, apparently also in the model, the serpent has a spotted back, dark underside, and bears a vermilion comb and beard. In the Vivian Bible, he also has teeth. The peculiar features of this creature are those of the mythical python-like beast described in ancient writings and named δράκων.[48] In the section on poisonous snakes in Nicander's *Theriaca*,[49] for example, this dragon is described, "radiant indeed does he appear, but in his jaw above and below are arrayed rows of teeth; gleaming eyes are below his brows, and lower down beneath his chin there is ever a beard of yellow stain." In his *De venenatis animalibus* Philumenus also noted that the dragon has projections

[47] The watching angels in the Grandval and Vivian Bibles and in the Millstatt Genesis are not to be confused with the personifications of the days that appear in scenes from the first chapter of Genesis in the Cotton Genesis (cf. Marie-Thérèse D'Alverny, "Les anges et les jours," *Cahiers Archéologiques*, IX [1957], 271ff. and T. Klauser, "Engel in der Kunst," *Reallexikon für Antike und Christentum*, V, col. 314). Judging from the Millstatt Genesis, we may conclude, as Köhler did, that the single angel of the Vivian Bible is a more accurate replication of the model. Pickering's identification of this angel as the Holy Spirit is not based on a study of the history of the pictorial tradition and is unconvincing ("Genesis," LXXXIII, 107).

[48] Cf. Pauly-Wissowa, *Realencyclopädie der classischen Altertumswissenschaft*, V², 164f. and second series, II¹, 508f.

[49] Nicander of Colophon, *The Poems and Poetical Fragments*, ed. A. S. F. Gow and A. F. Scholfield (Cambridge, 1953), lines 438f.

above his eyes and a beard.[50] Representations of the dragon in such manuscripts as the Morgan Library Dioscurides (Cod. 652, fol. 352ʳ)[51] confirm that the Grandval and Vivian serpent is the classical δράκων.

It must have been the ancient association of the dragon with the serpent that guarded the tree of the Hesperides that prompted the illustrator of Genesis to depict Satan in the form of a δράκων. Both Pherekydes and Euripides mention the δράκων in their accounts of the Hercules saga,[52] and the creature is represented in numerous works of art, including an antique pelike in Turin (Fig. 46).[53] The dragon entwined around the tree in the Hercules scene provided a perfect model for the representation of the Fall of man.[54]

The source of the other extra-biblical elements in the Carolingian depictions can now be identified as the *Vita Adae et Evae*, an apocryphon wrongly called the *Apocalypsis Mosis* in its Greek version, which was written in Hebrew or Aramaic during the first century.[55] Passages from the *Vita* describe many of the extra-biblical elements of the miniatures:

> When God blew into thee (Adam) the breath of life and thy face and likeness was made in the image of God, Michael also brought thee and made (the angels) worship thee in the sight of God... (*Vita,* XIII, 2).[56]

> When God made us, me and your mother, and placed us in paradise and gave us every tree bearing fruit to eat, he laid a prohibition on us concerning the tree of knowledge of good and evil which is in the midst of paradise (saying) "Do not eat of it" (*Vita,* XXXII, 1).[57]

> ... the leaves showered down from all the trees in my part, except the fig tree only. But I took leaves from it and made myself a girdle and it was from the very same plant of which I had eaten (*Apoc. Mos.,* XX, 4–5).[58]

[50] *Corpus medicorum Graecorum,* ed. Wellmann (Berlin, 1908), chapter 30.

[51] Pedanii Dioscurides Anazarbei, *De materia medica* (Paris, 1935), fol. 352ʳ.

[52] Pherekydes, fragment 33 and Euripides, *Hercules,* lines 394ff.

[53] Cf. F. Brommer, *Herakles* (Münster and Cologne, 1953), and *idem,* "Herakles und die Hesperiden auf Vasenbildern," *Jahrbuch des kaiserlichen deutschen archäologischen Instituts,* LVII (1942), 105ff. The engraving of the Turin vase is from E. Gerhard, *Abbildungen und kleinen Schriften* (Berlin, 1868), pl. XXI, 1.

[54] A bearded serpent also appears in the scene of the Fall of Man on a fourth-century sarcophagus in Verona. Cf. S. Esche, *Adam und Eva* (Düsseldorf, 1957), p. 28 and text illustration VI. For the influence of Hercules iconography in Christian art, cf. Esche, p. 11 and M. Simon, *Hercule et le christianisme* (Paris, 1955).

[55] Because the paraphrase must be reconstructed from the several translations, it is cited here in English. R. H. Charles, *The Apocrypha and Pseudepigrapha of the Old Testament* (Oxford, 1913) and O. Eissfeldt, *Einleitung in das Alte Testament* (Tübingen, 1964), pp. 822ff.

[56] L. Reygers, "Adam und Eva," *Reallexikon zur deutschen Kunstgeschichte,* I, cols. 126ff., correctly observed that the angel at the Creation of Adam is mentioned in the *Vita Adae et Evae.*

[57] The presence of Eve at the forbidding is also described by Josephus, *Antiquitates Judaicae,* I, 40.

[58] For a detailed discussion of the fig tree in Genesis iconography, including references to other literary sources, cf. O. Goetz, *Der Feigenbaum* (Berlin, 1965), pp. 18ff. Gen., III, 7 does report that "they stitched fig-leaves together and made themselves loincloths."

After I had worshipped the Lord, straightway Michael, God's archangel, seized my hand and cast me out of the paradise of the vision and of God's command. And Michael held a rod in his hands . . . (*Vita*, xxviii, 3–4). When they were driven out from Paradise they made themselves a booth and spent seven days mourning and lamenting in great grief (*Vita*, i, 1).[59]

For he (Abel) was unburied since the day when Cain his brother slew him: for wicked Cain took great pains to conceal (him) but could not, for the earth would not receive him for the body sprang up from the earth and a voice went out of the earth saying, "I will not receive a companion body till the earth which was taken and fashioned in me cometh to me" (*Apoc. Mos.*, xlvii, 3).[60]

Only Cain's club is not mentioned. The weapon used in the first fratricide was, however, the subject of extended rabbinical discussion.[61] The favored opinion seems to have been that Abel died from a stoning;[62] but at least one school of thought held that he was struck with a club:

"With what did he kill him?" Rabbi Simeon said: "He killed him with a staff: 'And a young man for my bruising' (Gen., iv, 23) implies a weapon which inflicts a bruise."[63]

Elements based on Jewish legend and exegesis were features not only of the Carolingian frontispieces but of the archetype as well.[64] The fig tree and Cain's bludgeon appear throughout the pictorial family, the praying angel is found in the Millstatt Genesis, and Eve is present at the Admonition in the Hortus Deliciarum.[65] If the archetype of the Cotton Genesis family was so rich in extra-biblical elements, why is the most extensive reflection of it, the San Marco cycle, relatively free of them? Weitzmann has demonstrated that the thirteenth-century mosaicists had introduced Christian elements into the sixth-century source cycle.[66] It is also possible that the Cotton manuscript itself was a Christianization of the archetype. The Creator's cross scepter and

---

[59] The similar bower in the Ashburnham Pentateuch has been associated with the *Vita Adae et Evae* by H.-L. Hempel, "Jüdische Traditionen in frühmittelalterlichen Miniaturen," *Beiträge zur Kunstgeschichte und Archäologie des Frühmittelalters* (*Akten zum VII. internationalen Kongress für Frühmittelalterforschung*, 1958) (Graz and Köln, 1962), pp. 53ff.

[60] Kessler; "Unnoticed Scene," p. 118. The Bible implies that Cain buried Abel when it reports that the "brother's blood that has been shed is crying out to me from the ground," but only the *Vita Adae et Evae* accounts fully for the unusual scene in the Bamberg Bible.

[61] L. Ginzberg, *The Legends of the Jews* (Philadelphia, 1909ff.), v, 139ff.

[62] In the Octateuchs, he is stoned. Cf. Weitzmann, "The Question of the Influence of Jewish Pictorial Sources on Old Testament Illustration," *Studies*, pp. 82ff.

[63] *Midrash Rabbah*, trans. and ed. H. Freedman and M. Simon (London, 1939 and 1961), p. 188.

[64] Weitzmann has discovered the penetration of legend elsewhere in the Cotton Genesis illustrations, "Jewish Pictorial Sources," pp. 88ff.

[65] Cf. Green, *op. cit.*, p. 344. The fact that the Admonition was omitted in all other reflections of the Cotton Genesis archetype suggests that the scene may have been deleted because it included Eve.

[66] "The Mosaics of San Marco and the Cotton Genesis," *Venezia e l'Europa XVIII Congresso Internazionale di Storia dell'Arte* (Venice, 1955), pp. 152f.

cross nimbus were certainly features of the Cotton manuscript (cf. Fig. 16); but the Touronian Bibles raise doubts that they were also details of the archetype. The Carolingian frontispieces thereby gain importance as independent witnesses of the Cotton Genesis tradition, possibly of an early state.

The use of Jewish sources to supplement the Bible text raises the complex question of whether the archetype was of Jewish or Christian origin.[67] An extensive penetration of Jewish legendary elements in Christian Old Testament art has been discovered in recent decades. There is no agreement among scholars, however, as to whether the transmission of Jewish exegesis and legend was primarily a literary phenomenon[68] or whether the elements were derived from a Jewish pictorial tradition.[69] The evidence of the Carolingian Bibles must now be added to this continuing discussion of the Jewish contribution to Christian art.

Because the legends in the *Vita Adae et Evae* were the common property of Jews and Christians, they do not provide evidence of the origin of the archetype.[70] Cain's bludgeon is also not strong proof of a Jewish origin. It should be noted, nonetheless, that Christians were never as interested in Old Testament paraphrases as were the Jews.

The anthropomorphic Creator is an element of the Genesis cycles that suggests a Christian rather than a Jewish origin of the prototype. In San Marco and in the Millstatt Genesis, the nimbus identifies the Creator as Christ. In the Carolingian Bibles, the Creator is a beardless young man with long dark hair. He wears a tunic and long mantle, carries a scroll, and bears a simple gold halo.[71] Even without the *tituli*, the Creator in the ninth-century illustrations would certainly have been identified as Christ. Incarnation distinguishes the Christian from the Jewish conception of the Creator-Logos.[72] Even Philo, whose writings became the basis of the Christian formulation of

---

[67] Cf. *No Graven Images*, ed. J. Gutmann (New York, 1971).

[68] H. Strauss, "Jüdische Quellen frühchristlicher Kunst: Optische oder literarische Anregung," *Zeitschrift für die Neutestamentliche Wissenschaft*, LVII (1966), 114ff. and J. Gutmann, "The Illustrated Jewish Manuscript in Antiquity," *Gesta*, V (1966), 39ff. Gutmann accepts the possibility that the Ashburnham Pentateuch may have had a Jewish model.

[69] O. Pächt, "Ephraimillustration, Haggadah und Wiener Genesis," *Festschrift Karl M. Swoboda* (Vienna, 1959), pp. 218ff.; H.-L. Hempel, "Zum Problem der AT Illustration," *Zeitschrift für die Alttestamentliche Wissenschaft*, LXIX (1957), 122ff. and "Jüdische Traditionen"; Weitzmann, "Jewish Pictorial Sources."

[70] For a discussion of related problems see: G. Kretschmer, "Ein beitrag zur Frage nach dem Verhältnis zwischen Jüdischer und Christlicher Kunst in der Antike," in *Abraham unser Vater, Festschrift für Otto Michel* (Leiden, 1963), pp. 300ff. and C.-O. Nordström, "Rabbinic Features

in Byzantine and Catalan Art," *Cahiers Archéologiques*, XV (1965), 179ff.

[71] As in the Cotton Genesis, the Creator in the Vivian Bible holds a scepter, but it is not possible to ascertain whether this attribute also appeared in the prototype. In the Grandval and San Paolo Bibles and in the Hildesheim reliefs, the Creator is depicted holding a book, an attribute also found in the Salerno Antependium.

[72] For discussions of the concept of the Logos in Judaism and the early church consult: A. Aall, *Geschichte der Logosidee* (Leipzig, 1896); G. Armstrong, *Die Genesis in der alten Kirche* (Tübingen, 1962); H. Hegermann, *Die Vorstellung vom Schöpfungsmittler im hellenistischen Judentum und Urchristentum* (Berlin, 1961); J. Jervel, *Imago Dei* (Göttingen, 1960); W. Kelber, *Die Logoslehre von Heraklit bis Origenes* (Stuttgart, 1958); G. Lindeskog, *Studien zum Neutestamentliche Schöpfungsgedanken* (Uppsala, 1952); and H. Wolfson, *The Philosophy of the Church Fathers* (Cambridge, Mass., 1956).

the Creator-Logos, did not conceive of the Logos as a corporeal being.[73] He states this clearly in his *Questions on Exodus*, "But the divine Logos, which is established over all things, is immaterial, being, as it were, not impressed upon them but expressed, for it is external to all substances and to all corporeal and incorporeal elements."[74] Christians, however, attempting to merge the Creator-Logos of Philonic philosophy with the incarnate Logos of St. John, espoused its corporeality and identified it with Christ.[75] The Christian origin of the prototype cannot be doubted.

It is possible, nevertheless, that in its earliest stage, the cycle of illustrations did not include the anthropomorphic Creator. The Christ-Logos could have been inserted at a subsequent time. He appears only at the beginning of the cycle; and following the Expulsion, God is represented exclusively by the heavenly hand. Perhaps in the archetype, as in the Vienna Genesis and the Octateuchs, the Hand of God was used throughout the cycle. If it was, then the ultimate model may well have been Jewish.[76] A final decision about the origin of the "Jewish" elements, however, must await a full study of the Cotton Genesis family.[77]

Köhler assumed that the Latin verses accompanying the Genesis scenes in the Grandval and Vivian Bibles were the source of the illustrations; and he used them to determine the relative authority of each depiction, "Wenn bei Unterschieden zwischen den beiden Fassungen die eine dem Wortlaut des zugehörigen Titulus mehr entspricht als die andere, hat sie Anspruch darauf als die zuverlässigere Wiedergabe der Vorlage zu gelten."[78] Clearly, however, the illustrations were based on the Bible and certain exegetic texts. Their closeness to these is the best index of their faithfulness to the model.

In fact, the relationship of the Grandval and Vivian representations to the Latin *tituli* is very general. The verses follow the main action.

ADAM PRIMUS UTI FINGITUR ISTIC

CUIUS COSTA SACRAE CARPITUR EVAE

CHRISTUS EVAM DUCIT ADAE, QUAM VOCAT VIRAGINEM

[73] For an analysis of Philo's philosophy see: H. Wolfson, *Philo* (Cambridge, Mass., 1947). E. R. Goodenough (*Introduction to Philo Judaeus* [New York, 1963], pp. 103ff.) has pointed out the error in Colson's translation of Philo's term "logos" by the English "word." He suggests that the "reader of Philo or of the early Christian thought must first of all wipe that meaning from his mind and use the untranslated logos."

[74] *Philo*, trans. F. Colson and G. Whitaker (London, 1929).

[75] Theophilus, *To Autolycus*, II, 10, 22; Justin Martyr, *Dialogue with Typho*, 62; Clement of Alexandria, *The Instructor*, I, 10; Athenagoras, *A Plea for the Christians*, 10; Origen, *Against Celsus*, V, 37; Irenaeus, *Against Heresies*, XX.

[76] In Jewish art, the Hand of God was used to avoid representing God. Cf. H. Stern, *Le Calendrier de 354* (Paris, 1953), pp. 150ff. and T. Klauser, "Der Beitrag der orientalischen Religionen inbesondere des Christentums zur spätantiken und frühmittelalterlichen Kunst," *Atti del Convegno Internazionale sul tema: Tardo e Alto Medioevo* (Rome, 1967), pp. 31ff.

[77] The same problem faces students of the Ashburnham Pentateuch wherein the original dual-Creator also derives from Christian exegesis but where the narrative is rich in "Jewish" features. Cf. Narkiss, *op. cit.*, pp. 45ff.; Gutmann, "Illustrated Jewish Manuscript," p. 40; and Weitzmann, "Jewish Pictorial Traditions," pp. 91ff.

[78] *Kar. Min.*, I₂, 118.

AST EDANT NE POMA VITAE PROHIBET IPSE CONDITOR

SUADET NUPER CREATAE ANGUIS DOLO PUELLAE

POST HAEC AMOENA LUSTRANS ADAM VOCAT REDEMPTOR

UTERQUE AB UMBRIS PELLITUR INDE SACRIS

ET IAM LABORI RURA COLUNT HABITI.[79]

They do not, however, refer to numerous details in the illustrations: the onlooking angels, fig tree, the Eating of the Fruit,[80] the angel-expeller, Eve's child and booth. These, like the other elements of the miniatures, were derived from the Bible or other texts. It is possible that the verses were actually composed from the pictures. This is indicated by the reference to the couple in the Admonition caption.

The illuminators of the Grandval and Vivian Bibles apparently used the verses, not as the source of the illustrations, but as the means for selecting the scenes from their richly illustrated model. Thus, to represent the first line, the Grandval illuminator chose the scene of Enlivenment and the Vivian artist selected the Animation. To depict the next two lines, they copied the same scenes. Only the Grandval illustrator represented the Admonition; but for the Temptation, the two illuminators again drew upon the same compositions. For the Calling and Expulsion, the Grandval and Vivian illuminators copied different narrative phrases, but for Labor after Expulsion their model was once more the same. As a result of this process, sometimes the Grandval Bible and in other cases the Vivian Bible is closer to the *tituli*.[81]

The *tituli* in the Bamberg Bible are closer to the miniatures than are the Grandval-Vivian captions.

FORMAVIT IGITUR D(OMI)N(U)S ADAM DE LIMO TERRAE

ET ADDUX(IT) EI CUNCTA ANIMANTIA NOMINA INPONENDI.

MULIERE(M) DE COSTA FACTA(M) ADDUX(IT) D(OMI)N(U)S AD ADA(M)

P(RAE)VARICATIO GUSTU(S) LIGNI P(ER) SERPEN(T)E(M)

APERTIS OCULIS CONSUER(UNT) FOL(IA) FICI.

INCREPAN(T)E D(OMI)NO ADA(M) SUPER EVA(M) CRIM(EN)

INPONIT ET EVA SUP(ER) SERP(EN)T(EM)

EICIUNT(UR) AMBO DE PARADISO P(RO)PT(ER) CRIM(EN).

CONPELLIT(UR) ADA(M) OPERARE TERR(AM)

HIC CAIN INT(ER)FECTU(M) ABEL ABSC(ON)DIT HUMO

EVA NUTRIT INFANTES.[82]

The close relationship between the pictures and *tituli* is the result of the direct dependence of each on the Bible text.

[79] *Kar. Min.*, I₂, 119ff.

[80] Köhler had noted this, *Kar. Min.*, I₂, 122f.

[81] Grandval is closer in the Creation of Adam and Admonition; Vivian is closer in the Calling.

[82] The Alcuinian *tituli* adduced by Corssen have little relationship to the Bamberg verses. Cf. K. Menzel *et al., Die Trier Ada-Handschrift* (Leipzig, 1889), p. 75. Dr. Diane LeBerrurier and Dr. Wilhelm Schleicher graciously helped to prepare the transcription of the Bamberg Bible *tituli*.

The closeness of the *tituli* and pictures in the San Paolo Bible, on the other hand, seems to be due to the fact that the verses were based on the illustrations.[83]

> HIC HOMO FORMATUR PULCHRO SUB AGALMATE PRIMUS.
>
> CELSITHRONI VERBO DICTU MIRABILE CUNCTIS.
>
> DENIQUE SPIRATUR PRORSUSQ: SOPORE GRAVATUR
>
> AC LATERALIS EI SOCIATUR HABENDA VIRAGO
>
> SICQUE SUA LAETUS GAUDET DE VIRGINE VIRGO
>
> ATTAMEN HANC SERPENS VICIAVIT FRAUDE MALIGNA
>
> EXHINC ILLA VIRUM VETITI PER MUNERA POMI.
>
> SIC MANET AEQUALIS PRIMAE SUGGESTIO FRAUDIS.
>
> PELLERIS HIC ADAM PARADYSI SEDE RELICTA.
>
> FLAMMEUS ET GLADIUM TIBI CLAUSERAT ANTRA SALUTIS.
>
> SUBDERE TERRENIS IMPRESSO VOMERE SULCIS
>
> HIS MERITO SERVIS, QUI SPONTE SUPERNA RELINQUIS.[84]

It is possible that the lost Touronian model of the San Paolo frontispiece was built on the Grandval-Vivian captions. Although the specific phases differ, the San Paolo miniature follows the same sequence: Creation of Adam, Creation of Eve, Introduction, Admonition (missing as in the Vivian Bible), Temptation, Calling, Expulsion, and Labor.

The Hildesheim sequence conforms to none of the known *tituli*.

CONCLUSIONS

The four ninth-century Genesis frontispieces and the Touronian model of the Hildesheim door were independent reflections of the same prototype. Each preserves some aspect of that model which is missing in the other copies and each deviates from it in an individual manner. A careful comparison of the five cycles, however, leads to a reasonably accurate reconstruction of the source.

The model that was available in ninth-century Tours must have been an extensively illustrated Book of Genesis. Nineteen scenes from chapters two through four alone were copied onto the Bible frontispieces. These were certainly not arranged on a single page but were interspersed throughout the text. The model was closely related to the family of manuscripts associated with the Cotton Genesis; but it was independent of the known members of this family. The richness of extra-biblical features and the almost total absence of specifically Christian elements suggest that the model may have been a fairly pure witness of the archetype.[85] Iconographic purity is not in itself an indication of date. Only an analysis of style can possibly suggest the date and origin

[83] Gaehde, "Bible Manuscript," II, 132 and "Turonian Sources," pp. 365ff.

[84] Gaehde, "Bible Manuscript," II, 137.

[85] Of the extant members of the Cotton Genesis family, the Klagenfurt manuscript is closest to the Carolingian Bibles.

of the model; but attempting to read the style of the model through the copies has proven to be hazardous.[86]

Carolingian artists, not a fifth- or sixth-century illuminator were responsible for constructing full-page frontispieces from the column-picture model. They selected scenes from the picture source, arranged them on horizontal registers, and added captions to help explain the scenes that were now divorced from the text. Often, the artists chose the same scenes from the model; frequently, they made somewhat different selections. Their purpose seems to have been the same, however; to reduce the cycle in an extensive, narrative model to a format that was better suited to a full pandect.

[86] Köhler tried to show that the model was fifth century (*Kar. Min.*, I₂, 164ff.). Schmid proposed a date almost one hundred years later (*Bibel von Moutier-Grandval*, p. 174).

III. THE GOSPEL FRONTISPIECES

UNLIKE the Genesis pages, the frontispieces to the Gospels differ considerably in the four Bibles. They do share certain elements with one another. They are all designed as full-page compositions organized by a rhomboid frame set in a rectangle, and they all include evangelist symbols and portraits of the four major prophets. The Bamberg page (Fig. 47),[1] however, is focused on the Lamb of God within a green clipeus. The clipeus also contains a book roll and chalice and is crossed by a lance and a sponge-pole. In the Grandval Bible (Fig. 48),[2] a youthful Christ, enthroned on a globe within a blue mandorla, occupies the center of the page; while in the Vivian (Fig. 49)[3] and San Paolo Bibles (Fig. 50),[4] Christ is bearded and the four evangelists are represented in the corners of the page.

Depictions of Christ served as frontispieces in earlier Gospelbooks and the theme had entered Touronian art during the abbacy of Fridigus.[5] The pages in the Bibles share features with these precursors; it is clear that they were derived from pre-existent sources. In form and meaning, however, the compositions in the Bible manuscripts are more complex than the known examples that preceded them. Apparently, the Touronian illuminators freely transformed their prototypes to create appropriate New Testament frontispieces for their great pandects. The variations within the several manuscripts indicate that the artists did not immediately develop a satisfactory composition but continued to experiment with the *Majestas* theme for some time.

MAJESTAS DOMINI

Although it is not certain that the Grandval frontispiece predates the Bamberg page, because it is closely related to depictions produced during the abbacy of Fridigus and because the *Majestas Domini* became the standard theme in the later Bibles, it is best to begin with the Grandval composition.

The earliest surviving *Majestas* page from Tours contains the essential elements of the Grandval frontispiece. This is the opening page in the Weingarten Gospels of c. 830 (Stuttgart, Württembergische Landesbibliothek, Cod. H.B. II, 40, fol. 1ᵛ, Fig. 51)[6]

[1] Fol. 339ᵛ. Köhler, *Kar. Min.*, I₂, 102ff.

[2] Fol. 352ᵛ. Köhler, *Kar. Min.*, I₂, 132ff.; Schmid, *Bibel von Moutier-Grandval*, pp. 157ff.

[3] Fol. 329ᵛ. Köhler, *Kar. Min.*, I₂, 132ff.

[4] Fol. 259ᵛ. Gaehde, "Bible Manuscript," I, 374ff. and "Turonian Sources," pp. 381ff.

[5] Of the numerous studies of the *Majestas Domini*, the most useful are: F. van der Meer, *Maiestas Domini: theophanies de l'Apocalypse dans l'art chrétien* (Rome, 1938); H. B. Meyer, "Zur Symbolik frühmittelalterlicher Majestasbilder," *Das Münster*, XIV (1961), 73ff.; F. Rademacher, *Der thronende Christus der Chorschrank-* en aus *Gustorf* (Cologne, 1964); U. Nilgen, "Der Codex Douce 292 der Bodleian Library zu Oxford" (Unpublished doctoral dissertation, Bonn: Rheinischen Friedrich-Wilhelms Universität, 1967); M. Werner, "The Majestas Domini and the Eastern Penetration of Hiberno-Saxon Art" (Unpublished doctoral dissertation, New York, New York University, 1967); C. Nordenfalk, *Codex Caesareus Upsaliensis* (Stockholm, 1971), pp. 103ff. and G. Schiller, *Ikonographie der christlichen Kunst*, III (Kassel, 1971).

[6] Köhler, *Kar. Min.*, I₂, 240ff.

which represents Christ, enthroned on a pale blue globe within a large blue mandorla. In one hand, Christ holds an open book which bears the inscription: ΦWC-ZWH; in the other, he holds a cross-staff. Symbols of the four evangelists, holding books, are depicted above and below, to the left and to the right of Christ within the mandorla.

Köhler argued that the Stuttgart and Grandval *Majestas* pages had been derived from different models—the latter from the hypothetical "Leo Bible" and the former from his model Y, a Roman Gospelbook presumably produced between 650 and 750.[7] The general agreement of the two representations and the close parallels between the Christ figures, the evangelist symbols, the globe thrones and mandorlas suggest, instead, that the Grandval page is an elaboration of the same pictorial prototype of which the Weingarten Gospels is an independent replica.

Later Touronian Gospel frontispieces seem also to reflect the same model. The *Majestas Domini* in the Prüm Gospels (Berlin, Staatsbibliothek, Theol. lat. fol. 733, fol. 17ᵛ, Fig. 52)[8] is one that represents the youthful Christ on a globe holding an open book. As in the Grandval Bible, the book is blank and the evangelist symbols are outside the mandorla; the rendering of Christ's garments is remarkably alike in the two manuscripts. In the Prüm *Majestas*, Christ holds a gold disk in his right hand, his feet rest on an arc, and the evangelist symbols occupy the four corners of the page. Köhler believed that the Prüm *Majestas* was a fusion of the two models represented, respectively, by the Weingarten and Grandval frontispieces. It is likelier that all three compositions are variations on the same model.

The origins of that model are difficult to determine. Christ surrounded by the evangelist symbols was a popular frontispiece theme in the earliest Carolingian Gospelbooks. It is found in the Gundohinus Gospels of A.D. 754 (Autun, Bibliothèque Municipale, MS. 3, fol. 12ᵛ. Fig. 53)[9] and it is represented in a number of other eighth- and ninth-century manuscripts.[10] These, however, present Christ seated on a throne within a clipeus and they depict the evangelist symbols in circular medallions at the corners of the page. Of the earlier Carolingian Gospel pages, only the *Majestas Domini* in the Xanten Gospels (Brussels, Bibliothèque Royale, MS. 18723, fol. 16ᵛ, Fig. 54)[11] shares specific features with the Touronian frontispieces. Christ sits on a blue orb and half-length evangelist symbols emerge from an atmospherically rendered landscape.

Christ in Majesty was also depicted in Apocalypse manuscripts and the representations of the theme in the early ninth-century Trier Apocalypse (Stadtbibliothek, Cod. 31)[12] are especially close to the Touronian pages. On folio 15ᵛ (Fig. 55) for example,

[7] Köhler, *Kar. Min.*, I₂, 238ff.

[8] Köhler, *Kar. Min.*, I₂, 240ff.

[9] E. H. Zimmermann, *Vorkarolingische Miniaturen* (Berlin, 1916), pp. 182ff.; *Charlemagne*, p. 243.

[10] Codex Amiatinus (Florence, Biblioteca Medicea-Laurenziana, Cod. Am. 1), fol. 796ᵛ; Echternach Gospels (Trier, Cathedral Library, Cod. 61) fol. 1ᵛ; Sainte-Croix Gospels (Poitiers, Bibliothèque Municipale, MS. 17), fol. 31ʳ; and Lorsch Gospels (Bucharest, National Library), p. 36. The enthroned Christ without evangelist symbols was also a popular frontispiece theme; cf. Werner, *op. cit.*, pp. 290ff.

[11] Köhler, *Kar. Min.*, II, 72ff. and F. Mütherich, "Buchmalerei am Hofe," *Karl der Grosse*, III, 49.

[12] *Charlemagne*, pp. 301ff.; B. Bischoff, "Panorama der Handschriftenüberlieferung aus der Zeit

Christ is shown seated on a globe amid the four beasts. The Trier manuscript was apparently copied from an early Roman model.[13] Certainly, the globe-throne is an Italic feature. In Rome, Christ enthroned on a globe was depicted during the fourth century in the apse of Sta. Costanza.[14] Subsequently, the globe-throne was used in S. Teodoro, S. Agata dei Goti, and S. Lorenzo f.l.m.[15] In San Lorenzo as in the Weingarten Gospels, Christ holds a cross-staff. Christ enthroned on a heavenly sphere was also depicted in the apse of San Vitale in Ravenna[16] and in the Basilica Eufrasiana at Parenzo.[17] The globe-throne entered Byzantine art during the tenth century,[18] but it remained exceedingly rare in the East.

Although the motif may have originated in monumental art, the orb-throne had migrated to other media by the fifth century. It is an element in the scene of Christ and the Widow's Mite on an ivory diptych in Milan (Cathedral Treasury),[19] and it appears in the frontispiece to the third book of St. Ambrose's *De fide catholica* in a late fifth-century Italian manuscript preserved in St. Paul in Lavanttal (Cod. 1, 1, fol. 72ᵛ, Fig. 56).[20] The latter does not include the four evangelist symbols and therefore is not strictly a *Majestas Domini*, but the St. Paul in Lavanttal page constitutes important evidence that the illustrations in the Brussels Gospels and the Trier Apocalypse were based on an early Roman prototype. It is likely that the Touronian frontispieces were derived from the same type of model.

Certain elements of the Touronian *Majestas* compositions originated, not in Italy, but in Byzantium. Of these, the mandorla is the most significant. Distinct from the round clipeus, the oval mandorla appeared first in eastern art where it was commonly used in representations of the Ascension of Christ.[21] The mandorla was also a feature

---

des Karls des Grossen," *Karl der Grosse*, II, 240; P. Klein, "Der Kodex und sein Bildschmuck," *Trierer Apokalypse* Kommentarband (Graz, 1975). Klein concluded that "Entstehung im ersten Viertel des 9. Jahrhunderts, vermutlich in der Zeit nach Alkuins Tod .... in einem westfränkischen (nordfranzösischen?) Skriptorium im Einflussgebiet von Tours entstanden; eine Herkunft aus Tours selbst ist unwahrscheinlich, aber nicht völlig auszuschliessen." pp. 59 and 69.

[13] W. Neuss, *Die Apokalypse des Hl. Johannes in der altspanischen und altchristlichen Bibelillustration* (Münster, 1931), pp. 365ff.; J. Snyder, "The Reconstruction of an Early Christian Cycle of Illustrations for the Book of Revelation—The Trier Apocalypse," *Vigiliae Christianae*, XVIII (1964), 146ff.; Klein, *op. cit., passim*.

[14] C. Ihm, *Die Programme der Christlichen Apsismalerei vom Vierten Jahrhundert bis zur Mitte des Achten Jahrhunderts* (Wiesbaden, 1960), pp. 129ff.

[15] *Ibid.*, pp. 140f., 153f., 138f.

[16] *Ibid.*, pp. 163f.

[17] *Ibid.*, pp. 167f.

[18] Cf. the Ascension ivory in Florence (Museo Nazionale); A. Goldschmidt and K. Weitzmann, *Die byzantinischen Elfenbeinskulpturen* (Berlin, 1930–34), II, no. 58.

[19] F. Volbach, *Elfenbeinarbeit der Spätantike und des frühen Mittelalters* (Mainz, 1952).

[20] *Charlemagne*, pp. 230f. For an eleventh-century representation of the globe-throne that may reflect a sixth-century Ravennate depiction, consult B. Bischoff and W. Köhler, "Eine illustrierte Ausgabe der spätantiken Ravennater Annalen," *Medieval Studies in Memory of A. Kingsley Porter* (Cambridge, Mass., 1939), pp. 125ff. E. Rosenbaum has argued that the mosaics of San Vitale were derived from an illustrated Gospels, cf. "The Evangelist Portraits of the Ada School and their Models," *Art Bulletin*, XXXVIII (1956), 84ff.

[21] W. Cook, "The Carolingian Globe-Mandorla," *Art Bulletin*, VI (1923–24), 47ff.; A. Baumstark, "Die karolingische-romanische Majestas Domini und ihre orientalische Parallelen," *Oriens Christianus*, Ser. 3, I (1926–27), 242ff.

in eastern depictions of the Vision of Ezekiel. The seventh-century Emmanuel Icon from Syria or Palestine on Mt. Sinai (Fig. 57),[22] presents Christ enthroned within a blue oval that, as in the Weingarten and Prüm Gospels, is decorated with rosette stars. The Sinai icon is badly damaged, but the remains indicate that originally the four evangelist symbols were depicted emerging from behind the aureole. The winged man and vestiges of the eagle are still visible at the upper left and right. The inscription on Christ's book can also be deciphered. It is the passage from the eighth chapter of John, "he shall have the light of life," the very passage that is abbreviated in the Weingarten depiction.

The most famous eastern representation of the theme is the fifth-century apse mosaic in Hosios David in Saloniki.[23] Christ is beardless in the Greek mosaic and, in addition to the four evangelist symbols, the composition includes representations of the fountain of life, Ezekiel, and Habakkuk. Christ in Majesty was especially popular in Coptic and Cappadocian art;[24] and the theme occasionally was depicted in Byzantine manuscripts. A *Majestas Domini* serves as a frontispiece in the early twelfth-century Gospelbook from Constantinople in the Marciana in Venice (Cod. Z. 540, fol. 11[v], Fig. 58).[25] The Marciana composition is distinctly eastern: Christ sits on a rainbow with his feet on an arc and the evangelist symbols emerge from behind the aureole. (Ezekiel and Isaiah are also portrayed.) The parallels with the Carolingian compositions, especially with the Prüm frontispiece, are striking.

The Eastern version of the *Majestas Domini* may have been known in the West even before the Carolingian period. It was used to decorate one side of the sarcophagus of Agilbert at Jouarre (Fig. 59), which has been assigned to the seventh century.[26] The Merovingian sculptor copied his model faithfully, although he neglected to indicate the throne on which Christ is sitting.

The Touronian *Majestas* compositions merge features from both the eastern and western versions of the theme. The Greek inscription in the Weingarten manuscript, the evangelist symbols that turn their backs to Christ in the Grandval Bible, and the arc footrest in the Prüm Gospels are indications that the merger of the two sources was undertaken independently several times in the scriptorium of St. Martin's. The most important hybrid element, the globe-mandorla, was known earlier and may have been derived from a mixed model. The globe-mandorla appears in the Trier Apocalypse (fol. 14[v], Fig. 60), in the Stuttgart Psalter (Württembergische Landesbibliothek, Cod.

---

[22] K. Weitzmann, *The Icons in the St. Catherine Monastery on Mount Sinai* (Princeton, 1976), pp. 41ff.

[23] Ihm, *op. cit.*, pp. 182f. and Van der Meer, *op. cit.*, pp. 255ff.

[24] J. Lafontaine-Dosogne, "Théophanies-Visions auxquelles participent les prophètes dans l'art byzantine après la restauration des images," *Synthronon* (*Bibliothèque des Cahiers Archéologiques*,

II), pp. 135ff. and Werner, *loc. cit.*

[25] *Byzantine Art, An European Art* (catalogue of an exhibition, Athens, 1964), no. 316 and P. Bloch and H. Schnitzler, *Die Ottonische-Kölner Malerschule* (Düsseldorf, 1967ff.), II, 88f.

[26] B. Brenk, "Marginalien zum sog. Sarkophag des Agilbert in Jouarre," *Cahiers Archéologiques*, XIV (1964), 95ff.

fol. 23, fols. 22ʳ and 127ᵛ),[27] and in the Utrecht[28] and Troyes Psalters[29] (Utrecht, Bibliotheek der Rijksuniversiteit and Troyes, Cathedral, MS. 12, fol. 41ᵛ). When and where the globe-throne was first merged with the mandorla remains uncertain. The combined motif is unknown before the ninth century, however, and there is every reason to believe that it was a Carolingian innovation.[30]

The *Majestas Domini* was derived from two biblical texts:

I saw a storm wind coming from the north, a vast cloud with flashes of fire and brilliant light about it; and within was a radiance like brass, glowing in the heart of the flames. In the fire was the semblance of four living creatures in human form. . . . Their faces were like this: all four had the face of a man and the face of a lion on the right, on the left the face of an ox and the face of an eagle (Ezek., I, 4ff.).

There in heaven stood a throne and on the throne sat one whose appearance was like the gleam of jasper and cornelian; and round the throne was a rainbow, bright as an emerald. In the circle about this throne were twenty-four other thrones, and on them sat twenty-four elders, robed in white and wearing crowns of gold. . . . In the center, round the throne itself, were four living creatures, covered with eyes, in front and behind. The first creature was like a lion, the second like an ox, the third had a human face, the fourth was like an eagle in flight. The four living creatures, each of them with six wings, had eyes all over, inside and out; and by day and by night without pause they sang: "Holy, holy, holy is God the sovereign Lord of all, who was, and is, and is to come" (Rev., IV, 1ff.).

The Touronian illuminators also drew upon Isa. LXVI, 1, "Heaven is my throne and earth my footstool."

In choosing the *Majestas Domini* as the theme of their Gospel frontispieces, medieval illuminators must have been guided by Jerome's Gospel preface that begins *Plures fuisse*.[31] This prologue is included in all the Touronian manuscripts,[32] and is

---

[27] B. Bischoff *et al.*, *Der Stuttgarter Bilderpsalter* (Stuttgart, 1965), fols. 22ʳ and 127ᵛ.

[28] E. T. Dewald, *The Illustrations of the Utrecht Psalter* (Princeton, 1933), fols. 4ᵛ, 5ʳ, 7ᵛ, 11ʳ, 11ᵛ, 16ʳ, 20ᵛ, 27ʳ, 30ʳ, 40ᵛ, 47ʳ, 48ʳ, 51ᵛ, 55ᵛ, 56ʳ, 56ᵛ, 57ʳ, 58ᵛ, 60ᵛ, 63ᵛ, 64ᵛ, 76ᵛ, 77ᵛ, 79ᵛ, 82ᵛ, 86ᵛ, 88ʳ, and 89ᵛ.

[29] S. Dufrenne, "Deux psautiers carolingiens à Oxford et à Troyes," *Synthronon*, pp. 167ff. The fact that Christ and the globe-mandorla are not represented in the Douce Psalter (Oxford, Bodleian, Douce 59, fol. 51ᵛ) is good evidence that they were not in the prototype. Dufrenne has argued that the Douce manuscript is the best witness of the Early Christian archetype and that the Utrecht and Troyes Psalters were based on a modified intermediary.

[30] Cook, *op. cit.*, pp. 47ff. and Van der Meer,

op. cit., pp. 328ff.

[31] D. de Bruyne, *Les préfaces de la Bible latine* (Namur, 1920), pp. 155f. and *PL*, XXVI, cols. 15ff. For the influence of biblical prefaces on other Carolingian manuscripts, cf. R. Walker, "Illustrations to the Priscillian Prologues in the Gospel Manuscripts of the Carolingian Ada School," *Art Bulletin*, XXX (1948), 1ff. and P. Underwood, "The Fountain of Life in Manuscripts of the Gospels," *Dumbarton Oaks Papers*, V (1950), 43ff. Underwood connected the Soissons Gospels Fountain of Life page (Paris, Bibliothèque Nationale, Cod. lat. 8850, fol. 6ᵛ, Fig. 86) with the *Plures fuisse*.

[32] It is found in the Weingarten, Prüm, Lothar, Dufay, and Le Mans Gospels and in the Bamberg, Grandval, and Vivian Bibles. It also appears in the San Paolo Bible.

associated with earlier depictions of the theme.[33] In the *Plures fuisse*, Jerome set out to affirm the authenticity of the four Gospels and he used as his principal authorities precisely those Bible passages that were the bases of the *Majestas* pictures, the Vision of Ezekiel and the fourth chapter of Revelation.

> Haec igitur quattuor Evangelia multum ante praedicta, hiezechielis quoque volumen probat, in quo prima visio ita contexitur: "Et in medio sicut similitudo quattuor animalium: et vultus eorum facies hominis, et facies leonis, et facies vituli, et facies aquilae" (Ezek., I, 5). Prima hominis facies Mattheum significat, . . . Secundum Marcum, . . . Tertia vituli, quae evangelistam Lucam a Zacharia sacerdote sumsisse initium praefiguravit. Quarta Joannem evangelistam, . . . Unde et Apocalypsis Joannis, post expositionem viginti quattuor seniorum qui tenentes citharas et phialas, adorant Agnum Dei, introducit fulgura, et tonitrua et septem spiritus discurrentes, et mare vitreum et quattuor animalia plena oculis (Apoc., IV, 4–6), dicens: "Animal primum simile leoni, et secundum simile vitulo, et tertium simile homini, et quartum simile aquilae volanti" (Apoc., IV, 7). Et post paululum: "Plena erant, inquit oculis et requiem non habebant die ac nocte, dicentia: sanctus, sanctus, sanctus Dominus Deus omnipotens qui erat, et qui est, et qui venturis est."[34]

Jerome's preface explains the popularity of the *Majestas Domini* as the theme of Gospel frontispieces. In the prologue, the theophanic visions of Ezekiel and St. John are cited as the primary evidence of the authenticity and unity of the four Gospels. Depictions of these visions, therefore, are not merely powerful portraits of the celestial Christ; they are appropriate harmony pictures, testifying to the divine concord of the holy writings.

During the abbacy of Vivian, a number of changes were introduced into the Touronian *Majestas* compositions. In the Lothar Gospels (Paris, Bibliothèque Nationale, Cod. lat. 266, fol. 2ᵛ, Fig. 61),[35] in the Dufay Gospels (Paris, Bibliothèque Nationale, Cod. lat. 9385, fol. 179ᵛ, Fig. 62),[36] and in the Le Mans Gospels (Paris, Bibliothèque, Cod. lat. 261, fol. 18ʳ, Fig. 63),[37] as in the Prüm Gospels, the symbols are depicted in the corners of the page and Christ holds a disk in his right hand. With the exception of the Prüm frontispiece, the *Majestas* pages produced under Abbot Vivian all show Christ holding a closed book and all depict the mandorla as a pointed oval contiguous at the bottom with the globe-throne. In the Lothar Gospels, Christ is bearded; in the Dufay manuscript St. John's eagle grasps a scroll rather than a codex.

Except for the book roll and the disk, the differences between the Vivian pages and the earlier *Majestas* compositions are insignificant. As Meyer Schapiro has argued, the use of the roll form of book in place of the codex may have its origin in the con-

---

[33] E.g., Codex Amiatinus, Gundohinus Gospels, Lorsch Gospels, and Xanten Gospels.
[34] De Bruyne, *op. cit.*, pp. 155f.

[35] Köhler, *Kar. Min.*, I₂, 243f.
[36] *Ibid.*
[37] *Ibid.*

temporary belief in the superiority of John among the evangelists.[38] The disk is more difficult to identify and explain. First Leitschuh and then Leprieur, Cook, Köhler, Schapiro, Gaehde and others[39] identified the disk in Christ's hand as a eucharistic wafer; and attempts were made to relate its inclusion in the Touronian frontispieces to the ninth-century controversy over the nature of Christ's body in the eucharist.[40] There is neither textual nor pictorial support for this identification. The gold color and red ornament indicate that the disk is not a wafer. It should be identified, instead, as an image of the world. Cook and Van der Meer favored this identification and Schade and Hinkle have presented detailed arguments in favor of it.[41] A similar tiny orb, held by King David on a Carolingian ivory in Florence (National Museum, Fig. 164) certainly symbolizes the world.[42] The textual and theological evidence also supports this interpretation.[43]

Whereas the frontispieces in the five Touronian Gospelbooks display considerable variety, they conform generally to the same iconographic scheme and must have been derived from the same pictorial sources. These sources seem to have included both a Byzantine and a Roman *Majestas Domini*. It is possible that the two sources had already been amalgamated in a single model; but the fact that the canonical composition was known first at Tours and the considerable experimentation evident in the Touronian frontispieces themselves strongly indicate that the ninth-century illuminators worked from more than one prototype.

MAJESTAS AGNI

One Touronian Gospelbook, the St. Gauzelin Gospels of c. 830 in Nancy (Cathedral Treasury, fol. 3[v], Fig. 64),[44] contains a different type of *Majestas* frontispiece. The

[38] "Two Drawings in Auxerre and Some Iconographical Problems," *Studies in Art and Literature for Belle da Costa Greene* (Princeton, 1954), pp. 331ff.

[39] F. Leitschuh, *Karolingischen Malerei* (Berlin, 1894), p. 380; Cook, *op. cit.*, pp. 57f.; Köhler, *Kar. Min.*, I₂, 135ff.; Schapiro, *op. cit.*, p. 342 and *idem*, "A Relief in Rodez and the Beginnings of Romanesque Sculpture in Southern France," *Romanesque and Gothic. Studies in Western Art (Acts of the Twentieth International Congress of the History of Art)* I (Princeton, 1963), pp. 59ff.; Gaehde, "Turonian Sources," p. 382.

[40] Cf. Köhler, *Kar. Min.*, I₂, 135; Schapiro, "Drawings," pp. 341ff. and "Relief," pp. 59f.; and Gaehde, "Turonian Sources," p. 383.

[41] Cook, *op. cit.*, pp. 57f.; Van der Meer, *op. cit.*, pp. 333f.; H. Schade, "Der Wäger der Welt," *Das Münster*, II (1958), 389ff.; and W. Hinkle, "The Iconography of the Apsidal Fresco at Montmorillon," *Münchner Jahrbuch der bilden-*

den Kunst, XXIII (1972), 38ff.

[42] Goldschmidt, *Elfenbeinskulpturen*, I, no. 113.

[43] Schade, *op. cit.*, p. 392 and Hinkle, *op. cit.*, pp. 40f. cite the most important texts: the caption of the *Majestas* frontispiece in the San Paolo Bible, "Sedet throni residens mundum qui ponderat omnem . . ." and the caption of the *Majestas* in the Codex Aureus of St. Emmeram, "Christus . . . librat tetragonum miro discrimine mundum." They also cite verses around the *Majestas* miniature of the Codex Viglianus of A.D. 976 in the Escorial (Cod. D.i.2, fol. 16[v]), "Dominus in tribus digitis dextere molem arbe (orbe) libravit . . . omnia enim in celo et in terra et subtus terra equanimiter per ipsum dominata sunt," and they refer to the *Majestas* in the Beatus of Gerona (Cathedral Archive, fol. 2[r]) where the disk is labeled MUNDUS. Cf. also E. Delaruelle, "Le Christ élevant l'Hostie," *Congrès de Rodez 14–16 Juin 1958*, pp. 193ff.

[44] Köhler, *Kar. Min.*, I₂, 94ff.

Nancy page, which focuses on the *Agnus Dei*, also has clear significance for the development of the New Testament frontispieces in the full Bibles. At the center of the page, the Lamb of God, a chalice and a lance are represented within a clipeus. The clipeus, in turn, occupies the center of a silver and gold rhombus at the angles of which are the four evangelist symbols. Two cherubim flank the lozenge and the four major prophets[45] are depicted in medallions in the triangular fields formed by the rhombus and the frame of the page.

Like the *Majestas Domini*, the *Majestas Agni* is an apocalyptic theme that had entered art as an independent subject during the Early Christian period.[46] It is based on the fifth chapter of Revelation, "Then I saw standing in the very middle of the throne, inside the circle of living creatures and the circle of elders, a Lamb with marks of slaughter upon him. . . . And the Lamb went up and took the scroll from the right hand of the One who sat on the throne" (6–7). This passage was, of course, illustrated in the Carolingian Apocalypse manuscripts, for example, in the Trier Apocalypse (fol. 17ᵛ, Fig. 65).[47] It was also used for Gospel frontispieces. In the early ninth-century Soissons Gospels (Paris, Bibliothèque Nationale, Cod. lat. 8850, fol. 1ᵛ, Fig. 66),[48] the Lamb of God is shown standing on a book roll in a clipeus. It is worshipped by the twenty-four "elders" while below, in medallions beneath the Sea of Glass, the evangelist symbols are depicted. In the St. Amand Gospels (Valenciennes, Bibliothèque Municipale, fol. 138ᵛ)[49] the Lamb and symbols are presented in a decorative, circular frame. And in the Codex Aureus of St. Emmeram (Munich, Bayerische Staatsbibliothek, Cod. Clm. 14000)[50] two full-page compositions focus on the Agnus Dei. Fol. 6ʳ presents the Adoration of the Lamb as described in the Apocalypse text;[51] and fol. 65ᵛ, the frontispiece to the Gospel of Luke (Fig. 67), depicts the Lamb with the book roll in a central clipeus and represents the evangelist symbols in medallions at the corners of the page.

The more abstract Luke frontispiece in the Codex Aureus, which is closer than the narrative depictions to the St. Gauzelin composition, has precursors in pre-Carolingian art. The clipeate Lamb and evangelist symbols appeared c. 400 on an Italian ivory now in Milan (Cathedral Treasury).[52] During the Merovingian period, the Lamb and evangelist symbols were used to decorate the sixth-century desk of Radegund (Poitiers, Cloister of Ste. Croix),[53] and in the eighth-century Orosius manuscript in Laon (Bibliothèque Municipale, MS. 137, fol. 1ᵛ),[54] the Lamb and the symbols are arranged in a

[45] The captions identify them as Ezekiel, Isaiah, Jeremiah, and Daniel.

[46] Cf. Van der Meer, *op. cit.*, pp. 93ff. and H. Schnitzler, "Das Kuppelmosaik der Aachener Pfalzkapelle," *Aachener Kunstblätter*, XXIX (1964), 12ff.

[47] Also fols. 18ᵛ, 19ᵛ, 20ᵛ, 23ᵛ, and 24ᵛ.

[48] Köhler, *Kar. Min.*, II, 70ff.

[49] J. Porcher, *Carolingian Art* (London, 1970), Fig. 171.

[50] G. Leidinger, *Der Codex Aureus der Bayer-* *ischen Staatsbibliothek in München* (Munich, 1925), pl. 11 and Schnitzler, *op. cit.*, pp. 22ff.

[51] Leidinger, *op. cit.*, pl. 11.

[52] Volbach, *op. cit.*, pl. 37.

[53] L. Palustre, "Le pupitre de Sainte Radegonde," *Bulletin Monumentale*, XLIV (1878), 258ff.

[54] Zimmermann, *Vorkarolingische Miniaturen*, pl. 144 and O.-K. Werckmeister, *Irisch-northumbrische Buchmalerei des 8. Jahrhunderts und monastische Spiritualität* (Berlin, 1967), p. 13.

cross. What may have been the most significant precursor of the Carolingian pages is known only indirectly. An eighth-century Anglo-Saxon Gospel fragment in the British Library (Royal I.E. VI)[55] contains a description of a frontispiece that no longer exists, "Haec est speciosa quadriga luciflua animae spiritus gratia per os agni Dei inlustrata in quo quattuor proceres consona voce magnalia Dei ca(ntant)." McGurk was certainly right to conclude that these verses must have accompanied "an illuminated page showing the Lamb of God in the centre with four evangelists or their symbols in the corners of the page. One thinks of the similar scenes introducing the four Gospels in the Bamberg Bible or in the Nancy Gospels of St. Gauzelin. . . ."[56] He could also have cited the St. Amand Gospels or the Codex Aureus of St. Emmeram as Carolingian parallels.

The composition in the Nancy manuscript was certainly derived from the tradition represented by these Merovingian frontispieces. It differs from the predecessors, however, in a number of significant details. In the St. Gauzelin Gospels page, the evangelist symbols are arranged in a cross pattern at the angles of a rhombus; and cherubim and the four major prophets are portrayed. Where did these elements come from and what is their meaning in the composition?

Of the several precursors of the Nancy page, the one that is closest to it in date and origin also shares certain of its peculiar features. This is Figura xv in Hrabanus Maurus' *De laudibus sanctae crucis*.[57] Written about 810 and revised before 840, Hrabanus' commentary is best known in the copy now in Vienna (Nationalbibliothek, Cod. 652, fol. 20ʳ, Fig. 68) which was produced at Fulda toward the middle of the century.[58] For stylistic and iconographic reasons, it has been argued that the Vienna manuscript was copied from a Touronian exemplar produced about the same time as the Grandval Bible.[59] There can be no doubt that this popular treatise by a prominent disciple of Alcuin was known at Tours even earlier.

Figura xv of Hrabanus' tract, *De quatuor evangelistis et agno, in crucis specie constitutis*, like the St. Gauzelin Gospels frontispiece, depicts a Lamb amid the four evangelist symbols arranged in a cross pattern. The order of the creatures is identical in the two compositions. Hrabanus explained the pictorial configuration as an emblem of the harmony of the four Gospels. Like Jerome, he began the commentary by referring to the visions of Ezekiel and John. Then he continued, "Agnum vero qui in medio sedis est, quid aliud quam mediam crucem tenere intelligimus? Ipse enim in ea confixus est qui abstulit peccata mundi. Quatuor quippe haec animalia quatuor evangelistas significant, ut Ecclesiae tradit auctoritas, hoc est, Matthaeum, Marcum, Lucam, Joannem, qui jure in sanctae crucis specie conscribuntur, quia passionem

[55] P. McGurk, "An Anglo-Saxon Bible Fragment of the Late Eighth Century," *Journal of the Warburg and Courtauld Institutes*, xxv (1962), 18ff.

[56] *Ibid.*, p. 23.

[57] *PL*, cvii, cols. 207ff.

[58] *Charlemagne*, no. 497 and *Codex Vindobonensis 652* (Graz, 1972).

[59] P. Bloch, "Zum Dedikationsbild im Lob des Kreuzes des Hrabanus Maurus," *Das erste Jahrtausend* (Düsseldorf, 1962), I, 471ff.

Domini et resurrectionem in libris sancti Evangelii omnes concorditer testantur."[60] Whether the illuminator of the Nancy page had Hrabanus' interpretation specifically in mind when he depicted the *Majestas Agni* as a Gospel frontispiece or whether he was simply following the *Plures fuisse* which also cites the adoration of the lamb, cannot definitely be decided. There are reasons, however, for believing that Hrabanus' commentary was his inspiration.

First, in his discussion of Figura xv, Hrabanus emphasized Christ's passion and this may account for the depiction of the lance and chalice in the Nancy composition.[61] More significantly, Hrabanus' treatise interprets the *Majestas Agni* as an allegory of the fountain of four rivers. "Quatuor ergo Evangelia a quatuor evangelistis conscripta, quatuor flumina paradisi de uno fonte procedentia significant, quia sicut ipsa ex una matrice fontis procedentia totam terram rigaverunt, ita ab uno vero fonte, hoc est, Christo, a quo qui semel bibet, non sitiet in aeternum, quatuor Evangelia emanantia, et per praedicatorum ora diffluentia, totum mundum ad virtum fructus germinandum irrigant."[62] The *titulus* of the Nancy frontispiece states this interpretation more directly:

QUATTUOR HIC RUTILANT UNO DE FONTE FLUENTES
MATTHEI, MARCI, LUCAE LIBRI ATQ: JOHANNES[63]

The association of the *Agnus Dei* with the rivers of paradise derives ultimately from the Book of Revelation.

> They will never again feel hunger or thirst, the sun shall not beat on them nor any scorching heat, because the Lamb who is at the heart of the throne will be their shepherd and will guide them to the springs of the water of life (Rev., VII, 7).

> Then he showed me the river of the water of life, sparkling like crystal, flowing from the throne of God and of the Lamb down the middle of the city's street. On either side of the river stood a tree of life (Rev., XXII, 1–2).

The Lamb on a hill from which four streams issue was represented in monumental art as early as the fifth century when it was depicted in the apse of the basilica at Nola.[64] The Lamb, the tree of life, and four streams are also represented on the sixth/seventh-century "Sedia di San Marco" in Venice (San Marco, Treasury).[65] In both these monuments, the Lamb and four rivers were connected to the four Gospels. Paulinus of Nola interpreted the apse decoration:

[60] *PL*, CVII, col. 209. Also Hrabanus Maurus, *De universo*, XI, 9 (De fontibus) and XI, 10 (De fluminibus); *PL*, CXI, cols. 317ff.; and *Comment. in Genesim* (*PL*, CVII, col. 479).

[61] Cf. V. Elbern, *Der eucharistische Kelch im frühen Mittelalter* (Berlin, 1964), pp. 109ff. and "Die Stele von Moselkern," *Bonner Jahrbuch*, 155/56 (1955/56), 184ff.

[62] *PL*, CVII, col. 210.

[63] Elbern (*Kelch*, p. 110) considers the St. Gauzelin Gospels frontispiece to be nothing other than the fountain of life itself.

[64] Ihm, *op. cit.*, pp. 179ff.

[65] A. Grabar, "Le trône des martyrs," *Cahiers Archéologiques*, VI (1952), 31ff.

PETRAM SUPERSTAT IPSE PETRA ECCLESIAE,
DE QUA SONORIS QUATTUOR FONTES MEANT,
EVANGELISTAE VIVA CHRISTI FLUMINA.[66]

The symbols of the four evangelists are depicted on the sides of the San Marco chair.

The allegory that likens Christ and his four evangelists to the fountain of life in the Garden of Eden can be traced back to the fourth century.[67] It is alluded to in the *Plures fuisse*, "Ecclesia autem . . . similis a ammulae hinnuloque cervorum, quattuor flumina paradisi instar eructans, quattuor et angulos et anulos habet, per quos quasi arca Testamenti et custos legis domini, lignis mobilibus vehitur." And it soon became associated with the *Majestas Domini* theme. Four rivers emerge from beneath Christ's globe in the mosaic of Hosios David and the streams are represented beneath Christ's throne in other Early Christian representations.[68] The allegory of the *fons vitae* was especially popular during the Carolingian period when it was depicted in a literal fashion,[69] was applied to the *Majestas Domini*, and was given schematic realization in the Nancy Gospels frontispiece. It remained popular. Rivers of life were depicted in Ottonian evangelist portraits, in an eleventh-century *Majestas Domini* (Munich, Bayerische Staatsbibliothek, Cod. lat. 4454, fol. 20ᵛ) and, with the *Agnus Dei*, on a twelfth-century Mosan book cover in Paris (Musée Cluny).[70]

The frontispiece in the St. Gauzelin Gospels is not, of course, a literal representation of the Lamb-river allegory. The rivers are not depicted or personified. The fountain is alluded to, instead, through a complex juxtaposition of figures, symbols, and words. The cross, lance, chalice, and cherubim—even the prophets and the lozenge frame— seem to be elements of the allegorical program.

Following John VII, 38, medieval theologians associated the streams of blood and water that flowed from Christ's side with the *fons vitae*,[71] "If anyone is thirsty, let him come to me; whoever believes in me, let him drink. As Scripture says, 'Streams of living water shall flow out from within him.' " This idea, which is reiterated in Hrabanus Maurus' discussion of Figura XV, may explain the inclusion of the lance in the Nancy miniature.

Through an extension of the same idea, the chalice also came to be regarded as the fountain of living waters.[72] As early as the third century, St. Cyprian presented that metaphor:

[66] Ihm, *op. cit.*, pp. 179ff.

[67] Cf. Ambrose, *De Paradiso*, III, 16; Augustine, *De Genesis Contra Manichaeos*, II, 10–14; Cyprian, *Epistles*, LXX, 10, 3. The theme was especially popular during the Carolingian period: cf. Underwood, *op. cit.*; Elbern, *Kelch*, pp. 90ff.; and A. Thomas, "Ikonographische Studien zur Darstellung des Lebensbrunnens in trierischen Handschriften des Mittelalters," *Kurtrierisches Zeitschrift*, VIII (1968), 59ff.

[68] E.g., Pignatta Sarcophagus (Ravenna, Braccioforte), Silver Book Cover (Vatican, Museo Sacro).

[69] In the Godescalc Lectionary (Paris, Bibliothèque Nationale, nouv. acq. lat. 1203, fol. 3ᵛ) and in the Soissons Gospels (fol. 6ᵛ, Fig. 86). Cf. Underwood, *op. cit.*, pp. 46ff.

[70] Schiller, *op. cit.*, II, no. 404.

[71] H. Rahner, "Flumina de ventre Christi," *Biblica*, XXII (1941), 367ff.

[72] Elbern, *Kelch, passim.*

. . . et calicis manifestaverit veritatem, qui aquam illam fidelem, aquam vitae aeternae, praeceperit credentibus in baptismo dari, calicem vero docuerit exemplo magisterii sui vini et aquae conjunctione misceri. Calicem eternim sub die passionis accipiens, benedixit et dedit discipulis suis dicens: "Bibite ex hoc omnes. Hic est enim sanguis novi testmenti, qui pro multis effundetur in remissionem peccatorum. . . ."[73]

The allegory was especially popular during the ninth century. It is stated in the refrain couplet of the *Liber de fonte vitae*, a poem composed by the Touronian monk Audradus Modicus:

INCIPE NUNC MECUM CAELESTIS GRATIA CARMEN
AETERNI FONTIS SCYPHI PASCHALIS ET HORAE.[74]

And the same idea was given visual expression in the illustration of the Canticle of Isaiah in the Utrecht Psalter.[75] To illustrate the verse, "And so you shall draw water with joy from the springs of deliverance" (Isa., XII, 3), the illuminator represented men drinking from chalices out of the paradisical fountain whose source is Christ.

It is uncertain whether or not the Lamb, the chalice, and the *fons vitae* had been united in art before the St. Gauzelin Gospels. Ciampini's watercolor after the apse mosaic in Old St. Peter's shows the *Agnus Dei* bleeding into a chalice beneath Christ's throne from which the four rivers issue.[76] Ciampini's copy, however, reflects the restoration of the mosaic undertaken by Pope Innocent III (1198–1216).[77] Its reliability as a source of the Early Christian iconography, therefore, is questionable. The Lamb and chalice may also have been represented in the dome of the Palatine Chapel in Aachen.[78] As in the case of the apse of St. Peter's, however, the original state of the Aachen dome decoration is not certainly known. From the evidence it seems likeliest that the chalice was added by the Touronian illuminator to emphasize the eucharistic implications of his schematic *fons vitae*.

The cherubim that flank the central image of the Nancy frontispiece may also have been intended to convey the idea of the *fons vitae*. Cherubim and a flashing sword were stationed outside Eden "to guard the way of the tree of life" (Gen., III, 24). Medieval representations of the fountain of paradise commonly include cherubim. Cherubim are shown in a representation of the Earthly paradise in the tenth-century Codex Vigilanus (Escorial, Cod. D.I.2, fol. 16ᵛ);[79] and perhaps more significantly, cherubim are depicted in the eleventh-century copy of Hrabanus Maurus' *De universo* at Montecassino (Cod. 132, p. 297, Fig. 69).[80] The Montecassino illustration, which seems to have

[73] Epistola LXIII (*PL*, IV, col. 392).

[74] *MGH. Poetae latini*, III, pp. 73ff. Cf. Elbern, *Kelch*, pp. 92ff.

[75] *Ibid., loc. cit.*

[76] S. Waetzoldt, *Kopien des 17. Jahrhunderts nach Mosaiken und Wandmalereien in Rom* (Wien, 1964), p. 71.

[77] Elbern's arguments that the chalice was depicted before the restoration are not compelling (cf. *Kelch*, p. 115).

[78] Schnitzler, *op. cit.*, p. 22.

[79] P. Guillermo Autolin, *Catalogo de los Códices Latinos* (Madrid, 1910), I, 368ff.

[80] A. Amelli, *Miniature sacre e profane dell'anno 1023* (Montecassino, 1896), pl. LXXII.

been based on a ninth-century model,[81] shows two cherubim flanking the four rivers of paradise.

According to the Bible, cherubim also guarded the ark of the covenant. During the ninth century, they were depicted beside the ark in the apse of Germigny des Pres[82] and were included in the tabernacle frontispiece of the San Paolo Bible (fol. 32ᵛ).[83] It is possible, therefore, that the illuminator of the St. Gauzelin Gospels had these guardians of the ark in mind when he represented cherubim on the Gospels frontispiece. He could have been inspired to include them by the *Plures fuisse* which, after the four rivers of paradise, likens the Church to the ark of the covenant.[84]

It is also possible that the cherubim of the Nancy page are no more than vestiges of a *Majestas Domini* model. Isaiah's vision, which was the third major textual source of the *Majestas Domini*, describes the majestic Lord surrounded by seraphim, "And about him were attendant seraphim and each had six wings . . . and they were calling ceaselessly to one another, 'Holy, holy, holy is the Lord of Hosts; the whole earth is full of his glory' " (Isa., VI, 1ff.). Seraphim are included in Byzantine depictions of the vision[85] and cherubim quite similar to those in the St. Gauzelin Gospels are represented on the Prophets frontispiece in the San Paolo Bible (fol. 117ᵛ, Fig. 70).[86] It may also have been from the Vision of Isaiah that angels entered *Majestas* imagery. Ministering angels are depicted in the Codex Amiatinus (Florence, Biblioteca Medicea-Laurenziana, Cod. Am., I, fol. 796ᵛ, Fig. 71) and in the Gundohinus Gospels (Fig. 53); and cherubim are represented in a number of ninth-century *Majestas Domini* compositions.[87] Neither cherubim nor angels seem to appear in another *Majestas Agni* composition, however, until the tenth century when they were depicted in the Fulda Lectionary (Aschaffenberg, Hofbibliothek, MS. 2, fol. IV).[88] The cherubim of the Nancy frontispiece may only be vestiges of a *Majestas Domini*; it is possible, however, that they were included as a reference to the *fons vitae* theme.

Like the cherubim, the prophets of the Nancy frontispiece can also be traced to early representations of the *Majestas Domini*. Prophets are portrayed, for example, in Byzantine Majesty depictions. Ezekiel and Habakkuk are presented in the mosaic of Hosios David and Ezekiel and Isaiah are portrayed in the Marciana Gospels (Fig. 58). The four major prophets, however, were represented in no known eastern repre-

[81] Cf. D. LeBerrurier, "Un fragment inédit d'une copie du XIVᵉ siècle de l'encyclopédie de Raban Maur," *Cahiers Archéologiques*, XXII (1972), 47ff.

[82] P. Bloch, "Das Apsismosaik von Germigny-des-Pres," *Karl der Grosse*, III, 234ff.

[83] Gaehde, "Bible Manuscript," I, 210ff. and *idem*, "Carolingian Interpretations of an Early Christian Picture Cycle to the Octateuch in the Bible of San Paolo Fuori Le Mura in Rome," *Frühmittelalterliche Studien*, VIII (1974), 358ff. Seraphim and cherubim were often confused with one another. Cf. Bloch, "Apsismosaik," pp. 244f.

and Gaehde, "Bible Manuscript," I, 231ff.

[84] See above.

[85] Lafontaine-Dosogne, *op. cit.*, figs. 6, 8, and 9.

[86] Gaehde, "Bible Manuscript," I, 305ff.

[87] E.g., Paris, Bibliothèque Nationale, Cod. lat. 1141, fol. 6ʳ and two ivories, Goldschmidt, *Elfenbeinskulpturen*, I, nos. 23 and 163a. For an analysis of the Codex Amiatinus, cf. Werner, *op. cit.*

[88] E. H. Zimmermann, *Die fuldaer Buchmalerei in Karolingischer und Ottonischer Zeit* (Halle, 1910), pp. 33ff.; Elbern, *Kelch*, pp. 110f.; Rademacher, *op. cit.*, p. 47.

sentation of the theme; and in Western *Majestas Domini* compositions, the four prophets did not appear prior to their inclusion in the Grandval Bible. The analogous figures of the Codex Amiatinus are certainly evangelists and the prophets in Ottonian frontispieces were derived from Carolingian models.[89] Excluding the Touronian examples, the first known appearance of prophets with the Lamb of God is the early tenth-century stole of Frithistan,[90] which is independent of Touronian sources.

The relevance of Ezekiel, Isaiah, and Daniel to the *Majestas Domini* is not difficult to discern. Together with St. John, Ezekiel was the principal author of the *Majestas* image and he is cited in the *Plures fuisse*. Daniel, too, reported a vision of the four beasts, "In my visions of the night, I, Daniel, was gazing intently and I saw a great sea churned up by the four winds of heaven and four huge beasts coming up out of the sea, each one different from the others" (Dan., VII, 2–3). Isaiah's vision (Isa. VI, 1ff.) does not refer to the beasts. It does, however, account for the cherubim in certain Majesties and its seraphic refrain was paraphrased by St. John as the chant of the four living creatures in the Apocalypse (Rev., IV, 8). Jeremiah, alone, had no vision directly related to the *Majestas*. He may have been included simply to complete the series.

The significance of the major prophets for the *Majestas Agni* is not more certain. Isaiah foretold the sacrifice of the Lamb, "He was afflicted, he submitted to be struck down and did not open his mouth; he was led like a sheep to slaughter, like a ewe that is dumb before the shearers" (Isa., LIII, 7). Jeremiah wrote, "I had been like a sheep led obedient to the slaughter; I did not know that they were hatching plots against me" (Jer., XI, 19).[91] Ezekiel and Daniel, however, are not easy to connect to the *Agnus Dei*. Alcuin related Ezekiel's reference to "commerce in lambs" (Ezek., XXVII, 21) to the Apocalyptic vision.[92] Daniel's comment, "As in holocausts of rams and bullocks and as in thousands of fat lambs, so let our sacrifice be made in thy sight this day that it may please thee" (Dan., III, 40), could conceivably account for his inclusion in a *Majestas Agni*.

It is possible that the four prophets were represented in the Touronian frontispieces, not because of their theophanic visions, but because they made references to the fountain of living waters. All four prophets commented, in one way or another, on the *fons vitae*. Isaiah's canticle (XII, 3) is one such comment. Another is in Isa., XXXIII, 21, "There we have the Lord's majesty: it will be a place of rivers and broad streams, but no galleys shall be rowed there, no stately ships sail by. For the Lord our judge, the Lord our law-giver, the Lord our king—he himself will save us." Jeremiah twice referred to God as the fountain of life:

> Two sins have my people committed: they have forsaken me, a spring of living water, and they have hewn out for themselves cisterns, cracked cisterns that can hold no water (Jer., II, 13).

[89] Bloch and Schnitzler, *op. cit.*, pp. 85ff.
[90] C. Hohler, "The Iconography of the Stole and Maniples," in Battiscombe *et al.*, *The Relics of St. Cuthbert* (Oxford, 1956), pp. 396ff.
[91] *Ibid.*, pp. 400f.
[92] *Comment. in Ezekielem*, X. PL, CX, col. 779.

For they have rejected the Lord, the fountain of living waters (Jer., XVII, 13).

These passages from Isaiah and Jeremiah were quoted by Hrabanus in his discussion, *De fontibus*, in *De universo*.[93] Ezekiel's reference to the living waters is even more closely related to the majestic vision:

> He brought me back to the gate of the temple, and I saw a spring of water issuing from under the terrace of the temple towards the east. . . . When any one of the living creatures that swarm upon the earth comes where the torrent flows, it shall draw life from it. . . . Beside the torrent on either bank all trees good for food shall spring up. Their leaves shall not wither, their fruit shall not cease; they shall bear early every month. For their water comes from the sanctuary; their fruit is for food and their foliage for enjoyment (XLVII, 1–12).

Only Daniel made no direct comment on the *fons vitae*. His Susanna story, however, was incorporated into commentaries on the fountain at an early date. Hippolytus' exegesis of Dan., I, 16–18, for example, interpreted Susanna's garden as Eden and her bath as the fountain at the center of paradise:

> "She entered as was her habit, accompanied only by her two servants, intending to bathe," that is to say . . . the garden which had been planted in Eden is the figure and, in a certain way, the model of the true garden. . . . There runs in this garden an inexhaustible river. Four rivers flowing from it water the whole earth. It is like the church: Christ, who is the river, is announced to the entire world by those who believe in him, according to the words of the prophet: Out of his belly shall flow rivers of living water (John, VII, 38).[94]

The motivation behind the inclusion of the prophets in the *Majestas* compositions remains in question. Relevant passages bearing on the *Majestas Domini*, the *Majestas Agni*, and the *fons vitae* can, however, be adduced from their writings.

Pictorial models for the prophets are also difficult to specify. One is tempted to argue that the prophets were based on figures similar to the evangelists in the Codex Amiatinus. Prophets holding books and scrolls, however, do appear in Byzantine *Majestas* compositions which may have been the source (cf. Fig. 58). Old Testament figures similar to those in the Touronian manuscripts also appear in the Syriac Bible in Paris (Bibliothèque Nationale, Cod. Syr. 341, fol. 180ʳ, Fig. 72)[95] and on the Frithestan Stole.[96] The prophets could also have been adapted at Tours from such a model as the portrait of St. Luke in the Nancy manuscript itself (fol. 111ᵛ, Fig. 73).[97]

The prophets of the St. Gauzelin frontispiece occupy four circles, somewhat smaller than the central clipeus. Five-circle compositions similar to this one had been used for

[93] *PL*, CXI, col. 317ff.

[94] Cf. Hippolyte, *Commentaire sur Daniel*, trans. M. Lefèvre (Paris, 1947).

[95] H. Omont, *Peintures de l'ancien testament dans un manuscrit syriaque* (*Monuments et Mémoires. Fondation Eugene Piot*, XVII. [Paris, 1909]) and J. Leroy, *Les manuscrits syriaques à peintures* (Paris, 1964), pp. 208ff.

[96] Hohler, *op. cit.*, pp. 396ff.

[97] Köhler, *Kar. Min.*, I, pl. 37a.

both the *Majestas Domini* and the *Majestas Agni* from earliest times and, hence, the format of the Nancy page may have been derived from the basic model. The page in the manuscript at St. Paul in Lavanttal (Fig. 56) is an early example of the five-circle *Majestas Domini*; while the frontispieces in the Gundohinus Gospels (Fig. 53), in the Landevennec Gospels (New York, Public Library, Harkness Ms., fol. 13ᵛ),[98] in the Cambrai Apocalypse (Bibliothèque Municipale, Ms. 386, fol. 11ᵛ),[99] and in the Stuttgart Psalter (Württembergische Landesbibliothek, fol. 23, fol. 77ʳ)[100] are Carolingian examples of the same scheme. The Lamb of God occupies the center circle of a five-circle composition on the fifth-century Milan ivory and the format was popular in Carolingian and Ottonian depictions of the *Majestas Agni*. The Luke frontispiece in the Codex Aureus of St. Emmeram (Fig. 67) is one example; the frontispiece in the Lectionary from Fulda is another; and other versions can be cited. In these compositions, however, evangelist symbols always occupy the corner circles. The prophets are never portrayed. This raises the possibility that the Touronian illuminator began, not with a five-circle figural model but with a purely abstract source. At least two manuscripts, the seventh-century Orosius in Milan (Ambrosiana, Cod. D. 23, fol. 1ᵛ)[101] and the ninth-century Bible in Cava dei Tirreni (fol. 1ᵛ, Fig. 74)[102] contain non-figural frontispieces decorated with five circles. At Tours, this design was adapted for the portrait of Raganaldus in the Marmoutier Sacramentary (Autun, Bibliothèque de la Ville, MS. 19 bis, fol. 173ᵛ, Fig. 208)[103] and it is possible that the illuminator of the St. Gauzelin Gospels introduced the scheme for the *Majestas Agni* frontispiece.

The lozenge may also have come from the same source. A fourth-century belt-buckle in Budapest (Hungarian National Museum)[104] is decorated with five circles and a rhombus. The scheme is virtually identical to that of the Nancy page. And the map of the world in an early ninth-century astronomical manuscript in Vienna (Nationalbibliothek, Cod. 387, fol. 134ʳ, Fig. 75)[105] is similar in format; only the central clipeus is missing.

The Vienna manuscript suggests that the lozenge of the Nancy page may be a meaningful element of the pictorial program. The rhombus represents the earth. As Victor Elbern,[106] Hans Meyer,[107] and A. A. Schmid[108] have argued, the rhomboid frame in the Carolingian frontispieces may have been intended as an emblem of the world, the

[98] C. R. Morey *et al.*, "The Gospel-Book of Landevennec in the New York Public Library," *Art Studies*, VIII (1931), 225ff. and Rademacher, *op. cit.*, pp. 37f.

[99] H. Omont, *Manuscrits illustrés de l'Apocalypse* (Paris, 1924).

[100] Bischoff *et al.*, *op. cit.*, II, 90.

[101] Werckmeister, *op. cit.*, p. 31.

[102] M. Vieillard-Troiekouroff, "Les Bibles de Theodulphe et la Bible Wisigothique de la Cava dei Tirreni," *Synthronon*, pp. 153ff.

[103] Köhler, *Kar. Min.*, I₂, 96ff.

[104] J. Hampel, *Altertümer des frühen Mittel-alters in Ungarn* (Braunschweig, 1905), I, p. 65 and Werckmeister, *op. cit.*, p. 31.

[105] Apparently written in Salzburg c. 818. Cf. H. Hermann, *Die illuminierten Handschriften und Inkunablen der Nationalbibliothek in Wien* (Leipzig, 1923), III¹, 145.; P. E. Schramm, *Sphaira, Globus, Reichsapfel* (Stuttgart, 1958), pp. 44f.; E. J. Beer, *Die Rose der Kathedrale von Lausanne* (Bern, 1952); Meyer, *op. cit.*, pp. 75ff.; Werckmeister, *op. cit.*, pp. 155ff.

[106] "Stele," pp. 204ff.

[107] *Op. cit.*

[108] *Bibel von Moutier-Grandval*, pp. 159ff.

tetragonus mundus. Both Alcuin and Hrabanus identified the lozenge as the world. In Alcuin's figural poem on the cross (Bern, Stadtbibliothek, Cod. 212, fol. 123ʳ, Fig. 76),[109] the text written as a rhombus reads:

SALVE SANCTA RUBENS FREGISTI VINCULA MUNDI
SIGNA VALETE NOVIS RESERATE SALUTIBUS ORBI.

In his *De universo,* Hrabanus' discussion *De orbe* includes the following analysis of the lozenge: "Quatuor autem cardinibus eam formari dicit; quia quatuor cardines quatuor angulos quadrati significant, qui intra praedictum terrae circulum continentur."[110]

Although rhomboid frames were common elements in Early Christian art, their significance before the ninth century is difficult to establish. On the Budapest buckle, on the consular diptych of Filoxenus (Washington, Dumbarton Oaks),[111] and in the portrait of Julia Anicia in the Vienna Dioscurides (Nationalbibliothek, Cod. Med. gr. 1, fol. 6ᵛ),[112] the lozenge seems to serve a purely decorative function. Even in the fourth-century gold glass in the British Museum (Fig. 77),[113] the lozenge may be an insignificant element of design. Whether the central lozenge of the John frontispiece in the Book of Kells (Dublin, Trinity College Library, MS. 58 A.I.6., fol. 290ᵛ)[114] has cosmic meaning is also questionable.

No doubt can exist, however, that in Carolingian art, the lozenge had symbolic meaning. The rhombus was a central element in the monograms of Charlemagne and Charles the Bald.[115] It was inscribed, for example, on Charles' orb in the San Paolo Bible dedication portrait (fol. 334ʳ, Fig. 197).[116] A lozenge also frames the portrait of a ruler, possibly Charles the Bald, in the Cambrai Gospels (Bibliothèque Municipale, Cod. 327, fol. 16ᵛ, Fig. 78).[117] In format, the Cambrai page resembles the Vienna map of the world. The ruler occupies the center of the earth and personifications of the virtues replace the four elements. This suggests that the Cambrai portrait may have been based on an idea of Alcuin who likened the ruler (microcosm) and the four virtues to the world and the four elements, "Quatuor sunt elementa, quibus mundi ornatus constat maxime. Quatuor sunt virtutes, quibus minor mundus, id est homo, ornari debet."[118] The *tetragonus mundus* mentioned in the *titulus* of the *Majestas Domini* in the Codex Aureus of St. Emmeram (fol. 6ᵛ, Fig. 85) seems to refer, not to the lozenge,

[109] *MGH. Poetae latini,* I, 225.

[110] *PL,* CXI, col. 333 and Meyer, *op. cit.,* p. 76.

[111] Dumbarton Oaks, Washington, D. C., *Handbook of the Collection* (Washington, 1967); Meyer, *op. cit.,* p. 73; Rademacher, *op. cit.,* p. 46; Schmid, *Bibel von Moutier-Grandval,* p. 160; and K. Weitzmann, *Catalogue of the Byzantine and Early Mediaeval Antiquities in the Dumbarton Oaks Collection* (Washington, 1972), no. 17.

[112] H. Gerstinger, *Der Wiener Dioscurides* (Graz, 1965); Meyer, *op. cit.,* p. 73; Schmid, *op. cit.,* p. 160.

[113] O. M. Dalton, *Catalogue of the Early Christian Antiquities* (London, 1901), no. 630; Meyer, *op. cit.,* p. 73; Werckmeister, *op. cit.,* p. 31; and Schmid, *Bibel von Moutier-Grandval,* p. 159.

[114] Elbern, "Stele," pp. 203f.; Meyer, *op. cit.,* p. 73; Werckmeister, *op. cit.,* pp. 155ff. *et passim.*

[115] K. Hoffmann, *Taufsymbolik im mittelalterlichen Herrscherbild* (Düsseldorf, 1968), pp. 17ff.

[116] Gaehde, "Bible Manuscript," I, 454ff. See Chapter IX.

[117] Hoffmann, *op. cit.,* p. 18.

[118] *MGH. Epistolae,* IV, 124. Cf. Meyer, *op. cit.,* p. 75.

but to the disk held by Christ.[119] The cosmic significance of the rhombus on the lid of the contemporary Ellwangen reliquary (Collegiate Church of St. Vitus) however, seems undeniable.[120]

The *tetragonus mundus* may have been introduced into the *Majestas Agni* of the St. Gauzelin Gospels to designate the paradisical world watered by the streams of living water. That would be consonant with the interpretations presented by Hrabanus Maurus in his discussion of Figura xv and by Alcuin in one of his letters, "Quatuor de uno paradisi fonte ad inrigandam profluunt flumina terram. Quatuor evangelia de uno fonte, qui est Christi, procedunt ad inriganda corda arida, ut virtutum floribus vernent."[121]

Although its individual elements have precedents in earlier compositions, the frontispiece in the Nancy Gospels appears to be an original and complex assemblage from a variety of sources. The basic model was a *Majestas Agni*, similar to the lost frontispiece of the British Library Gospel fragment, the depiction in the Trier Apocalypse (Fig. 65), or Figura xv of Hrabanus Maurus' poem (Fig. 68). The selection of this theme, like the choice of the *Majestas Domini*, was apparently inspired by Jerome's *Plures fuisse* which cites St. John's vision of the Lamb as a primary source for the canonicity of the four Gospels. To the basic prototype, the Touronian illuminator added the cross, the lance, the chalice, cherubim, and four prophets, and he organized the elements in five circles separated by a rhomboid frame. These modifications were made, it seems, to emphasize the harmony of the Gospels through references to the *fons vitae* allegory stated in the *titulus*. As in Hrabanus' *De laudibus sanctae crucis*, the Lamb and the evangelist symbols on the Nancy page symbolize the fountain of living waters. The lozenge represents the paradisical world which is guarded by cherubim and which is nourished by these waters; and the prophets recall the foretelling of Christ's sacrifice and of this source of eternal life.

THE FULL BIBLES

It is possible that the illuminator of the St. Gauzelin Gospels derived the lozenge and the portraits of the prophets from the Grandval Bible frontispiece (Fig. 48) or its model. The Nancy and London compositions are clearly related to one another;[122] and because the dates of their creation remain uncertain, the nature of this relationship cannot be easily established. The Grandval frontispiece, however, is a variation on a well-established *Majestas Domini* tradition—represented at Tours by the Weingarten, Prüm, Lothar, Dufay, and Le Mans Gospels—that did not include the lozenge or the prophets. It is likelier, therefore, that the rhombus and the Old Testament figures

---

[119] See note 43, above.

[120] W. Volbach, "Das Ellwanger Reliquien- kästchen," *Ellwangen 764–1964* (Ellwangen, 1964), pp. 767ff. See also: K. Christ, "Karoling- ische Bibliothekseinbände," *Festschrift Georg*

Leyh (Leipzig, 1937).

[121] *MGH. Epistolae*, iv, 123f.; cf. Meyer, *op. cit.*, p. 75.

[122] This was emphasized by B. Fischer, *Die Alkuin-Bibel* (Freiburg im Breisgau, 1957).

were added to a traditional composition from a coherent schematic depiction such as the Nancy page than that the illuminator of the St. Gauzelin Gospels distilled the *Majestas Domini* elements from a Bible frontispiece and retained only the prophets and lozenge.

Moreover, a *Majestas Agni* frontispiece, almost identical to the page in the St. Gauzelin Gospels, was incorporated into one of the Touronian pandects, the Bible in Bamberg (Fig. 47). The differences between the two compositions are minor. The symbols of Luke and John have been interchanged; the cherubim and the caption have been omitted; and a book roll and sponge-pole have been added. The sponge-pole reinforces the allusion to the Crucifixion made by the lance. The scroll is a narrative element described in Rev., v, 7 and may have been derived from the Apocalypse model. The Lamb is shown standing on a book in the Trier Apocalypse (Fig. 65), in the Soissons Gospels (Fig. 66), and in the Codex Aureus of St. Emmeram (Fig. 67).

With the fusion of the *Majestas Domini* and *Majestas Agni* compositions in the Grandval manuscript, the Touronian illuminator created an impressive and appropriate Gospels frontispiece for the full Bible. It was this composition that became the basis for the later development. Centered on an imposing icon of the celestial Christ, the new frontispiece composition expressed the harmony of the four Gospels through the evangelist symbols placed at the corners of the *tetragonus mundus* and alluded to the unity of the Old and New Testament through the four prophets.[123]

The evolution of the Touronian *Majestas* composition was completed by the introduction of seated evangelists in the Vivian Bible frontispiece (Fig. 49). The source of these portraits was a Gospelbook. The nearly contemporary Lothar Gospels, for example, presents especially close parallels.[124] The Lothar Matthew (fol. 22ᵛ, Fig. 79), a seated, frontal figure with raised pen, is quite like Mark in the Vivian *Majestas*. The profile figures of Mark and John in the Lothar manuscript (fols. 75ᵛ and 171ᵛ, Figs. 80 and 82) resemble the Vivian St. John; and the Lothar Luke (fol. 112ᵛ, Fig. 81) recalls the Vivian St. Matthew. Even the thrones are similar. Only the figure of Luke in the Vivian frontispiece is a type not found in the Lothar Gospels; but evangelists who sit frontally with books on their knees and who dip their pens in preparation for writing are depicted in other Touronian Gospel manuscripts: Weingarten Mark,[125] Nevers Luke,[126] and the Prüm Mark (fol. 79ʳ, Fig. 83).

To accommodate the seated portraits, the prophets were reduced to bust-images placed in medallions at the angles of the rhombus. The evangelist symbols, displaced by the prophets, were, in turn, relocated around Christ's mandorla. It may have been to make room for these symbols within the lozenge that the Vivian master squeezed the

[123] In depicting the prophets with scrolls and the evangelist symbols with codices, the illuminator may have intended to distinguish the Old from the New Testament. The prophets wear gold helmets, probably the result of a misunderstand-ing of nimbi in the model.

[124] Köhler, *Kar. Min.*, I₂, 240ff.

[125] Fol. 65ᵛ. Köhler, *Kar. Min.*, I, pl. 21.

[126] Fol. 109ᵛ. Köhler, *Kar. Min.*, I, pl. 25.

mandorla into a figure eight. H. Meyer, however, has adduced interesting textual evidence that suggests that even this modification was meaningful.[127] Meyer proposed that the illuminator of the Vivian Bible refashioned the globe-mandorla to accord with the exegetical interpretation of Ezek., I, 27, "I saw what might have been brass glowing like fire in a furnace from the waist upwards; and from the waist downwards I saw what looked like fire with encircling radiance." The Vivian Master also provided the Majestic Christ with a beard, a disk, and a closed book.

In the Vivian *Majestas*, the standard five-page system for illustrating Gospelbooks— a *Majestas Domini* or *Majestas Agni* and four full-page evangelist portraits—was consolidated on a single frontispiece.[128] This consolidation, like the gathering of individual column pictures onto a single Genesis page, provided a suitable frontispiece for a pandect. It also served to emphasize the harmony theme by increasing the prominence of the evangelists.

The *titulus* of the Grandval and Vivian Gospels pages does not explicitly express the *fons vitae* idea:

REX MICAT AETHEREUS CONDIGNE SIVE PROPHETAE

HIC, EVANGELICAE QUATTUOR ATQUE TUBAE.[129]

There is reason to believe, however, that the theme still underlies these conceptions. At Tours, even the simpler *Majestas Domini* frontispieces in Gospelbooks were interpreted as allegories of the fountain of living waters, just as was the *Majestas Agni* of the Nancy manuscript. The *Majestas* pages in both the Lothar and Le Mans Gospels (Figs. 61 and 69) bear the *titulus*,

HAC SEDET ARCE DEUS MUNDI REX GLORIAE CAELI

QUATTUOR HIC RUTILANT UNO DE FONTE FLUENTES.[130]

In the Vivian Bible, the harmony idea is expressed visually. Beneath each of the seated evangelists is a rolling blue band full of long-legged birds and aquatic plants. These bands were intended to represent the paradisical streams.[131] Similar streams full of birds and plants are depicted beneath each of the evangelists in the mosaics of San Vitale in Ravenna (cf. Luke, Fig. 84).[132] It is also possible that the greenish-blue strips beneath each evangelist in the full-page portraits of the San Paolo Bible (cf. Mark, fol.

[127] *Op. cit.*, pp. 76ff. Meyer quoted Hrabanus and earlier exegetes.

[128] Köhler, *Kar. Min.*, I₂, 232ff.

[129] Köhler, *Kar. Min.*, I₂, 132. The idea of harmony is expressed by the reference to trumpets sounding together. That these trumpets are not depicted is additional evidence that the illuminators of the Grandval and Vivian frontispieces were not illustrating the caption. Trumpet-blowing evangelist symbols appear in Hiberno-Saxon art (cf. E. Kitzinger, "The Coffin-Reliquary" in Bat-

tiscombe *et al.*, *Relics of St. Cuthbert*, pp. 237f. and R. Bruce-Mitford, "Decoration and Miniatures," *Codex Lindisfarnensis* [Olten, 1960], pp. 161f.). In the Touronian Apocalypse pages, the symbol of Matthew is shown blowing a trumpet. Cf. Underwood, *op. cit.*, pp. 118ff. See Chapter V.

[130] Köhler, *Kar. Min.*, I₂, pp. 416f.

[131] Cf. Underwood, *op. cit.*, p. 129.

[132] F. Deichmann, *Frühchristliche Bauten und Mosaiken von Ravenna* (Baden-Baden, 1958), pls. 332-35.

270^r)[133] represent streams. There is no doubt that in Ottonian evangelist portraits reference to the fountain of life was intended.[134]

A *Majestas* frontispiece, nearly identical to the Vivian page, precedes the Gospels in the San Paolo Bible (Fig. 50). In a number of details, the San Paolo page is more traditional than the Vivian Bible depiction. The mandorla is oval and the evangelist symbols are placed directly above the seated authors. This suggests that the Touronian model of the San Paolo page may have predated the Vivian manuscript.

The *titulus* of the San Paolo *Majestas* reads:

SEDET THRONI RESIDENS MUNDŪ QUI PONDERATIŌNE

CORDA REPLET VATUM. UT NOB. ARCHANA REVELENT

ALTIUS ESAIA HIEREMIAS HIEZECHIELQUE

AFFLATI DANIHELQ: VIDENS MISTERIA TECTA

QUATTUOR ASSIGNANT NOBIS ANIMALIBUS ALMIS

ALMIGRAPHOS XPI VIRTUTUM QUATTUOR AEQUE.[135]

Although this caption is important for identifying the disk held by Christ as *mundus*, it is otherwise of little value in interpreting the miniature. Like the Grandval and Vivian verses, the San Paolo titulus makes no reference to the *fons vitae* theme. There is, however, reason to believe that even at the close of the Carolingian period, the fountain allegory was still recognized in the *Majestas Domini*. The San Paolo frontispiece or its Touronian model was copied in 870 in the Codex Aureus of St. Emmeram (fol. 6^v, Fig. 85).[136] In the Munich manuscript, the *Majestas* precedes a set of canon tables copied from the concordance tables of the Soissons Gospels.[137] The *Majestas Domini* of the Codex Aureus, therefore, is a substitution for the frontispiece to the canon tables in the early ninth-century Gospel book, the handsome depiction of the fountain of life on folio 6^v (Fig. 86).[138] It is difficult to believe that the illuminator of the Munich manuscript was unaware of the appropriateness of his substitution when he replaced the literal depiction of the *fons vitae* with a *Majestas Domini* of Touronian origin.

Touronian *Majestas Domini* pictures exerted a strong influence on Ottonian art.[139] In only one eleventh-century frontispiece, however, is the fountain of life explicitly expressed. This is in the Bamberg Cathedral Gospels (Munich, Bayerische Staatsbibliothek, Cod. lat. 4454, fol. 20^v)[140] where Christ stands before the tree of life and the evangelist symbols are supported by female personifications of the four rivers.

---

[133] Cf. Gaehde, "Bible Manuscript," I, 396ff.; and "Turonian Sources," pp. 395ff.

[134] K. Hoffmann, "Die Evangelistenbilder des Münchner Otto-Evangeliars," *Zeitschrift des Deutschen Vereins für Kunstwissenschaft*, XX (1966), 17ff.

[135] Gaehde, "Bible Manuscript," II, 143.

[136] Leidinger, *op. cit.*, pl. 12. Gaehde, "Bible Manuscript," I, 378ff.

[137] A. M. Friend, Jr. "Carolingian Art in the Abbey of St. Denis," *Art Studies*, I (1923), 67ff.; Leidinger, *op. cit.*, pls. 7ff.; Underwood, *op. cit.*, p. 128.

[138] Köhler, *Kar. Min.*, II, 70ff. and Underwood, *op. cit.*, p. 127.

[139] Bloch and Schnitzler, *op. cit.*, II, 85ff.

[140] G. Leidinger, *Meisterwerke der Buchmalerei* (Munich, 1920), p. 26.

CONCLUSIONS

The Touronian illuminators retained for their pandects the *Majestas* themes that had been traditional frontispiece subjects in earlier Carolingian Gospelbooks. The choice of these subjects had been inspired by Jerome's preface *Plures fuisse* and, like the prologue, the frontispieces were intended to express the unity of the four Gospels through the visions of Ezekiel and St. John. The Touronian artists abandoned the medallion composition, found in the Gundohinus Gospels and favored in the court atelier of Charlemagne, and fashioned new pictures from sources available at Tours. The *Majestas* pages in the full Bibles resulted from a fusion of the *Majestas Agni* and *Majestas Domini* compositions found in earlier Touronian Gospelbooks. The *Majestas Agni* expressed the unity of the Gospels not only in the terms from Revelation quoted by Jerome but also by alluding to the allegory of the *fons vitae*. The allegorical reference is presented most clearly in the Gospels of St. Gauzelin. The Lamb of God with the chalice at the center of the Nancy page is the *fons vitae*; the evangelist symbols at the corners of the lozenge are the four rivers that irrigate the world. The Nancy scheme was adopted with slight modifications in the Bamberg Bible. In the Bamberg manuscript, however, it is part of a full Bible program. To contrast with the Old Testament Eden at the head of the Book of Genesis, it depicts the Christian paradise offered by the Gospels. The *Majestas* was also used in the Grandval Bible. There, however, the *Agnus Dei* was replaced by the figure of Christ from a different type of Touronian Gospel page. The Vivian and San Paolo *Majestas* pictures mark the final stage of the evolution. Evangelist portraits, also copied from a Touronian Gospel manuscript, were added to the image. The streams depicted beneath these author portraits in the Vivian Bible prove that, even in these elaborate compositions, the metaphor of the fountain of living waters was an underlying concept.

The origins and purpose of the Gospel frontispieces are wholly unlike those of the Genesis pages. No single pictorial model was used. Instead, elements from several sources—most notably an Italian Apocalypse or Gospelbook and a Byzantine theophanic representation—were gradually fused and then amalgamated with schematic devices from the *Majestas Agni*. How advanced the merger of several traditions was in the basic model known at Tours is difficult to determine. Certainly, the combination of the *Majestas Domini* with schematic elements from the *Majestas Agni* was a mid-ninth century innovation. Schmid has argued on the basis of style that the Touronian illuminators used two late antique models for their *Majestas* frontispieces: one from the first half of the fifth century and the other from the beginning of the sixth.[141] Whatever the origin of their models, however, the conception of the Touronian *Majestas* compositions is without true precedent.

In the *Majestas* frontispieces, the Touronian illuminators created complex images that convey on several levels the idea of the harmony of the Gospels. Exegeses of the

---

[141] *Die Bibel von Moutier-Grandval*, pp. 164f.

visions of Ezekiel and St. John influenced the artists. The *Plures fuisse* appears to have been the basic text, but later commentaries, specifically the writings of Hrabanus Maurus, may also have guided the illuminators. In a sense, the *Majestas* pictures are themselves a kind of exegesis. With figures, symbols, and abstract schemata, they argue the authenticity of the four Gospels in terms of Old and New Testament allegories.

For the Genesis pages, the ninth-century illustrators relied confidently on Early Christian sources; for the Gospel frontispieces, they created new images that presage the art of the High Middle Ages.

IV. THE COVENANT OF THE
OLD TESTAMENT

A FULL-PAGE miniature depicting Moses Receiving the Commandments and Moses Addressing the Israelites precedes the Book of Exodus in the Grandval[1] and Vivian[2] Bibles (Figs. 87 and 88) and a related depiction is placed before Leviticus in the San Paolo manuscript (Fig. 89).[3] The Moses frontispiece is lacking in the Bamberg Bible. The close similarity of the three frontispieces leaves no doubt that they were derived from the same model.[4] As is the case with the Genesis and *Majestas* frontispieces, however, the relationship of the Moses pages to one another is more complicated than has generally been supposed.

MOSES RECEIVING THE COMMANDMENTS

Each frontispiece is divided horizontally into two scenes. In the upper composition, Moses is shown reaching up to receive the tablets of the law[5] which are extended to him in the right hand of God emerging from the clouds. Joshua, wearing a tunic and paludamentum and carrying a staff, observes the scene from the left, partly concealed by the mountain. Sinai is depicted as a mound of overlapping hillocks on which sprout bushlike flames. In the two Touronian books, the mountain reaches into the clouds and Moses is silhouetted against it. In the San Paolo Bible, the prophet stands atop the mountain and receives the tablets in veiled hands. As in the Vivian Bible, the San Paolo Moses is nimbed and like the Grandval figure, he wears sandals;[6] in the San Paolo Bible as in the Vivian manuscript, Mount Sinai is covered with daisy-like flowers; it also has trees similar to those in the Grandval illustration. These details indicate that the San Paolo frontispiece was derived, not from the Grandval or Vivian manuscript but from their model—presumably through a Touronian intermediary.[7]

The Carolingian frontispieces illustrate Exod., XXIV, 12–XXXI, 18:

> The Lord said to Moses, "Come up to me on the mountain, stay there and let me give you the tablets of stone, the law and the commandment, which I have written down that you may teach them." Moses arose with Joshua his assistant and went

[1] Fol. 25ᵛ. Köhler, *Kar. Min.*, I₂, 22ff. and 129ff.

[2] Fol. 27ᵛ. Köhler, *Kar. Min.*, I₂, 39ff. and 125ff.

[3] Fol. 31ᵛ. Gaehde, "Bible Manuscript," I, 188ff. and "Turonian Sources," pp. 370ff.

[4] Cf. Köhler, *Kar Min.*, I₂, 129f.; C. Nordenfalk, *Early Medieval Painting* (New York, 1957), p. 148; Gaehde, "Bible Manuscript," I, 188ff. and "Turonian Sources," pp. 370ff.; Schmid, *Bibel von Moutier-Grandval*, pp. 174ff.

[5] In the Grandval and Vivian Bibles they appear in the form of a roll.

[6] Exod., III, 5 and Acts VII, 33 report that God commanded Moses to remove his shoes when in his presence on Mount Horeb. God also bade Joshua to remove his shoes when standing on a holy place (Jos., V, 15). It is not surprising, therefore, that this reverential gesture was projected to Moses on Sinai. In Byzantine art, Moses is shown removing his sandals before he ascends Sinai to receive the law. Cf. Mosaics in St. Catherine's Monastery, Mt. Sinai.

[7] Gaehde, "Bible Manuscript." I, 191ff. and "Turonian Sources," *passim*.

up the mountain of God. . . . So Moses went up the mountain and a cloud covered it. The glory of the Lord rested upon Mount Sinai, and the cloud covered the mountain for six days; on the seventh day he called to Moses out of the cloud. The glory of the Lord looked to the Israelites like a devouring fire on the mountain-top. Moses entered the cloud and went up the mountain; there he stayed forty days and forty nights. . . . When he had finished speaking with Moses on Mount Sinai, the Lord gave him the two tablets of the Tokens, tablets of stone written with the finger of God.

Of the basic iconographic details, only the angels that descend from a cloud to empty fiery cornucopias on Mount Sinai in the Grandval Bible are not mentioned in this text. Reminiscent of the angels of the Apocalypse (Rev., xvi), these figures may have been inspired by Deut., xxxiii, 2, "The Lord showed himself from Mount Paran and with him were myriads of holy ones streaming along at his right hand." More likely, the angels were based on the New Testament recapitulations of the Exodus episode:

You have betrayed him and murdered him, you who received the Law as God's angels gave it to you, and yet have not kept it (Acts, vii, 53).

The law was promulgated through angels (Gal., iii, 19).

The exegetes also refer to angels at the giving of the law.[8]

Despite their literalness, the Carolingian miniatures contain elements that were seldom depicted in art. Joshua, for example, was rarely represented with Moses on Mount Sinai. He is present in the scene of Moses Receiving the Commandments on several Early Christian sarcophagi[9] and perhaps on an ivory pyxis in the Hermitage, Leningrad.[10] Joshua (with Aaron) is also represented in the illustration of Moses Receiving the Laws that accompanies Psalm LXXVIII in the eleventh-century Hamilton Psalter in Berlin.[11] The relationship of the Carolingian manuscripts to these isolated and reduced illustrations is difficult to determine. The scene of Moses Receiving the Laws in the Bible of A.D. 960 in Leon (Cathedral Library, Cod. 2, fol. 46[r], Fig. 90),[12] which Köhler adduced,[13] is more significant. It shows Moses, atop the mountain of

[8] *Midrash Rabbah* (Exod., xxix, 2) and numerous Christian commentaries including Pseudo-Dionysius' *De coelesti hierarchia*, iv, 2 and Augustine's *De civitate dei*, x, 13 and 17. Angels are depicted in an archivolt of the left portal of the west facade of St. Denis, in the frescoes of St. Savin, and in the enamel retable of Klosterneuburg.

[9] J. Wilpert, *I sarcofagi cristiani antichi* (Rome, 1929–36), i, pls. cxxvii (2), ii, pls. cxcviii (3), ccv (5), and ccviii (7).

[10] Cf. W. F. Volbach, *Elfenbeinarbeiten der Spätantike und des frühen Mittelalters* (Mainz, 1952), pl. 57; K. Weitzmann, "The Survival of

Mythological Representations in Early Christian and Byzantine Art," *Dumbarton Oaks Papers*, xiv (1960), fig. 30.

[11] Kupferstichkabinett, MS. 78.A.5. fol. 66[v].

[12] W. Neuss, *Die katalanische Bibelillustration um die Wende des ersten Jahrtausends und die altspanische Buchmalerei* (Bonn, 1922), pp. 72ff.; P. Galindo, "La 'biblia de Léon' del 960," *Gesammelte Aufsätze zur Kulturgeschichte Spaniens*, xvi (1960), pp. 37ff. I wish to thank Prof. John Williams of the University of Pittsburgh for supplying photographs of the Leon Bible for purposes of study.

[13] Köhler, *Kar. Min.*, i₂, 192.

hillocks, receiving the tablets from out of a cloud. Joshua stands at the left, half hidden behind the mountain. That the Touronian frontispieces and the tenth-century Spanish Bible were based on the same archetype seems likely and this hypothesis is buttressed by the connection between the Leon Bible and Exodus illustrations in the ninth-century Stuttgart Psalter.[14]

Although the Leon Bible, like the San Paolo frontispiece, represents Moses standing on the mountain, it is clear from the Grandval and Vivian Bibles that the model used at Tours showed him below the crest. Moses' position in the San Paolo manuscript is to be explained, not as the more faithful reflection of the basic model, but rather as the intrusion of a second source. For Moses' position, his energetic stride, and his veiled hands, the San Paolo illuminator consulted a Byzantine Octateuch.[15] The Octateuch manuscripts, for example Vatican gr. 747 (fol. 114^v, Fig. 91),[16] show Moses scaling the side of the mountain and accepting the laws in veiled hands. Gaehde has demonstrated that the illuminators of the San Paolo Bible based other frontispieces on a Greek Octateuch.[17] It is not surprising that the illustrator of the Leviticus page also consulted this Byzantine source.

MOSES ADDRESSING THE ISRAELITES

Compared to the scenes of Moses Receiving the Law in the upper panels of the frontispieces, the depictions in the bottom sections are quite varied. All three show Moses addressing a group of Israelites. But the details of action, setting, and costume differ considerably in the three compositions.

In the Grandval Bible, Moses speaks to a group of fifteen "filii Israhel" which is led by Aaron. Joshua stands behind him at the door of the columnar building in which the scene takes place.[18] Moses holds a diptych on which is written: "Hear, O Israel, the Lord is our God, one Lord, and you must love the Lord your God with all your heart and soul and strength" (Deut., VI, 4–5).[19]

---

[14] Cf. F. Mütherich, "Die Stellung der Bilder in der frühmittelalterlichen Psalterillustration," Bischoff et al., Die Stuttgarter Bilderpsalter (Stuttgart, 1968), pp. 171 et passim.

[15] Kessler, "Sources and Construction," p. 95 and Gaehde, "Turonian Sources," pp. 372f.

[16] According to K. Weitzmann, of the several Octateuch manuscripts, Vat. gr. 747, is generally the most faithful to the archetype. Cf. Weitzmann, Joshua Roll (Princeton, 1948), pp. 31ff.

[17] "Bible Manuscript," I, 493ff. et passim and idem, "Carolingian Interpretations of an Early Christian Picture Cycle to the Octateuch in the Bible of San Paolo Fuori Le Mura in Rome," Frühmittelalterliche Studien, VIII (1974), 351ff.

[18] The figures are labelled: Josue, Moys, Aaron, and filii Israhel.

[19] For a precise transcription of the verses, cf. Schmid, Bibel von Moutier-Grandval, p. 175. These verses from Deuteronomy were considered to be the essence of the Mosaic law. Cf. Matt., XXII, 40, " 'Master, which is the greatest commandment in the law?' He answered, 'Love the Lord your God with all your heart, with all your soul, with all your mind.' That is the greatest commandment. It comes first. The second is like it: 'Love your neighbor as yourself.' Everything in the Law and the prophets hangs on these two commandments."

The likeliest identification of the Grandval scene is the traditional one—Moses speaking to the Israelites following his second descent from Sinai:[20]

> At length Moses came down from Mount Sinai with the two stone tablets of the Tokens in his hands, and when he descended, he did not know that the skin of his face shone because he had been speaking with the Lord. When Aaron and the Israelites saw how the skin of Moses' face shone, they were afraid to approach him. He called out to them, and Aaron and all the chiefs in the congregation turned towards him. Moses spoke to them, and afterwards all the Israelites drew near. He gave them all the commands with which the Lord had charged him on Mount Sinai and finished what he had to say (Exod., XXXIV, 29–33).

Even though Moses' face neither shines nor bears the "cornutam Moysi faciem,"[21] the men of the congregation react with clear concern. These twelve men, in ranks behind Aaron and his ministers, may be delegates of the tribes, the "chiefs of the congregation."

The Grandval illuminator also incorporated elements described in the preceding passages of Exodus. Joshua, for example, was probably included because according to Exod., XXXIII, 11, "Joshua son of Nun never moved from inside the Tabernacle." The great emphasis in the miniature on Aaron and on the Tabernacle may result from the lengthy description of the priestly vestments and the Tabernacle in Exod., XXV–XXXI. Aaron is crowned and wears a tunic trimmed with gold bells and a pallium (Exod., XXVIII, 34) and he is flanked by two attendants, probably his sons Nadab and Abihu (Exod., XXIV, 1 and XXVIII, 1). He also holds a maniple which is an extra-biblical, in fact a Christian, intrusion that enhances Aaron's priestly demeanor.[22] The tabernacle does not follow the prescripts of Exod. XXVI. On the other hand, it does resemble the *tentorium Domini* shown from the outside in the Ashburnham Pentateuch (Paris, Bibliothèque Nationale, nouv. acq. lat. cod. 2334, fol. 127ᵛ, Fig. 92).[23]

Moses Teaching the Israelites had been incorporated into Carolingian Psalters as an illustration to Psalm LXXVIII. In the Utrecht Psalter (fol. 45ʳ), Moses stands at a lectern beneath the Hand of God and addresses a vast crowd of Israelites.[24] In the Stuttgart Psalter (fol. 90ʳ, Fig. 93),[25] the depiction, though less ambitious, is similar. Moses lectures the Israelites who constitute an animated gathering at the right. The

[20] Cf. Köhler, *Kar. Min.*, I₂, 130 and Schmid, *Bibel von Moutier-Grandval*, pp. 174ff. It is also possible, however, that the scene depicts the Calling of the Census (Num. I). Cf. Kessler, "Sources and Construction," pp. 97ff.

[21] Cf. R. Mellinkoff, *The Horned Moses in Medieval Art and Thought* (Berkeley, 1970).

[22] Cf. Leitschuh, *Malerei*, p. 111 and Köhler, *Kar. Min.*, I₂, 130f. For a history of the maniple see: J. Braun, *Die liturgische Gewandung* (Freiburg, 1907), pp. 515f.

[23] O. Gebhart, *The Miniatures of the Ashburnham Pentateuch* (London, 1883). The Grandval tabernacle is also quite similar to the tent structures in certain miniatures of the San Paolo Bible (fol. 32ᵛ and 40ᵛ). Cf. Gaehde, "Bible Manuscript," I, 216ff. and *idem*, "Carolingian Interpretations," pp. 358ff. It is apparent that the originator of the model that was used by the Grandval artist had adapted an architectural convention to his needs. Cf. Schmid, *Bibel von Moutier-Grandval*, p. 177.

[24] E. T. Dewald, *The Illustrations of the Utrecht Psalter* (Princeton, 1933), pl. 72.

[25] Mütherich, *op. cit.*, p. 111.

textual basis of these scenes is difficult to pinpoint. Mütherich has connected the Stuttgart Psalter miniature with Exodus XXIV, 7 which is one possibility. The Utrecht Psalter representation is certainly based on Deut., XXXIff., and it is quite possible that the Stuttgart Psalter picture also illustrates Moses' farewell. Comparisons with the representation of Moses Blessing the Israelites in the eleventh-century Aelfric Paraphrase (London, British Library, Cod. Cotton, Claudius, B IV, fol. 199ʳ, Fig. 94)[26] support the latter identification. The lectern is not depicted in the Aelfric manuscript, but the Hand of God, Moses, and the group of Israelites are similar to the elements in the ninth-century manuscripts. Even the leader of the Israelites who raises his arms in animated speech is alike in these depictions.

The connection between the ninth-century Psalters and the Grandval Bible is not direct. The Grandval manuscript includes neither the hand of God nor the lectern and the Stuttgart illustration lacks Joshua, Aaron, and the Tabernacle. The two illustrations may, nevertheless, be related to each other. The Moses figures and the Israelites (especially certain of their gestures) are alike in the two manuscripts and this may indicate that both ninth-century depictions were drawn from the same model. It is possible that the two illuminators copied different narrative moments from the picture source. That would account for the differences and the similarities.

In the Ashburnham Pentateuch, Moses is shown reading to the Israelites from an open diptych (fol. 76ʳ, Fig. 95).[27] There is no compositional similarity with the Grandval Bible, but it is interesting that in the Ashburnham Pentateuch, too, the group of Israelites is led by two priests wearing togas. In the scene of the Giving of the Laws and in the Tabernacle scene, Aaron is accompanied by Nadab and Abihu. Joshua accompanies Moses in the latter scene.

The depiction of Exod., XXXIV, 29–33 in the Aelfric Paraphrase (fol. 105ʳ, Fig. 96) is reasonably close to the Grandval representation although there is a great stylistic discrepancy in the two miniatures. Joshua is not included, but as in the Grandval frontispiece, Moses stands with the tablets before a curtained tabernacle and he addresses a group of men headed by Aaron. Moses is bearded and, like Aaron, he wears a toga. The Israelites, standing in ranks behind Aaron, exhibit considerable agitation. It is possible that the Grandval Bible and the Aelfric Paraphrase were based on the same pictorial archetype.

Exod., XXXIV, 29–33 is not illustrated in the Leon Bible. The Spanish manuscript does include representations of Moses' Charge to the Levites (Exod., XXXII, 26–27. fol. 46ʳ, Fig. 90) and Moses Ordering the Idolaters Slain (fol. 46ᵛ, Fig. 97). Those depictions are not inconsistent with the Grandval miniature.

The lower scene in the Vivian frontispiece is distinctly different from the Grandval

[26] Cf. C. R. Dodwell, "L'originalité iconographique de plusieurs illustrations anglo-saxonnes de la Ancien Testament," *Cahiers de Civilisation Médiévale*, XIV (1971), 319ff. and *idem*, *The Old English Illustrated Hexateuch* (eds. C. R. Dodwell and P. Clemoes, "Early English Manuscripts in Facsimile" [Copenhagen-London-Baltimore, 1974]). Moses' horns are represented, perhaps for the first time in the history of art, in the Aelfric paraphase. Cf. Mellinkoff, *op. cit.*, pp. 13ff.

[27] Gebhart, *op. cit.*, pl. 20.

composition. The action takes place outside the Tabernacle. Joshua does not guard the door but stands behind Moses and Moses hands the tablets to one of the priestly assistants as he reads from them.[28] The entourage has grown to nineteen men and they all wear fillets. Moses' action secures the identification of this scene. It is the Transferal of the Laws to the Levites:

> Moses summoned Joshua and said to him in the presence of all Israel, "Be strong, be resolute; for it is you who are to lead this people into the land which the Lord swore to give their forefathers, and you are to bring them into possession of it. The Lord himself goes at your head; he will be with you; he will not fail you or foresake you. Do not be discouraged or afraid." Moses wrote down this law and gave it to the priests, the sons of Levi, who carried the Ark of the Covenant of the Lord, and to all the elders of Israel (Deut., XXXI, 7–9).

> That day Moses wrote down this rule of life and taught it to the Israelites. The Lord gave Joshua son of Nun his commission. . . . When Moses had finished writing down these laws in a book, from beginning to end, he gave his command to the Levites who carried the Ark of the Covenant of the Lord: "Take this book of the Law and put it beside the Ark of the Covenant." (Deut., XXXI, 22–26).

Moses is about to die. Having appointed Joshua as his successor, he instructs the Levites and delivers the book to them. The high priest depicted in the Vivian frontispiece cannot be Aaron; he must be Aaron's successor, Eleazar, who wears the priestly crown and robes. Around his neck is the *ephod*, which resembles a medieval rationale more than the Old Testament breastplate.[29] The tabernacle, a curtained basilica, is quite similar to the structures in the Ashburnham Pentateuch.

Moses' farewell illustrated in the San Paolo Bible (fol. 50[v])[30] is one of the non-Touronian frontispieces and is not directly related to the Vivian page. In the Leon Bible, Deut., XXXII, 1 and Deut., XXXIII, 1 are illustrated with conventional compositions of Moses' farewell rather than the Transferal of the Law. They show Moses with his arm extended toward a group of "filii israhel" (fols. 87[r] and 87[v], Figs. 98 and 99).[31] In the Aelfric Paraphase, Moses' farewell occupies five miniatures. Fol. 136[v] (Fig. 100) represents at the top Moses encouraging Joshua before the Israelites and below, it shows the prophet writing the book which one Levite is about to accept (Deut., XXXI, 7–9). Fol. 137[r] depicts Moses and Joshua in the Tabernacle (Deut., XXXI, 14ff., Fig. 101); fol. 138[v] represents Moses Giving the Law (Deut., XXXI, 24–27, Fig. 102); and fol. 139[v] is a full-page miniature of Moses Blessing the Israelites (Deut., XXXII–XXXIII, Fig. 94).[32] Joshua is absent in the majority of these

---

[28] Inscribed: *Diliges Dominum Deum tuum ex toto corde.*

[29] Cf. Ex., XXVIII, 4–29.

[30] Cf. Gaehde, "Bible Manuscript," I, 250ff. and "Carolingian Interpretations," 371ff.

[31] In another Spanish manuscript, the eleventh-century Roda Bible (Paris, Bibliothèque Natio-nale, cod. lat. 6, fol. 73[r]), Moses sits writing and is about to place the book into the veiled hands of one of the three Levites who kneel before him.

[32] H. Swarzenski, *Monuments of Romanesque Art* (Chicago, 1953), p. 21. Swarzenski drew a connection between the Aelfric Paraphrase and the Deuteronomy frontispiece in the San Paolo

illustrations and in many, Moses is seated. The Levites wear fillets, however, and in other ways, they resemble the figures in the Vivian Bible. It is possible, therefore, that the Aelfric scenes and the Vivian Bible miniature were derived from the same archetype.

Iconographically closest to the Vivian frontispiece is the representation of Moses' Farewell in the mosaics of Sta. Maria Maggiore in Rome (Fig. 103).[33] Moses stands at the left and extends an open book to a group of togate men. Joshua is missing and Moses is beardless, but the mosaic composition is enough like the Vivian scene to confirm the identification of the latter as Moses Transferring the Book of the Laws to the Levites. It is not impossible that the Roman mosaics were derived from the same archetype as the Vivian frontispiece.

The lower scene of the San Paolo page differs from both Touronian frontispieces. The event which takes place outside a four-posted edifice is more casual and more animated than the others. Moses is engaged in an active debate with two young men who, like the other Israelites, are dressed in short tunics and paludamenta. A second debate, centering on the bearded man, fourth from the right in the composition, is also shown. Aaron is not present and it is not clear whether the togate figure behind Moses is Joshua.[34]

The San Paolo scene probably copies an illustration of the Spies Sent to Canaan, recounted in Num., XIII, 25–31:

> After forty days they returned from exploring the country, and came back to Moses and Aaron and the whole community of Israelites at Kadesh in the wilderness of Paran. They made their report to them and to the whole community, and showed them the fruit of the country. . . . Then Caleb called for silence before Moses and said, "Let us go up at once and occupy the country; we are well able to conquer it." But the men who had gone with him said, "No, we cannot attack these people; they are stronger than we."

The depiction of this event in the mosaics of Sta. Maria Maggiore (Fig. 104) is quite similar to the scene in the San Paolo Bible. Moses, accompanied by a robed assistant, converses with a band of spies in field dress. No scene from Numbers is illustrated in the Leon Bible, but in the Aelfric Paraphrase (fol. 117ʳ, Fig. 105), the depiction is even closer than the Roman mosaic to the ninth-century composition. The togate Moses instructs the spies who are dressed in tunics and who are arranged in groups quite like the San Paolo band. Two leaders confront Moses while several men at the far right conspire among themselves.

Bible (fol. 50ᵛ). This has been amplified by Gaehde ("Bible Manuscript," I, 255ff. and "Carolingian Interpretations," p. 373) but is contested by Mellinkoff, op. cit., pp. 14f.

[33] H. Karpp, Die frühchristlichen und mittelalterlichen Mosaiken in Santa Maria Maggiore zu Rom (Baden-Baden, 1966). The mosaics do not include the scene of Moses Receiving the Commandments.

[34] Gaehde, "Turonian Sources," pp. 373ff. identified the figures on the basis of the Touronian frontispieces. It is difficult to believe, however, that the figure addressing Moses in the San Paolo Bible is Aaron. He is entirely unlike the priest figures in the Grandval and Vivian frontispieces.

To construct their frontispieces, the ninth-century illuminators selected scenes from an illustrated Pentateuch. All three chose to represent Moses Receiving the Laws (Exod., XXIVff.) in the upper section of the page, but in the lower halves they selected different compositions. The Grandval illuminator copied the scene of Moses Instructing the Israelites after his second return from Sinai (Exod., XXXIV, 29–33); the Vivian master borrowed the composition of Moses Transferring the Laws to the Levites (Deut., XXXI); and the artist of the San Paolo Bible copied the depiction of the Return of the Spies (Num., XIII).

In selecting these scenes, the artists seem to have been guided by the *tituli*. The caption in the Grandval and Vivian Bibles reads:

> SUSCIPIT LEGEM MOYSES CORUSCA
>
> REGIS E DEXTRA SUPERI, SED INFRA
>
> IAM DOCET CHRISTI POPULUM REPLETUS
>
> NECTARE SANCTO[35]

These verses were not the textual source of the frontispieces. They do not specify numerous details in the scenes, details that were based on the Bible text itself. But they might have served as a general guide which led the illuminators to select from their model the scene of Receiving the Laws and an appropriate composition of Moses teaching. The San Paolo Bible *tituli* are more elaborate:

> E NUBIS MEDIO MOYSES FLAMMAEQUAE VOCATUS
>
> CONSCENDIT MONTEM. LONGES SISTENTE MINISTRO.
>
> AC PRECEPTA DI TABULIS BIS QUINA NOTATA
>
> SUSCEPIT LEGIS LUMEN PERFERRE PERITUS
>
> EXPERTI POPULO VIDEAT QUO NOSCERE VERUM
>
> ET LINQUENS CREDAT DNO SIMULACHRA NEFANDA.[36]

There is no reason to believe that these verses guided the creator of the Touronian model of the San Paolo frontispiece when he selected scenes from the pictorial prototype. They seem to have been invented after the images to explain the pictures.

THE MODELS OF THE MOSES FRONTISPIECE

The correct identification of the several scenes in the Carolingian Bibles suggests that the Touronian illuminators had access to a richly illustrated Pentateuch. The artists all copied the same composition from this Pentateuch to depict Moses on Mt. Sinai; but they chose different representations of Moses Addressing the Israelites. This was due, in part, to the vagueness of the second part of the *titulus*—at least in the Grandval and Vivian Bibles. It also probably resulted from the great number of very similar teaching scenes in the pictorial prototype.

Scenes of address or instruction, consisting of a single figure confronting an as-

[35] Köhler, *Kar. Min.*, I₂, 129. [36] Gaehde, "Bible Manuscript," II, 138.

sembled audience are common in medieval manuscripts. In the Byzantine codex of the works of Gregory Nazianzenus in Milan (Ambrosiana, MS. 49–50)[37] for example, the composition of Gregory teaching a group of monks is repeated more than thirty times. It is not surprising that similar compositions appeared in an illustrated Pentateuch where over and over Moses speaks to the Israelites. In the Ashburnham Pentateuch, for instance, Moses is shown confronting gatherings of Israelites on fol. 68[r], fol. 76[r], and fol. 127[v].[38] In the more conventionalized Leon Bible, virtually identical confrontation compositions appear on fol. 40[r] (Exod., XVI, 22–23), fol. 46[v] (Exod., XXXII, 26–29), fol. 87[r] (Deut., XXXII, 1) and fol. 87[v] (Deut., XXXIII, 1). The Aelfric Paraphrase is richest of all. It contains no fewer than twenty-four scenes of Moses Addressing the Israelites.[39] Only minor details distinguish many of these compositions from one another. If the depictions were seen out of context, it would be almost impossible to identify the specific events portrayed in these compositions.

The relationship of the Carolingian depictions to other Pentateuch illustrations is difficult to determine. Although they seem to share certain details with the Ashburnham Pentateuch, these are of a general nature. A scene to scene comparison, possible only with fol. 76[r], strongly indicates that the two manuscripts are not related to one another. The connections with the Leon Bible, the Aelfric Paraphrase, and the mosaics of Sta. Maria Maggiore are closer. Despite the stylistic differences, the similarities with the Leon Bible are most striking. The Leon Bible rendering of Moses Receiving the Laws shows Joshua and the scalloped mountain. Parallels between the Leon Bible and the Stuttgart Psalter constitute further evidence that the prototype of the Spanish manuscript was available to the Carolingian illuminators. Unfortunately the scenes of Moses Addressing the Israelites in the Leon Bible are too few and too conventional to allow detailed comparisons with the Bible compositions. Because of its pictorial richness, the Aelfric Paraphrase is also interesting. There are no good comparisons between it and the Touronian depictions of Moses on Mt. Sinai; but its representations of Moses Addressing the Israelites reveal numerous similarities to the Carolingian compositions.

Implied by these comparisons is the hypothesis that the Leon Bible and the Aelfric manuscript belong to the same pictorial family. The proof of this theory is impossible to test fully within the limits of this investigation. That it is plausible, however, can be indicated by a single comparison. To illustrate the Commission of Joshua (Deut., XXXI, 15), both manuscripts (Figs. 101 and 106)[40] represent Moses and Joshua in the arched doorway of the tent of meeting. Moses raises his right hand toward the pillar of cloud and his gesture is echoed by the diminutive Joshua standing behind him.

The mosaics in Sta. Maria Maggiore pose complex problems, but they, too, seem to belong to this pictorial family.

[37] A. Grabar, *Les miniatures du Grégoire de Nazianze de l'Ambrosienne* (Paris, 1943), I.

[38] Gebhart, *op. cit.*, pls. 17, 18, and 19.

[39] Fols.: 93[r], 93[v], 96[v], 97[r] (a and b), 99[v], 100[v], 105[v], 108[v], 111[v], 112[r], 113[v], 115[r], 115[v], 117[r], 118[v], 119[v], 121[r], 121[v], 122[r], 123[v], 136[v] (a and b), 139[v].

[40] Leon Bible, fol. 86[v]; Aelfric Paraphrase, fol. 137[r].

The ultimate origin of the model can be deduced only through very tenuous evidence. There is no indication that it was Byzantine.[41] It bears no similarity to the Byzantine Octateuchs and all the related monuments are Western. The earliest of these is Roman; and Rome seems to be the likeliest place of origin for the prototype. Rome is also suggested by the style of the Carolingian miniatures.[42] Until a thorough investigation of the Leon Bible, the Aelfric Paraphrase, and the Sta. Maria Maggiore mosaics sheds greater light, the origin of the model will remain in question.

The model seems certainly to have been a Christian creation. The angels in the representation of Moses Receiving the Law in the Grandval Bible and the Christian liturgical details in the Grandval and Vivian compositions were probably aspects of the model and indicate a Christian origin.

In the San Paolo Bible, a second model influenced the illuminator. The effect of this Byzantine Octateuch, however, is apparent only in the upper composition and is of only secondary significance.

CONCLUSIONS

The three Moses frontispieces are analogous to the Genesis pages in the Carolingian Bibles. Like the latter, they were constructed from a richly illustrated narrative model and each represents a somewhat different selection from the prototype. Few changes appear to have been introduced into the original compositions; but it is possible that the Christian and liturgical elements were Carolingian additions.

The model appears to have been Western, related to the mosaics of Sta. Maria Maggiore, the Leon Bible, and the Aelfric Paraphrase. The prototype certainly included Exodus, Numbers, and Deuteronomy. Whether it was a full Pentateuch, a Heptateuch, or another similar compilation cannot be determined with precision. It is unlikely that the source of the Genesis frontispiece in the Carolingian Bibles was more extensive than the first book of the Pentateuch.[43] What is more, connections between the Cotton Genesis and the Roman mosaics, Leon Bible, or Aelfric Paraphrase are difficult to identify.[44] This makes it very unlikely, therefore, that the same Pentateuch model supplied the ninth-century illuminators with material for both their Genesis and Exodus frontispieces. One must conclude that at least two illustrated Old Testaments were available at ninth-century Tours: a Genesis manuscript and a Pentateuch or similar collection.

[41] O. Pächt, *The Rise of Pictorial Narrative* (Oxford, 1962), p. 5, has asserted that the source of the Aelfric Paraphrase was Greek but he gives no proof. C. R. Dodwell, "L'originalité," pp. 319 and *Hexateuch*, pp. 65ff. maintained that it is a fresh creation.

[42] Cf. Schmid, *Bibel von Moutier-Grandval*, pp. 176ff.

[43] Cf. Chapter II.

[44] G. Henderson, "Late-Antique Influences in Some English Mediaeval Illustrations of Genesis," *Journal of the Warburg and Courtauld Institutes*, xxv (1962), 171ff.

V. REVELATION

THE problems posed by the Apocalypse illustrations of the Grandval (Fig. 107),[1] Vivian (Fig. 108),[2] and San Paolo Bibles (Fig. 109),[3] are more fundamental and more complex than those presented by the other Touronian frontispieces. For these pages alone is there serious difficulty in identifying the subject matter itself and from this difficulty of iconographic identification follow the more significant questions of sources and interpretation.

Fortunately, the similarity of the basic images depicted on the three miniatures permits a reasonably precise reconstruction of their common model. That model must have focused on two depictions. The first represented a nimbed lamb breaking the seal of an enormous codex propped up on a throne or altar. The second depicted a bearded man enthroned and holding above his head a great cloth. An eagle was perched on top of the cloth, a winged ox and winged lion tugged at its ends, and a winged man blew into it through a long trumpet.

Correspondences among the frontispieces permit the restoration of other details. Judging from the Grandval and Vivian Bibles, the first image included a lion as well as a lamb. There is little basis for deciding with certainty whether the lion participated in the action or simply stood at the side. A twelfth-century fresco at Münstereifel (Monastic church, Fig. 110),[4] which may have been copied from the lost Prüm Bible,[5] suggests that the Grandval lion is more authentic. The model must also have represented the four evangelist symbols—as in the Grandval and Vivian Bibles, half-length figures holding open codices. From the Vivian and San Paolo pictures, it is clear that the great book was sealed with seven straps, the first of which was already loosed by the lamb's raised right foreleg. Apparently, the book was decorated with almond rosette patterns. The altar/throne is more difficult to reconstruct. It seems to have consisted of a slab supported on columns as in the San Paolo Bible. The slab is a feature in the Grandval picture and the columns are visible in the Vivian frontispiece. A curtain, decorated with clusters of three dots must have hung from the slab; and a similar curtain was suspended behind the altar/throne as in the Grandval and Vivian pages.

In the second representation, the man must have been seated on a massive throne rather than a faldstool and the beasts must have had nimbi and wings. These are features that distinguish the Grandval and Vivian depictions from the San Paolo fron-

---

[1] Fol. 449[r]. In the Grandval Bible, the Apocalypse miniature is placed after the text of Revelation. Cf. Köhler, *Kar. Min.*, I₂, 136ff. and Schmid, *Bibel von Moutier-Grandval*, pp. 178ff.

[2] Fol. 415[v]. Köhler, *Kar. Min.*, I₂, 136ff.

[3] Fol. 331[v]. Cf. Gaehde, "Bible Manuscript," I, 443ff. and "Turonian Sources," pp. 392ff.

[4] P. Clemen, *Die romanische Monumentalmalerei in den Rheinlanden* (Düsseldorf, 1916),

I, 200f.; II, pl. XIV and R. Schmitz-Ehmke, "Zum Programm der Apsis Malerei in der Ehemaligen Stiftskirche St. Chryzanthus und Daria in Münstereifel," *Beiträge zur Rheinischen Kunstgeschichte und Denkmalpflege. Festschrift R. Wesenberg* (Düsseldorf, 1970), pp. 103ff.

[5] Cf. Chapter I. Münstereifel was a priory of Prüm. This was suggested by Schmitz-Ehmke, *op. cit.*, p. 111.

tispiece. In showing the eagle actually clawing and lifting the cloth and the lion tugging at it, the San Paolo Bible may be the most accurate reflection of the model.[6] An active eagle appears also in the Vivian Bible and a prancing lion is depicted on the Grandval page.

THE SOURCES OF THE PRIMARY IMAGES

The textual basis of the lamb images is Revelation:

In the center, round the throne itself, were four living creatures, covered with eyes, in front and behind. The first creature was like a lion, the second like an ox, the third had a human face, and the fourth was like an eagle in flight. (Rev., IV, 6–8)

Then I saw in the right hand of the One who sat on the throne a scroll with writing inside and out, and it was sealed up with seven seals. . . . But one of the elders said to me: "Do not weep; for the Lion from the tribe of Judah, the Scion of David, has won the right to open the scroll and break its seven seals." Then I saw standing in the very middle of the throne, inside the circle of living creatures and the circle of elders, a Lamb with the marks of slaughter upon him. He had seven horns and seven eyes, the eyes which are the seven spirits of God sent out over all the world. And the Lamb went up and took the scroll from the right hand of the One who sat on the throne. . . . Then I watched as the Lamb broke the first of the seven seals. (Rev., v, 1–7; vi, 1).

The lamb breaking the seal on the book, the throne, the lion, and the "four living creatures" are clearly based on these passages although they differ from the biblical text in numerous details.[7]

The pictorial origin of the images is less clear than the textual sources. In the Carolingian Apocalypse manuscripts at Cambrai (Bibliothèque Municipale, MS. 386, fol. 12ᵛ)[8] and Trier (Stadtbibliothek, MS. 31, fols. 17ᵛ, 18ᵛ, 19ᵛ, and 20ᵛ, cf. Fig. 65),[9] the lamb is represented in a clipeus and the four creatures are shown full-length and holding closed codices. A similar image serves as the frontispiece in the Soissons Gospels (Paris, Bibliothèque Nationale, Cod. lat. 8850, fol. 1ᵛ, Fig. 66),[10] although in this early ninth-century miniature, the evangelist symbols hold open books. Only in the

[6] This is also proposed by Gaehde, "Turonian Sources," p. 393.

[7] The Münstereifel fresco includes verses based on Revelations v: S VDA LEO VIC/T . . . A. Cf. Schmitz-Ehmke, op. cit., p. 109.

[8] F. van der Meer, Maiestas Domini (Rome and Paris, 1938), passim.

[9] Van der Meer, op. cit., passim.; J. Snyder, "The Reconstruction of an Early Christian Cycle of Illustrations for the Book of Revelation—The

Trier Apocalypse," Vigiliae Christianae, XVIII (1964), 146ff.; Charlemagne, pp. 304f.; Trierer Apokalypse (Graz, 1975).

[10] Köhler, Kar. Min., II, pl. 67. The Beatus manuscripts conform to this type. Cf. W. Neuss, Die Apokalypse des Hl. Johannes (Münster, 1931). For example, in the Gerona Apocalypse (Sancti Beati a Liebana in Apocalypsin Codex Gerundensis [Olten, 1962]).

ninth-century Apocalypse in Valenciennes (Bibliothèque Municipale, MS. 99, fol. 12, Fig. 111),[11] is there a depiction of the lamb on a throne. The absence of the books, the depiction of the symbols in clipei, and the presence of two angels, however, distinguish the Valenciennes representation from those in the Touronian Bibles. The Valenciennes illustration can only be cited as the type of Apocalypse page that may have served as the fundamental source of the Bible miniatures.

Peter Klein has adduced interesting parallels to the Carolingian frontispieces in two twelfth-century manuscripts, Haimo's *Commentary on the Apocalypse* in Oxford (Bodley Cod. 352) and the *Liber Floridus* in Wolfenbüttel (Herzog August Bibliothek, Cod. Guelf. 1 Gud. lat. 2°, Fig. 112).[12] Among other features, these manuscripts share with the Carolingian Bibles the heraldic placement of the Lamb and Lion. Klein has contended that the ninth-century Bibles, the Oxford *Haimo*, and the Wolfenbüttel *Liber Floridus* are a subgroup of the vast Apocalypse recension that originated in fifth-century Rome and underwent repeated revisions during subsequent centuries. He has argued that the prototype of this subgroup probably was created during the sixth century.[13]

Curiously, some of the closest parallels to the Touronian lamb images appear in a seventeenth-century Byzantine manuscript, the so-called Maximos Apocalypse in Chicago (University of Chicago Library, MS. 931, fols. 48^v, 51^r, and 52^v, cf. Figs. 113 and 114).[14] The lamb, the codex, the throne, and the evangelist symbols recall the Carolingian frontispieces. Because the origin of the Byzantine illustrations remains unknown, their relationship to the Touronian frontispieces cannot be specified. Nevertheless, the Chicago manuscript, like the Valenciennes codex, helps to establish the likelihood that the lamb images in the ninth-century Bibles were copied from an illustrated Apocalypse. The Chicago Apocalypse also sheds light on a detail of the Carolingian frontispieces that has puzzled many commentators: the altar-like throne. Köhler had argued that the Grandval and Vivian pictures refer to the altar of the Old Covenant described in Exod., xxx, 1–10; and his view is supported by the appearance of the altar in the San Paolo Bible.[15] Schmid considered the altar/throne a "mehrschichtig" image.[16] Klein, on the other hand, maintained that the Touronian frontispieces depict the throne and reflect the intrusion of the *Hetoimasia* into Apocalypse imagery.[17] Klein may be correct. Nevertheless, the alternation of a backed and an altar-like throne in the Chicago Apocalypse (Figs. 113 and 114) suggests that there may

[11] F. Juraschek, *Die Apokalypse von Valenciennes* (Linz, 1954); *Charlemagne*, p. 271.

[12] "Der Kodex und sein Bildschmuck," in *Trierer Apokalypse*, pp. 105ff. I wish to thank Dr. Klein for sending me the proofs of his essay before it appeared. Cf. also: P. Klein, "Der Apokalypse-Zyklus der Roda-Bibel und seine Stellung in der ikonographischen Tradition," *Archivio Español de Arqueologia*, XLV–XLVII (1972–74), 267ff.

[13] "Der Kodex," p. 111.

[14] H. Willoughby, *The Elizabeth Day McCormick Apocalypse* (Chicago, 1940) and *Illuminated Greek Manuscripts from American Collections. An Exhibition in Honor of Kurt Weitzmann* (Princeton, 1973), pp. 215ff.

[15] *Kar. Min.*, I₂, 138.

[16] *Bibel von Moutier-Grandval*, p. 182.

[17] "Der Kodex," pp. 108ff.

be no special significance to the form. It should be noted that Rev., VIII, 3 describes an altar in front of the throne and that the altar appears in many miniatures of the Trier Apocalypse.

A nearly contemporary reflection of the Apocalypse source used by the Touronian illuminators may be preserved in the Stuttgart Psalter (Württembergische Landesbibliothek, Bibl. fol. 23).[18] On fol. 51ᵛ (Fig. 115), the illuminator depicted a lamb beside an altar on which a closed book lies. The representation illustrates Psalm, XL, 6–7:

> IF THOU HADST DESIRED SACRIFICE AND OFFERING THOU WOULDST HAVE
> GIVEN ME EARS TO HEAR.
> IF THOU HADST ASKED FOR WHOLE-OFFERING AND SIN-OFFERING I
> WOULD HAVE SAID, "HERE I AM."

The book and the raised left foreleg of the lamb strongly suggest that the depiction was copied from an illustration of Rev., V.[19] The parallels with the Apocalypse frontispiece in the San Paolo Bible are particularly striking.

Whether the evangelist symbols also were derived from the same source is difficult to determine. They are referred to in the text and they are depicted in the Apocalypse illustrations (cf. Fig. 65). However, the fact that they find their closest parallels in the Touronian evangelist portraits, for example in the Prüm Gospels (Berlin, Staatsbibliothek, Cod. theol. lat. fol. 733)[20], suggests that the creator of the Bible pages may have supplemented his Apocalypse model with motifs copied from a Gospel book.[21]

The lamb images in the Touronian Bibles refer to passages in Rev., IV, V, and VI. Although they do not conform to the illustrations of these verses in the well-known Carolingian Apocalypse manuscripts, there is reason to believe that they were copied from an illustrated Book of Revelation.

Identification of the second principal subject is more difficult. Köhler's suggestion that the illustration depicts the Elder of the Apocalypse[22] is most obvious:

> And among the lamps one like a son of man, robed down to his feet, with a golden girdle round his breast. The hair of his head was white as snow-white wool, and his eyes flamed like fire; his feet gleamed like burnished brass refined in a furnace, and his voice was like the sound of rushing waters (Rev., I, 13–14).

> There in heaven stood a throne, and on the throne sat one whose appearance was like the gleam of jasper and cornelian (Rev., IV, 3–4).

---

[18] F. Mütherich, "Der Inhalt der Bilder" and "Die Stellung der Bilder in der frühmittelalterlichen Psalterillustration," in B. Bischoff et al., *Der Stuttgarter Bilderpsalter* (Stuttgart, 1968), pp. 88 and 189.

[19] *Ibid.*, p. 189.

[20] Köhler, *Kar. Min.*, I₁, 256ff. and I₂, 333f.

[21] Cf. Schmid, *Bibel von Moutier-Grandval*, p. 183. The symbols in the Vivian Bible are closer to those in the Touronian Gospels than are the Grandval creatures.

[22] *Kar. Min.*, I₂, 139ff. This identification was also argued by the author in "Sources and Construction," pp. 113ff.

The elder of Revelation was traditionally identified as Christ and in the Carolingian Apocalypse manuscripts, he is represented as the youthful savior (Cf. Figs. 55 and 60). In the Roda Bible (Paris, Bibliothèque Nationale, Cod. lat. 6), in the Oxford *Haimo* and Wolfenbüttel *Liber Floridus* (Fig. 112) he is bearded. Again, it is the Maximos Apocalypse that comes closest to the Touronian images. Although it differs in numerous details from the ninth-century Bibles, the Greek manuscript includes depictions of a bearded, enthroned Christ (fols. 4^v, 35^v, 41^v, and 44^r, cf. Fig. 116).[23]

Of all the personages in the Book of Revelation, the Elder best fits the Touronian images. Nevertheless, this identification poses several questions. Why does the depiction follow the representation of the lamb rather than precede it as prescribed by the text? More important, why does the elder support a great cloth which is being pulled at by the symbols?

Several scholars, unable to reconcile the Touronian depictions with the Apocalypse text, have sought other identifications for the enthroned man. J. Croquison proposed that the man is St. John and that the image is a kind of author portrait.[24] This proposal poses more problems than it resolves. The man is quite unlike representations of St. John in Touronian Gospelbooks and in the Vivian and San Paolo *Majestas* pages; and he does not resemble the beardless evangelist on the Vivian Apocalypse frontispiece. Furthermore, Croquison's dismissal of the cloth as a vestige of classical imagery begs the question.

In creating an image of the Lord holding over his head the celestial cloth, the illuminator may simply have been referring to the description in Isa., XL, 22, "He stretches out the skies like a curtain, he spreads them out like a tent to live in." Isaiah's vision does not account for the evangelist symbols, however, nor does it explain the significance of the figure in the Carolingian Bibles.

Most convincing is the hypothesis that the elder is Moses and that the image represents the revelation of the Old Testament by the New in the form of the unveiling of Moses.[25] There is an unmistakable resemblance between the Apocalyptic man and Moses in all three Bibles (cf. Figs. 87–89) and the idea of revelation is conveyed by the action of the animals.[26] Presumably, the illustrator had in mind II Cor., III, 12–18, where the unveiling of Moses is used as an allegory of the abrogation of the Old Testament by the New:

> It is not for us to do as Moses did: he put a veil over his face to keep the Israelites from gazing on that fading splendor until it was gone. But in any case their minds had been made insensitive, for that same veil is there to this very day when the

[23] Willoughby, *op. cit.*, pls. IV, XIII, XIV, and XV.

[24] "Une vision eschatologique Carolingienne," *Cahiers Archéologiques*, IV (1950), 105ff.

[25] Van der Meer, *op. cit.*, pp. 161ff.; H. Schade, "Hinweise zur frühmittelalterlichen Ikonographie," *Das Münster*, XI (1958), pp. 387ff.; K. Hoffmann, *Taufsymbolik im mittelalterlichen Herrscherbild* (Düsseldorf, 1968), pp. 25f. and *idem*, "Sugers 'Anagogisches Fenster' in St. Denis," *Wallraf-Richartz Jahrbuch* XXX (1968); Gaehde, "Turonian Sources," pp. 392ff.; and Schmid, *Bibel von Montier-Grandval*, pp. 180ff.

[26] It is especially clear in the San Paolo Bible, cf. Gaehde, "Turonian Sources," p. 393.

lesson is read from the old covenant; and it is never lifted, because only in Christ is the old covenant abrogated. But to this very day, every time the Law of Moses is read, a veil lies over the minds of the hearers. However, as Scripture says of Moses, "whenever he turns to the Lord the veil is removed." Now the Lord of whom this passage speaks is the Spirit; and where the Spirit of the Lord is, there is liberty. And because for us there is no veil over the face, we all reflect as in a mirror the splendor of the Lord.

It seems quite possible that Moses is represented on the Apocalypse frontispieces. Conceivably, the illustrator began with a depiction of the Apocalyptic elder. If he did, however, he transformed it fundamentally, changing it into an image of Moses revealed by the New Testament.

THE MEANING OF THE APOCALYPSE PAGES

The identification of the second image as Moses Unveiled conforms better than any other interpretation to the *tituli* of the Bible pages. In the Grandval and Vivian Bibles, the verses read:

> SEPTEM SIGILLIS AGNUS INNOCENS MODIS
> SIGNATA MIRIS IURA DISSERIT PATRIS.
> LEGES E VETERIS SINU NOVELLAE
> ALMIS PECTORIBUS LIQUANTUR ECCE,
> QUAE LUCEM POPULIS DEDERE MULTIS.[27]

In the San Paolo Bible, the *tituli* are:

> INSONS PRO NOBIS AGNUS QUI VICTIMA FACTUS
> DETEXIT VICTOR SURGENS VELAMINA LEGIS.
> ATQ: LIBRI SEPTEM DIGNUS SIGNACULA SOLVIT.
> HIC SEPTEM STELLE FIDEI FUNDAMINE RECTAE
> DESIGNANT UNĀ SACRO MODULAMINE PROLEM
> QUAE GENERAT NATOS XPO SINE FINE BEATOS.[28]

Both sets of verses describe the images as allegories of the Old and New Testaments.

It was Köhler who first introduced into the discussion of these Apocalypse pages the exegesis of Revelation by Victorinus of Pettau;[29] and Köhler's insight has been substantiated by subsequent commentators.[30] Like the frontispiece images, the third-century church father presented the Apocalypse as an allegory of the unity of the Old and New Testaments. He identified the book of the seven seals as the Old Testament; he interpreted the lion and lamb of Rev., v, 5 as Christ prevailing over death; and most significantly, he related the fifth book of Revelation to the unveiling of Moses:

[27] Köhler, *Kar. Min.*, I₂, 136.
[28] Gaehde, "Bible Manuscript," II, 146.

[29] *Kar. Min.*, I₂, 138ff.
[30] In particular by van der Meer and Schmid.

"Ecce vicit leo de tribu Juda, radix David." Hunc leonem de tribu Juda vicisse in Genesi legimus, ubi Jacob patriarcha ait: "Juda te laudabunt fratres tui: recubuisti, et dormisti, et surrexisti tamquam leo, et tamquam catulus leonis." Ad devincendum enim mortem leo dictus est; ad patiendum vero pro hominibus, tanquam agnus ad occisionem ductus est. Sed quia mortem devicit, et praevenit carnificis officium, quasi occisus dictus est. Hic ergo aperit et resignat, quod ipse signaverat testamentum. Hoc significans Moses legislator, quod oportebat esse signatum et celatum usque ad adventum passionis ejus, velavit faciem suam, et sic est populo locutus: ostendens velata esse verba praedicationis usque ad adventum temporis ejus. . . . Ideo modo merito signatur per agnum occisum, qui tamquam leo confregit mortem, et quae de eo praenuntiata fuerant replevit, et hominem liberavit, id est carnem de morte, et accepit possessionem substantiam morientis, id est membrorum humanorum. Ut sicut per unum corpus omnes homines debito mortis suae ceciderant, per unum etiam corpus universi credentes renati in vitam resurgerent. Merito ergo facies Mosi aperitur et revelatur; ideoque Apocalypsis, Revelatio dicitur. Modo enim liber ejus resignatur, modo hostiae oblationis intelliguntur, modo sacerdotum chrismae fabricatio; sed et testimonia aperte intelliguntur.[31]

The correspondence of the ninth-century frontispieces to Victorinus' exegesis of Rev., v leaves little doubt of the meaning of the images. They are allegorical pictorializations of the Old Testament fulfilled by the New. The lamb breaking the seal on the great book is Christ revealing the Old Testament; the evangelist symbols lifting the cloth from the elder's face are the Gospels unveiling Moses.

Carolingian theologians also viewed the Book of Revelation as an allegory proclaiming the unity of the Scriptures. Alcuin, who apparently knew the writings of Victorinus, identified the "scroll with writing inside and out" as the Old and New Testaments.[32] In the Codex Aureus of St. Emmeram (Munich, Bayerische Staatsbibliothek, Cod. clm. 14000, fol. 65ᵛ, Fig. 67)[33] the Gospel of Luke is preceded by a frontispiece showing a Lamb on a book and four evangelist symbols. The inscription around the central clipeus reads:

HUNC MOYSES AGNUM MONSTRAVIT LEGE FUTURUM.

CUNCTIS PRO POPULIS SUFFERRI VULNERA MORTIS.[34]

During the ninth century, the allegorical interpretation of the Apocalypse was elaborated most fully by Haimo of Auxerre.[35] In the introduction to his *Expositionis in*

[31] *PL*, v, cols. 327f.

[32] *PL*, c, col. 1120.

[33] G. Leidinger, *Der Codex Aureus der Bayerischen Staatsbibliothek in München* (Munich, 1925), pl. 130.

[34] *Ibid.*, p. 137.

[35] Almost nothing is known about Haimo of Auxerre. He was a monk at the Benedictine Abbey of St. Germain in Auxerre until his death c. 855. Until recently, he was almost entirely forgotten and his exegetical treatises, including his commentaries on the Apocalypse and II Corinthians (*PL*, CXVII) were attributed to Haimo of Halberstadt. Cf. J. Gross, "Ur- und Erbsünde bei

Apocalypsin B. Joannis, Haimo states clearly his views of the relationship of the two testaments, "Facta est autem haec ipsa revelatio per angelum, sed ipse angelus figuram Christi tenuit, qui loquebatur per illum, sicut et ille qui olim Moysi loquebatur. Unde idem Moyses aliquando dicit Deum ad se locutum fuisse, aliquando vero angelum."[36] For Haimo, as for Alcuin, the book of the seven seals is the Old and New Testaments united as a single work, the latter completing the former, "Liber autem in dextera sedentis Vetus et Novum Testamentum significat—Idcirco autem Vetus et Novum unus liber appellatur, quia nec Novum a Vetere, nec Vetus a Novo valet disjungi, sed quidquid praedictum est in Vetere, completum constat in Novo. Nam Vetus Testamentum nuntius est et velamen Novi, Novum vero revelatio et adimpletio est Veteris.[37] Haimo did not interpret the fifth chapter of Revelation as an allegory of Moses unveiled. He did, however, discuss at some length the revelation of Moses in his exegesis of II Cor., III. His interpretation is the traditional one. The veil of Moses represents the obscurity of the Old Testament which is lifted by Christ.[38]

The interpretation of the Apocalypse images as allegorical pictorializations of the unity of the Old and New Testaments is supported, not only by the ninth-century texts but also by the format of the frontispieces themselves. Of the eight Touronian frontispieces, only the Exodus and Apocalypse pages are divided into two picture areas. The others are either full-page miniatures or are composed of narrative registers. Furthermore, the *tituli* of the Grandval and Vivian Exodus and Apocalypse pages are related to each other. Both sets of verses conclude with references to the dispersion of sacred knowledge to the people.[39]

The Exodus and Apocalypse frontispieces may have been constructed as a unit. The first represents the giving of the laws—the central theological event of the Old Testament—and the latter depicts the revelation and abrogation of those laws by the New Testament. This interpretation would also help to explain a puzzling detail of the Grandval and Vivian Exodus pages. In the lower panels of both frontispieces, Moses' diptych is inscribed with a verse from Deut., VI, 5:

DILIGES DOMINUM DEUM TUUM EX TOTO CORDE.

The Grandval Bible also includes the preceding verse from Deut., VI, 4:[40]

AUDI ISRAHEL, DOMINUS DEUS NOSTER, DOMINUS UNUS EST.

Neither scene actually illustrates Deut., VI and hence, it is probable that these verses were added to make a special point. It is interesting, therefore, that these passages from the Pentateuch were adduced by Haimo of Auxerre in his exegetical com-

---

Haimo von Auxerre," *Zeitschrift für Religions- und Geistesgeschichte*, XI (1959), pp. 14ff. For the possible influence of Haimo in Carolingian art, cf. O.-K. Werckmeister, *Der Deckel des Codex Aureus von St. Emmeram* (Baden-Baden, 1963).

[36] *PL*, CXVII, col. 940.

[37] *Ibid.*, col. 1013.

[38] *Ibid.*, col. 618.

[39] Exodus: Iam docet Christi populum repletus nectare sancto. Cf. Hoffmann, "Anagogisches Fenster," pp. 61ff.

[40] See above Chapter IV.

mentary on the Book of the Seven Seals. For Haimo, the seals on the book described in Rev., VI, 1, symbolize the seven modes of expression used in the Scriptures. "Ipsa enim sacrae Scripturae locutio septiformis, quasi sub septem sigillis intelligentiae continetur, dum per septem modos distinguitur."[41] The first and simplest mode is characterized by the passage from Deut., VI, 4, "Inquirentibus enim nobis scripturas, primus gestae rei textus nobis occurrit, quia videlicet ea tantum Scripturarum eloquia comprehendit, quae nil mystice significant, sed tantum simpliciter rerum causas evolvunt, ut est: *Audi Israel, Dominus Deus tuus Deus unus est.*[42] The seventh and most complex is typified by the passage from Deut., VI, 5, Septimus modus est, qui geminam praeceptorum retinet qualitatem, id est vitae agendae vitaeque figurandae. Et quidem agendae vitae praecepta nunc usque manent, ut est: *Diliges Dominum Deum tuum ex toto corde, et proximum tuum* sicut *teipsum*, vel caetera talia, quae etiam nunc evangelica auctoritate servari jubentur."[43]

It is conceivable that the passages from Deuteronomy were included in the Carolingian Exodus miniatures as references to the modes of expression identified by Haimo in his exegesis of Rev., V. According to the ninth-century theologian, these concealed modes are revealed only through Christ, "Hos modos ante Redemptionis quidem tempus absconditos, ipso vero redemptoris tempore per Christum atque in Christo novimus revelatos.[44]

The angels descending from the clouds and emptying horns of fire in the upper scene of the Grandval Exodus frontispiece may also refer to the Apocalypse. Angels emptying fiery vials commonly illustrate Rev., XVI in Apocalypse cycles.[45]

The pairing of the Exodus and Apocalypse pages almost certainly was devised during the ninth century. Although as early as the third century, Victorinus had interpreted the sealed book as the Old Testament and even though his commentary seems to have been the basis of the second Apocalypse image, ninth-century exegesis seems to account for several specific elements on these pages. Furthermore, the Exodus pages were constructed at Tours from a narrative model containing several scenes.[46] Certainly, the Apocalypse miniatures were fashioned at the same time.

The Touronian illuminators also turned to a narrative model for their Apocalypse pages, but they treated it very freely. The depiction of the lamb breaking the seal may have been copied directly from an illustrated Apocalypse; but the image of the enthroned elder is essentially a fabrication.[47] To convey the idea of the unveiling of Moses, the artist gave the elderly man Moses' facial features and he provided him with a great cloth which is pulled, tugged, and inflated by the evangelist symbols. The illuminator may have based his representation directly on late antique models. Striking similarities are found in the depictions of Caelus on the breastplate of the Prima Porta

[41] *PL*, CXVII, col. 1014.
[42] *Ibid.*, col. 1014.
[43] *Ibid.*, col. 1016.
[44] *Ibid.*, col. 1016.
[45] Cf. Trier Apocalypse, fols. 49ᵛ, 50ᵛ, and 51ᵛ.

[46] See above, Chapter IV.
[47] Klein ("Der Kodex," pp. 105ff.) connected the upper, but not the lower scenes of the frontispieces to the narrative Apocalypse tradition.

Augustus,[48] the Junius Bassus sarcophagus (Fig. 117),[49] and a Gallo-Roman medallion in Lyon (Fig. 118).[50] It is likelier, however, that he drew upon a contemporary representation. The heavenly cloth is found in several ninth-century depictions. In the Madrid Aratea (Madrid, Biblioteca Nacional, Cod. A.16, fol. 55ʳ, Fig. 119),[51] Zeus is shown with a cloth billowing over his head as he ascends to heaven on an eagle; and in the Vivian Bible itself, Sol is shown with a heavenly scarf in the zodiac initial on fol. 8ʳ.[52] Even closer to the Apocalypse figures is the personification of Earth on fol. 54ʳ of the Stuttgart Psalter (Fig. 120).[53] Terra's frontality and the way she holds the cloth in her upraised arms are features that are particularly close to the figure in the San Paolo Bible.

The full-length evangelist symbols could have been taken from any number of sources. At Tours, similar creatures were represented in the Wolfenbüttel Gospels[54] and in the Vivian Bible itself.[55] Lively, tugging evangelist symbols appear in the canon tables of the Soissons Gospels[56] and numerous other parallels can be adduced. Even the trumpeting angel is found in early series of evangelist symbols.[57] It is likelier, however, that the angel was copied from one of the trumpeting angels repeatedly depicted in Apocalypse cycles (cf. Trier, Cod. 31, fol. 32ᵛ, Fig. 121).

The two principal images of the Touronian Apocalypse pages seem, then, to have been compiled during the ninth century from Apocalypse, Old Testament, and perhaps Gospel sources. They were designed to convey a complex allegory: the sealed book, the Old Testament, is revealed by Christ and Moses' face is unveiled by the Gospels.

THE SUPPLEMENTARY SCENES

On the Apocalypse pages of the Vivian and San Paolo Bibles, in addition to the primary images, other scenes are represented. The Vivian Bible includes three supplementary depictions. Above the book in the upper scene, a man is shown on a white horse. He wears a Phrygian cap and carries a bow and arrow. Clearly, he is the horseman described in Rev., VI, 1, "And there before my eyes was a white horse, and its rider held a bow. He was given a crown and he rode forth conquering and to conquer." In the upper left corner of the lower scene, a crowned man is shown consoling the tear-

[48] H. Kähler, *Die Augustusstatue von Prima Porta* (Köln, 1959). Cf. C. Morgan, "The Motive of a Figure Holding in Both Hands a Piece of Drapery which Blows Out Behind or Over the Figure," *Art Studies*, VI (1928), 163ff. and C. Tolnay, "The 'Visionary' Evangelists of the Reichenau School," *Burlington Magazine*, LXIX (1936), 257ff.

[49] F. Gerke, *Der Sarkophag des Iunius Bassus* (Berlin, 1936), p. 36f.

[50] H. Jucker, *Das Bildnis im Blätterkelch* (Olten, 1961), pl. 37.

[51] E. Bethe, *Das Buch und Bild in Altertum* (Leipzig, 1945).

[52] Köhler, *Kar. Min.*, I, pl. 79.

[53] Mütherich, *op. cit.*, p. 89.

[54] Köhler, *Kar. Min.*, I, pl. 41; I₁, 187ff. and 385ff.

[55] *Ibid.*, I, pl. 88e.

[56] Köhler, *Kar. Min.*, II, pls. 72–74, 77.

[57] Cf. E. Kitzinger, "The Coffin-Reliquary," *The Relics of Saint Cuthbert* (ed. C. Battiscombe. Oxford, 1956), pp. 239f. and R. Bruce-Mitford, "Decoration and Miniatures," *Evangeliorum Quattuor Codex Lindisfarnensis* (Olten, 1960), pp. 158ff.

ful John. This depiction illustrates Rev., v, 4–5, "I was in tears because no one was found who was worthy to open the scroll or to look inside it. But one of the elders said to me: 'Do not weep; for the Lion from the tribe of Judah, the Root of David, has won the right to open the scroll and break its seven seals.' " Whereas the horseman and the consolation of St. John relate directly to the upper image, the third supplementary scene in the Vivian Bible seems totally unconnected to the primary representations. It shows an angel standing on two heads and handing a book to John. John, who holds a rod in his right hand, raises the book to his mouth. The scene combines several events described in Rev., x, 2ff. and Rev., xi, 1:

> In [the angel's] hand he held a little scroll unrolled. His right foot he planted on the sea; and his left on the land. . . . Then the voice which I heard from heaven was speaking to me again and it said, "Go and take the open scroll in the hand of the angel that stands on the sea and the land." So I went to the angel and asked him to give me the little scroll. He said to me, "Take it and eat it. It will turn your stomach sour, although in your mouth it will taste sweet as honey." . . . I was given a long cane, a kind of measuring-rod, and told: "Now go and measure the temple of God, the altar, and the number of the worshippers."

Köhler argued that the Vivian artist copied these scenes from an Apocalypse cycle.[58] Their emphatically narrative qualities and parallels in Apocalypse manuscripts support this suggestion.

The first horseman is represented in virtually every illustrated Apocalypse. Usually he is shown with his bow already drawn,[59] but in the Trier Apocalypse (fol. 33^v, Fig. 122) and the Wolfenbüttel *Liber Floridus* (fol. 11^v, Fig. 123), as in the Vivian Bible, he simply holds the bow in his hand. The Phrygian cap is unique to the Vivian manuscript; but in the Wolfenbüttel *Liber Floridus* the third horseman sports the same headgear, a coincidence that ties the two representations to each other.

Like the Lion of Judah to which it is related, the scene of John Consoled by the Elder is rarely represented. It is omitted in the Valenciennes Apocalypse, in the Beatus volumes, and in the Gothic Apocalypses.[60] The scene is illustrated, however, in the Trier Apocalypse (fol. 17^v, Fig. 65), in the Wolfenbüttel *Liber Floridus* (Fig. 112), and in the Maximos manuscript (Fig. 116). In the Trier manuscript, John raises his arm to dry his eyes on his sleeve; and, although the elder is not crowned, as in the Vivian Bible, he is beardless and points his right arm at John. In the Wolfenbüttel depiction, the elder is bearded and is separated from the nimbed St. John by the image of the Enthroned. The elder is crowned, however, and he points toward the weeping

---

[58] *Kar. Min.*, I₂, 146.

[59] Cf. Valenciennes, fol. 12^v (Juraschek, *op. cit.*, fig. 4); Maximos Apocalypse, fol. 48^v (Willoughby, *op. cit.*, pl. XVI). He is shown with bow drawn in the Beatus manuscripts (cf. Gerundensis, fol. 126^r). In the Gothic Apocalypses, he usually holds the bow. Cf. Douce Apocalypse (Oxford, Bodleian, MS. Douce, 180, pt. 2, p. 131. M. R. James, *The Apocalypse in Latin and French.* [Oxford, 1922]).

[60] Cf. note 59.

John.[61] The representation in the Chicago manuscript is very different but it, too, depicts St. John raising his hand to his face.[62]

In most Apocalypse cycles, John Receiving the Book and John Receiving the Rod are illustrated as separate scenes. In the Trier Apocalypse, for example, fol. 32[r] (Fig. 121) shows the angel—with one foot on the sea and one foot on the land—handing the book to John. Fol. 33[r] (Fig. 124) shows John taking the rod.[63] Frequently, as in the Beatus manuscripts,[64] the two scenes are depicted on a single page. It was natural for artists to merge the two similar images. Such a merger appears in the eleventh-century Bamberg Apocalypse (Staatsbibliothek, Bibl. 140, fol. 26[v], Fig. 125),[65] where John is shown holding the rod as he receives the book from an angel. In the Gothic Apocalypses, three narrative phases are depicted. On page 33 of the Douce manuscript, for example, John is shown receiving the book from an angel, he is represented again eating it, and on page 34 he is shown receiving the rod. It is not unlikely, therefore, that the Vivian scene actually represents an amalgamation of three separate scenes from the model. Personifications of the land and sea, in place of more naturalistic renderings, appear only in the Vivian Bible.

In bands above and below the basic images, the San Paolo frontispiece presents seven angels seated before seven basilican churches. These angels, the seven stars referred to in the *titulus*, illustrate passages from Rev., I, 20 to Rev., III,

> The seven stars are the angels of the seven churches and the seven lamps are the seven churches. To the angel of the church of Ephesus, write: . . . to the angel of the church of Smyrna write: . . . to the angel of the church of Pergamum write: . . . to the angel of the church at Thatira write: . . . to the angel of the church at Sardis write: . . . to the angel of the church at Philadelphia write: . . . and to the angel of the church at Laodicea write: . . .

The angel at the center of the bottom row, who holds a disk with the monogram, is certainly the angel of the church at Pergamum who was given a stone on which was written "a new name, known to none but him who receives it" (Rev., II, 17).[66] The second angel from the left in the upper group is the angel of the church of Philadelphia, "a pillar in the temple of my God" (Rev., III, 12).[67]

Angels with or without seven buildings are frequently represented at the beginning of Apocalypse cycles. In the Beatus manuscripts and in the Gothic Apocalypses they occupy separate folios.[68] In the Trier Apocalypse, the seven angels and their churches

[61] Cf. Klein, "Der Kodex," p. 108.

[62] Willoughby, *op. cit.*, pl. XIV.

[63] In the Valenciennes Apocalypse (fol. 21), John is shown receiving the book; in the Maximos Apocalypse (fol. 88[v]), John eats the book and the angel holds the rod. Willoughby, *op. cit.*, pl. XXXIII.

[64] Cf. *Gerundensis*, fol. 161[v].

[65] *Die Bamberger Apokalypse*, ed. A. Fauser (Frankfurt, 1962).

[66] Gaehde, "Bible Manuscript," I, 448.

[67] Gaehde, "Turonian Sources," p. 394.

[68] *Gerundensis*, fols. 71[r], 76[r], 85[r], 89[v], 94[r], and 100[v]. Douce, pp. 2, 4–10. In the Valenciennes Apocalypse, only the basilican buildings and not the angels are represented on four folios (cf. Juraschek, Fig. 2). In the Maximos Apocalypse, four of the churches are depicted (cf. Willoughby, *op. cit.*, pls. VI, VIII, X, and XI).

are represented on a single leaf (fol. 5ᵛ, Fig. 126). Although the angels are standing and lack identifying attributes, their gestures and the buildings recall the San Paolo Bible. In the Wolfenbüttel *Liber Floridus* the seven angels stand behind the towered basilicas (Fig. 127).[69] They are arranged in bands of three and four and, as in the San Paolo Bible, the two angels in the lower left corner converse with one another. On the Wolfenbüttel page, the angel of the church of Ephesus holds a disk.

Whether the supplementary scenes were copied from the Apocalypse model used also as the basis of the primary images cannot be determined with certainty. One indication that they were is found in the Stuttgart Psalter. As noted above, the illuminators of the Stuttgart Psalter may have utilized the basic Apocalypse model for the depiction of the lamb and altar on fol. 51ᵛ. Presumably, they used this same source to illustrate Psalm, XLIV, 8 on fol. 56ʳ (Fig. 128).[70] The illustration is based on Rev., XIV, 10, "He shall be tormented in sulphurous flames before the holy angels and before the Lamb." Although the Touronian Bibles contain no parallel depiction, the angels and the turretted walls of the Heavenly City in the Stuttgart Psalter do resemble the San Paolo Bible depictions. If both of the Psalter scenes were taken from the same Apocalypse cycle then that cycle may also have served as the model for all of the Touronian depictions. The precise relationship of the Lamb image to the Wolfenbüttel *Liber Floridus* (Fig. 112) is not clear,[71] but the latter suggests that the primary and supplementary scenes were based on the same model.

Two of the supplementary scenes, the horseman and the Consolation of John in the Vivian Bible are directly related to the main image of the lamb breaking the seal. Their inclusion needs no special explanation. The illuminator simply embellished his basic image with closely connected representations. The inclusion of the scene of John Eating the Book in the Vivian Bible and the depiction of the seven angels and churches in the San Paolo Bible require further interpretation.

The *titulus* of the San Paolo page aids in the interpretation of the angels. They represent the universal church founded by Christ; and therefore, they are not unrelated to the main images which refer to the establishment of the new order.[72] The representation of John Eating the Book may be related to the lamb image. Contrary to the text which specifies that the book was open,[73] the Vivian scene shows John eating a closed codex similar in appearance to the enormous volume of the upper picture. Possibly the illuminator sought to convey the idea that by ingesting the book, John would be able to reveal and to preach the concealed meanings of the Scriptures.[74]

The supplementary elements of the Vivian and San Paolo Apocalypse frontispieces suggest the willingness of the Carolingian artists to embellish the symbolic images with

[69] Klein, "Roda-Bibel," pp. 283f.
[70] Mütherich, *op. cit.*, pp. 90 and 189.
[71] Klein, "Der Kodex," pp. 105ff.
[72] Gaehde, "Turonian Sources," p. 394.
[73] Cf. Alcuin (*PL*, c, 1144) and Haimo (*PL*,

cxvii, 1062). They identify the open book as the New Testament.
[74] Cf. Victorinus, *op. cit.*, p. 353.; Alcuin, *PL*, c, 1146 and Haimo, *PL*, cxvii, 1066.

narrative depictions.[75] They are further indications of the existence at Tours of an illustrated Apocalypse and they shed some light on the origin of this manuscript source.

Parallels in the Trier Apocalypse indicate that the illustrated Book of Revelation used at Tours was related to the known Carolingian cycles.[76] These parallel motifs include the first horseman, John Consoled, the seven angels and seven churches, and the trumpeting angel. Peculiar features of the Touronian depictions are, however, missing in the Trier manuscript: the Phrygian cap, the personifications of Land and Sea,[77] and the angels' attributes. The Phrygian cap and the angel's disk both appear in the Wolfenbüttel *Liber Floridus*, a later manuscript that represents a distinct branch of the Apocalypse recension to which the Trier volume also belongs.[78] The personifications have no precise counterparts in Apocalypse illustration. Similar busts, representing Land and Sea, are found on the Parabiago silver plate in Milan (Castello Sforzesco, Fig. 129).[79] There is no reason, therefore, to question Schmid's conclusion that the Touronian frontispieces were fashioned by the Carolingian illuminators from Early Christian models.[80] Schmid and Klein have independently concluded that the Apocalypse model post-dated the fifth century; but the evidence that they adduce for a sixth-century origin is not altogether compelling.[81]

The Apocalypse pages are among the most original of the Touronian frontispieces and, therefore, they are the most difficult to understand. They illustrate neither the Bible text nor a biblical prologue. They were devised, instead, to express a peculiar interpretation of Revelation that had first emerged during the third century in the writings of Victorinus of Pettau and that had been elaborated later by Carolingian exegetes. According to this interpretation, the Book of Revelation is an allegorical expression of the unity of the Old and New Testaments.

To express this interpretation pictorially, the Carolingian illuminators paired their Apocalypse illustrations with their Exodus frontispieces. In the latter, they depicted Moses receiving the law and reading it to the people; in the former they represented the law revealed by Christ and Moses' face unveiled by the Gospels.

For the Exodus miniatures, the Touronian artists found appropriate illustrations in an Old Testament narrative cycle. No illustrated Apocalypse could supply all the

---

[75] At Münstereifel an angel is also included. This angel certainly refers to Rev., v, 2, "And I saw a mighty angel proclaiming in a loud voice, 'Who is worthy to open the scroll and to break its seals?'"

[76] Cf. also Chapter III. According to Klein, ("Der Kodex," p. 69), the Trier Apocalypse was created under Touronian influence. Klein did not exclude entirely a Touronian origin for the manuscript.

[77] It should be noted that on folio 37ᵛ of the Trier Apocalypse the "woman robed in the sun" (Rev., XXII, 1) is shown standing on two heads

which personify the sun and the moon and on folio 63ʳ the "angel standing in the sun" (Rev., XIX, 17) is shown on a similar personification.

[78] Klein has shown in considerable detail that the Trier Apocalypse and the Wolfenbüttel-Oxford Revelation scenes derive ultimately from the same Italian cycle. Cf. "Roda-Bibel" and "Der Kodex."

[79] W. Volbach, *Early Christian Art* (New York, 1961), pl. 107.

[80] *Bibel von Moutier-Grandval*, pp. 183ff.

[81] *Ibid.*, p. 181 and Klein, "Der Kodex," p. 111.

motifs needed for their allegorical pictures and so they copied certain elements from a biblical model, but embellished and refashioned these in a completely original manner. The Touronian frontispieces are not unique, however. Three hundred years after they were devised, perhaps through the influence of the Vivian Bible itself, Abbot Suger used similar compositions to express the same ideas in one of the stained glass windows at St. Denis.[82]

Initially, the Apocalypse compositions may have been intended to serve as *explicit* pages rather than frontispieces. In the Grandval Bible, they occupy the last leaf; while in the Vivian and San Paolo Bibles—perhaps to make room for the dedication miniatures—they have been placed at the head of Revelation. The placement of the Apocalypse illustrations at the very end of the Bible better suits the interpretation of them as revelation motifs. It also conforms closely to the formulation of the ninth-century theologian Etherius of Osma, "Velata fuit Moysi usque ad Christum bibliothecae facies, et in fine huius bibliothecae revelata est. . . . Quae tota bibliotheca unus liber est, in capite velatus, in fine manifestus. Qui liber duo Testamenta dicuntur, Vetus et Novum."[83]

[82] Cf. Hoffmann, "Anagogisches Fenster," pp. 57ff.

[83] *PL*, XCVI, col. 956.

VI. JEROME PREPARES THE
VULGATE

JEROME'S letter to Paulinus and his preface to the Pentateuch are preceded in the Vivian[1] and San Paolo Bibles[2] by full page frontispieces depicting scenes from the life of St. Jerome (Figs. 130 and 131). These are among the most enigmatic ninth-century paintings. The subjects of the episodes depicted in them have not been precisely identified; their relationship to one another has not been fully established; and their textual and pictorial sources remain unknown. Joachim Gaehde has made the only detailed study of the two frontispieces; but his results are inconclusive. On the basis of his analysis of other frontispieces in the San Paolo Bible, Gaehde concluded that the Jerome page must also have depended on a Touronian source similar to, but not identical with, the frontispiece in the Vivian Bible. His arguments that the San Paolo illuminator adapted figures and compositions close to those in the Vivian Bible and interpolated elements from other sources do not follow from this conclusion. The lost Touronian model may have predated the Vivian manuscript and it may have included authentic features of the prototype that have been transformed in the Vivian page. Only a careful examination of each scene can disclose whether the Vivian illustrations or the San Paolo depictions are closer to the ultimate source.

THE INDIVIDUAL SCENES

Beginning with his departure from Rome and concluding with his dissemination of the completed Vulgate manuscripts, the frontispieces trace Jerome's intellectual activities in Palestine. The events are described in the *tituli*, but as in other frontispieces, these verses are only general captions that do not account for many details in the paintings.

The opening episode is depicted in like fashion in both manuscripts. Standing on the seashore outside the City of Rome, Jerome beckons toward a galley. In the Vivian Bible, he is alone and the ship is under sail; in the San Paolo Bible, he is accompanied by another monk and is about to board the ship on a runged gangway. The clear similarities of the two depictions, which extend to details of costume and architecture, leave no doubt that the two manuscripts are related to one another. Whether the San Paolo depiction was copied from the Vivian scene or from its model cannot, however, be determined from internal evidence.

The same is true of the second scene. Both manuscripts represent Jerome seated with a book in front of his Hebrew teacher to whom he tenders coins. In the Vivian Bible, the basilican schoolhouse is shown in front view; in the San Paolo manuscript

---

[1] Fol. 3ᵛ, Köhler, *Kar. Min.*, I₂, 50ff. and 214ff.   and "Turonian Sources," pp. 361ff.
[2] Fol. 3ᵛ, Gaehde, "Bible Manuscript," I, 109ff.

only its facade is rendered. The close relationship of the two representations is not in question.

More significant differences are apparent in the second registers. The Vivian Bible shows Jerome at the center of a bench-like throne that runs nearly the entire length of the register. He addresses the four women at his right while three monks behind him record his words. The second register in the San Paolo Bible is divided into two coherent scenes. In the first, Jerome—assisted by two companions—disputes two standing monks. In the second, the scholarly saint is shown teaching two women, one of whom holds an open book and inkpot and the other a scroll. Behind them, a monk records the dictation on a waxed tablet and outside the building, a second stenographer eavesdrops on the lessons and also takes notes. St. Jerome in the dispute scene is virtually identical in pose to the Vivian figure and the seated women in the second episode are mirror images of two figures in the earlier volume. The two frontispieces are thus closely related to one another. Either the Vivian artist merged separate episodes in his model to form a single composition or the San Paolo illuminator (or his Touronian predecessor) composed new subjects from elements excerpted from his Jerome model and from other sources.[3] The first is the likelier hypothesis. Conflations of several episodes can be identified in the Genesis and Epistles frontispieces of the Vivian Bible[4] and they seem to be a characteristic feature of the Touronian illuminator. The amalgamation of more than one composition would have been prompted, in this case, by the artist's desire to focus on the principal figure. Narrative expansion of the kind proposed in the second hypothesis cannot be demonstrated elsewhere in the San Paolo Bible. In other instances, the San Paolo illuminations present rich narrative sequences but these seem not to have been invented but, rather, to have been from the models. The sequence in the San Paolo Bible remains integral; the second register of the Vivian Bible, on the other hand, violates narrative logic. The role of the three monks behind Jerome is particularly mystifying. Two of them appear to pay no attention whatever to the proceedings at the left.

These monks seem to have been copied from yet another episode which, in the San Paolo Bible, is depicted at the beginning of the third register. The scene shows Jerome dictating the Vulgate to his disciples. Two of the monks debate a point with Jerome while the others transcribe his words into open codices. All three Vivian figures have counterparts in the San Paolo composition. The monks seated back to back in the Tours Bible appear to the right in the San Paolo scene while the monk who raises his pen and looks straight out has his counterpart at the far left of the San Paolo composition. The correspondence of these figures underlines the close relationship of the two manuscripts. It also tends to confirm the hypothesis that the second register of the Vivian Bible was compiled from several separate episodes still represented in their original form in the San Paolo Bible.

---

[3] This hypothesis is favored by Gaehde, "Turonian Sources," pp. 361ff.

[4] Cf. Chapters II and VIII.

Like the second band, the third register of the Vivian Bible frontispiece is devoted to a single action—St. Jerome distributing copies of the Vulgate. Seated on a faldstool at the center of the strip, Jerome is shown handing large codices to monks at the left and right. In cinemagraphic fashion, other monks are depicted carrying the enormous volumes into two buildings, apparently a church and a library. Additional tomes are stored in boxes at Jerome's feet. It is conceivable that, like Christ in a *Traditio legis*, Jerome was represented in the original presenting books to men on both sides. The strict symmetry and duplication of figures, however, suggests that the Vivian artist transformed a simple presentation bild miniature into this monumental composition. The dedication page in Hrabanus Maurus' *De laudibus sanctae crucis*, produced in Fulda between 831–840 (Vienna, Österreichische Nationalbibliothek, Cod. 652, fol. 2ᵛ, Fig. 132)[5] is an example of the type of composition found frequently. It shows a seated dignitary (Gregory IV) receiving a book from a subordinate (Hrabanus) who bows in deference. A similar formula was used to represent Jerome receiving a letter from Bonifatius on the cover of the Dagulph Psalter (Paris, Louvre, Fig. 133).[6] The model of the Vivian page may have included a simple composition not very different from these which the Touronian illuminator expanded by repeating several of the figures. For the figure of Jerome, he may have copied a simple author portrait similar to that in the Psalter of Charles the Bald (Paris, Bibliothèque Nationale, Cod. lat. 1152, fol. 4ʳ, Fig. 134)[7] or the portrait of Gregory in the Touronian Sacramentary at Autun (Bibliothèque de la Ville, MS. 19bis, fol. 5ʳ, Fig. 135).[8]

If this was the case, then again, the San Paolo Bible frontispiece is closer to the original. It represents Jerome standing and delivering a codex to one of his companions who receives it in covered hands. The incongruity of the two monks behind the main figures, however, requires explanation. They appear to be lifting volumes of the Vulgate over a high wall where other tomes have already been stored. Gaehde has observed that this wall was, in fact, an afterthought and that the first intention of the artist was to close the background with a curtain suspended from columns. One of which columns is still visible.[9] It is possible, therefore, that the original conception of the Distribution scene in the San Paolo Bible was to show the two monks carrying books into a building —similar in appearance perhaps to the one in the teaching scene above—and that this structure was subsequently walled up. The two figures do resemble the monks who carry books on their backs in the Vivian Bible and they may have been depicted in a like fashion in the model.

It is impossible, on the basis of internal evidence alone, to reconstruct precisely the scene of Distribution as it must have appeared in the model. The indications are, how-

[5] Cf. P. Bloch, "Zum Dedikationsbild im Lob des Kreuzes des Hrabanus Maurus," *Das erste Jahrtausend* (Düsseldorf, 1962), pp. 471ff. *Codex Vindobonensis 652* (Graz, 1972).

[6] Goldschmidt, *Elfenbeinskulpturen*, I, no. 14 and A. von Euw, "Studien zu den Elfenbeinarbeiten der Hofschule Karls des Grossen," *Aachener Kunstblätter*, XXXIV (1967), 36ff.

[7] V. Leroquais, *Les psautiers* (Macon, 1940–41), II, 67ff. and P. E. Schramm and F. Mütherich, *Denkmale der deutschen Könige und Kaiser* (Munich, 1962), p. 131.

[8] Köhler, *Kar. Min.*, I₁, 236f., 393ff. and I₂, 96ff.

[9] "Turonian Sources," p. 365, n. 28.

ever, that it showed Jerome presenting a volume to one monk while others carried copies of the Vulgate away.

The architectural elements in the San Paolo frontispiece may have been copied from the Touronian model and may reflect the ultimate prototype. A walled precinct, similar to those in which the scenes of Dispute and Dictation take place, is found in the scene of Ananias Healing Saul in the Vivian Bible Epistles frontispiece (Fig. 173). It is a common motif in Reimsian manuscripts such as the Utrecht Psalter, but as it does occur at Tours, it may well have been a feature of the Jerome model used by the San Paolo illuminator. The fact that similar walls enclose the city of Rome in depictions of Jerome's Departure in both the Vivian and San Paolo manuscripts tends to support this conclusion. The open, draped basilican facade in the second scene is similar to the Tabernacle in the Vivian Bible Moses page (Fig. 88). It, too, is common in Reimsian art. Only the arched house in the teaching scene has no known Touronian parallel. The curved-back throne in the same scene, however, does. It appears in the Vivian Majestas (Fig. 49) and in the Evangelist portraits of the Lothar and Le Mans Gospels (Fig. 80).

From an analysis and comparison of the Jerome pages in the Vivian and San Paolo Bibles, six scenes of the model can be reconstructed: Jerome Departs Rome; Jerome Pays his Hebrew Teacher; Jerome Disputes the Pelagians; Jerome Instructs the Women; Jerome Dictates the Vulgate; and Jerome Distributes the Bibles. The six scenes seem to have been copied almost without change in the San Paolo Bible which is, therefore, the more useful in the investigation of models. Elements of all six appear in the Vivian page. These have been rearranged, however, and new, centralized compositions, focusing on the saint, have been created from them. Both the Vivian and San Paolo frontispieces seem to have been derived from the same model.[10]

THE TEXTUAL SOURCES

The *tituli* that accompany the pictures in both manuscripts identify each episode. In the Vivian Bible, the verses emphasize Jerome's scholarly mission:

EXIT HIERONIMUS ROMA CONDISCERE VERBA

HIERUSALEM HEBRAEAE LEGIS HONORIFICE.

EUSTOCHIO NECNON PAULAE DIVINA SALUTIS

JURA DAT ALTITHRONO FULTUS UBIQUE DEO.

HIERONIMUS TRANSLATA SUI QUAE TRANSTULIT ALMUS

OLLIS HIC TRIBUIT QUIS EA CONPOSUIT.[11]

[10] P. Bloch and H. Schnitzler (*Die Ottonische-Kölner Malerschule* [Düsseldorf, 1967–70], II, p. 145) have also concluded that the San Paolo frontispiece is a close copy of the fifth century model and that the Vivian master altered the model to create symmetrical registers. See also:

H. Schnitzler, "Hieronymus und Gregor in der Ottonischen Kölner Buchmalerei," *Kunstgeschichtliche Studien für Hans Kauffmann* (Berlin, 1956), pp. 11ff.

[11] Köhler, *Kar. Min.*, I₂, 214.

The elaborate captions in the San Paolo Bible are less single-minded and more biographical:

HIERONIMUS VELIS SECAT AEQUORA SALSA SECUNDIS
ROMANUMQ: SOLUM LINQUIT LOCA SCA PETENDO
RELLIGIONE VIGENS HEBRAEO RITE LABORE
INSTRUITUR TALI REDIMENS ELEMENTA MAGISTRO
PELAGII PREMIT ERROREM COGITQ: FATERI
NON MERITIS HOMINUM CONFERRI DONA SUPERNA.
TE PAULAM CUM PROLE DOCET QUIBUS INTIMA XPĪ
GRATIA DIFFUSUM FIDEI DONUM DUPLICAVIT.
ARCHIVUM PENETRANS HEBRAEUM LAMPADE CORDIS
HIERONIMUS SACROS ADYTUS ET EBURNEA TEMPLA
DISCIPULIS RESERAT LATIO TRANSMITTIT HABENDA
IUDEMQ: NEMUS QUOD EATENUS INVIA NOSTRIS
SEPSERAT INGRESSUS CORDATO LUMINE LUSTRAT.
INGENIO MENTIS CAPIENS EXPONIT IN AURES
MOXQ: APERIT GEMINUM TRIPLEX QUOQUE SIDUS INORME
ATTICUS ATQUE STILUS HINC SURGIT ROBORE FORTI.[12]

Even these, however, do not account for such details in the representations as Jerome's companion when he departs Rome, the action of Jerome paying his teacher, the stenographers in the teaching scene, and the scene of dictation. The question must be asked: was the model of these two frontispieces based on other texts? If so, what were they?

The prefaces by St. Jerome that follow the illustrations are in no direct way related to the pictures. There is also no extant *Vita Hieronymi* that corresponds to the narrative depictions on these frontispieces.[13] Nevertheless, connections with Jerome's own writings indicate strongly that the Carolingian depictions were not adaptations of conventional formulae to suit Jerome's biography but are specific illustrations of his life story.

The account of Jerome's Departure from Rome in his *Apologia adversus libros Rufini*, for example, refers to his companions, "Mense Augusto, flantibus etesiis, cum sancto Vincentio presbytero, et adolescente fratre, et aliis monachis, qui nunc Hierosolymae commorantur, navim in Romano portu securus ascendi, maxima me sanctorum frequentia prosequente" (III, 22).[14] The monk who accompanies Jerome in the San Paolo Bible may be Vincentius or one of the monks mentioned in this text. If so, he may be considered as additional evidence of the reliability of the later manuscript.

The fact that Jerome paid for his Hebrew lessons is stressed in the writings. In Epistle

---

[12] Gaehde, "Bible Manuscript," II, 136.

[13] The three early *vitae* that survive (cf. *PL*, XXII, cols. 175ff.) were derived from Jerome's own writings, as was the account in the *Vitae Patrum* (*PL*, LXXIII, cols. 89ff.). Cf. Grützmacher, *Hieronymus* (Leipzig, 1901–1908), pp. 37ff.

[14] *PL*, XXIII, col. 493.

84, 3, Jerome complains of the cost, "Quo labore, quo pretio Baraninam nocturnum habui praeceptorem!"[15] And in his Preface to the Book of Job, Jerome again stated that he employed a Jew to instruct him, "Memini me ob intelligentiam hujus voluminis, Lyddaeum quemdam praeceptorem, quid apud Hebraeos primus haberi putabatur, non parvis redemisse nummis . . ."[16]

Jerome's dispute with Pelagius took place in 411, seven years after the death of Paula in 404. Its anachronistic placement in the San Paolo Bible raises the possibility, therefore, that in the model the scene depicted another of Jerome's numerous disputes such as his controversy with Atarbius.

The scene of Jerome teaching Paula and Eustochium presents other problems. Throughout his writings, Jerome referred with affection to these Roman women and to their erudition. The letter to Eustochium after the death of her mother is the best statement of Jerome's devotion to the holy ladies:

> Scripturas sanctas tenebat memoriter; et cum amaret historiam. . . . Denique compulit me: ut vetus et novum Instrumentum, cum filia, me disserente, perlegeret. Quod propter verecundiam negans, propter assiduitatem tamen et crebras postulationes ejus praestiti, ut docerem quod didiceram: non a meipso, id est a praesumptione, pessimo praeceptore, sed ab illustribus Ecclesiae viris. . . . Hebraeam linguam, quam ego ab adolescentia multo labore ac sudore ex parte didici, et infatigabili meditatione non desero, ne ipse ab ea deserar, discere voluit, et consecuta est: ita ut Psalmos hebraice caneret, et sermonem absque ulla latinae linguae proprietate personaret. Quod quidem usque hodie in sancta filia ejus Eustochio cernimus . . . (Epistle 108, v. 26).[17]

The illuminator seems also to have been acquainted with Jerome's actual methods of teaching. Because of failing eyesight and to increase his productivity, Jerome relied on dictation, employing stenographers to record his spoken words on waxed tablets which were later transcribed.[18] The man who stands behind Jerome and the women apparently refer to this practice.

The second stenographer, who eavesdrops on the lessons from outside Paula's house, requires a different explanation for she certainly does not reflect normal working procedures. Throughout his career, Jerome's association with Paula and Eustochium was widely criticized and the scholarly saint often became involved in hostile disputes. Soon after he settled in Bethlehem, for example, he learned that to cause dissension between him and the women, one of Jerome's enemies had supplied Paula and her daughters with treatises by Ambrose and Fortunation.[19] He was also rebuked for having translated Origen's homilies for them.[20] Later, Jerome's translation of Epiphanius'

---

[15] PL, XXII, col. 745.

[16] PL, XXVIII, col. 1140.

[17] PL, XXII, cols. 902f.

[18] For a discussion of Jerome's scholarly procedures, consult R. P. Evaristo Arns, La technique au livre d'après Saint Jerome (Paris, 1953).

[19] Cf. J. Steinmann, Saint Jerome and His Times (Notre Dame, 1959), pp. 185ff.

[20] Homily VII.

letter to John of Jerusalem was made public against his wishes and he complained angrily about this invasion of his privacy:

> Volo in chartulis meis quaslibet ineptias scribere; commentari de Scripturis, remordere laedentes, digerere stomachum, in locis me exercere communibus, et quasi limatas ad pugnandum sagittas reponere. Quamdiu non profero cogitata, maledicta, non crimina sunt: imo ne maledicta quidem, quae aures publicae nesciant. Tu corrumpas servulos, sollicites clientes: et, ut in fabulis legimus, auro ad Danaen penetres, dissimulatoque quod feceris, me falsarium voces . . . (Epistle 57, v. 4).[21]

It is possible that the illuminator had one of these clandestine attacks on St. Jerome in mind when he included a spying stenographer in the teaching scene.

The scene of Jerome dictating to his scribes may also reflect his actual working methods. Certainly, the normal procedure for preparing copies of a manuscript was to work from a written exemplar. Jerome, however, relied on dictation even for translations.[22] On the other hand, representations are known which show Gregory[23] and David[24] dictating to several scribes. The San Paolo representation, therefore, may reflect artistic convention rather than historical fact.

Convention seems also to have determined the final scene in the Bibles, Jerome Distributing the Vulgate. No text refers to Jerome's publishing activity, although this is implied in his work as author, translator, and editor. Actually, Jerome seems never to have produced a full edition of the Vulgate. The illuminator may have invented this episode to complete the sequence by transforming a traditional presentation composition.

The specificity of the events depicted indicates that the illuminator of the Jerome prototype consulted some text to create his narrative series, but no work is known which traces the biography of Jerome in a manner comparable to the sequence of scenes in the frontispieces. It is conceivable that a *Vita Hieronymi*, no longer extant, was the basis of these pictures. Lives of saints were recorded from the earliest times and it is not beyond question that the Touronian frontispieces were derived from an illustrated life of St. Jerome of which there is no longer any other trace.

The lives of the saints were illustrated almost as soon as they were written.[25] In addi-

---

[21] *PL*, XXII, col. 570.

[22] *Preface to Chron.* Cf. Arns, *op. cit.*, p. 41. In Ottonian frontispieces, Jerome is often shown dictating to a scribe. Cf. Bloch and Schnitzler, *op. cit.*, pp. 146ff.

[23] Cf. Paris, Bibliothèque Nationale, cod. lat. 1141, fol. 3 and cf. Bloch and Schnitzler, *op. cit.*, pp. 151ff.

[24] Of the many examples, the representation in the Folchard Psalter (St. Gall, Stiftsbibliothek, Cod. 23, fol. 9ʳ, Fig. 170) offers the best parallel

to the Jerome pages because it includes two scribes seated back to back. Cf. Chapter VII.

[25] F. Wormald, "Some Illustrated Manuscripts of the Lives of Saints," *Bulletin of the John Rylands Library Manchester*, XXV (1952), 248ff. Also: Life of St. Trudo of c. 870. *Mittelalterliche Schatzverzeichnisse*, ed. F. Mütherich (Munich, 1967), p. 88. O. Pächt also postulated the existence of illustrated *vitae* during the Late Antique period in *The Rise of Pictorial Narrative in Twelfth-Century England* (Oxford, 1962), p. 17.

tion to the great apostolic cycles of Early Christian Rome, a number of examples are known. On the walls of the cathedral of Tours itself, scenes from the life of St. Martin were painted during the fifth century;[26] and a fifth-century model may also lie behind the three episodes from the life of Cassianus and seven scenes of the martyrdom of Romanus, based on the Peristephanon, in the late ninth-century Prudentius manuscript in Bern (Stadtbibliothek, Cod. 264, fols. 60[r] ff.).[27] The life of St. Ambrose in the *vitae* of Paulinus and Gregory of Tours, may have inspired the twelve scenes on the Golden Altar of Milan during the ninth century;[28] and Hincmar's life of St. Remegius was the source of three depictions on a tenth-century ivory plaque in Amiens (Musée de la Picardie).[29] Undoubtedly, the Amiens plaque once served as the cover for a copy of Hincmar's *libellus*. These examples constitute ample proof of the popularity, during the Carolingian period and earlier, of illustrations based on the lives of the saints. Byzantium offers similar examples.[30] In all these cases, however, texts survive that are directly related to the pictures. That is not true of the Jerome illustrations for which no appropriate *vita* is known.

There are indications that the prototype of the Jerome pages was not a richly illustrated life of the saint. Unlike the Genesis and Epistles frontispieces in the Vivian and San Paolo Bibles, which can be shown to be excerpts from more extensive cycles, the Jerome pages seem to have been based on a model that was, itself, limited to six scenes. This raises the possibility that the ultimate prototype was not an illustrated *vita*. Rather, it seems to have been a restricted cycle that focused on Jerome's activity as the translator of the Bible. In other words, the model may have been a kind of narrative author portrait.

Author portraits are certainly the most common frontispiece subjects in early medieval manuscripts. Many of them are somewhat narrative in aspect. The evangelists are usually shown writing their inspired texts; Dioscurides is depicted at work on his Herbal while an artist paints one of the plants;[31] or several authors are shown in lively discussion, as in the ninth-century Agrimensores manuscript (Fig. 203).[32] Jerome was also portrayed in author frontispieces. He is depicted enthroned beneath an arch in the *Epistolae* of c. 800 in Leningrad (Public Library, lat. Q. v. I.N. 13, fol. 3[v]);[33] he is depicted in the mid-ninth century volume of Jerome's writings from Salzburg (Vienna, Nationalbibliothek, Cod. lat. 1332);[34] and he is represented in the Psalter of Charles

---

[26] J. von Schlosser, *Quellenbuch zur Kunstgeschichte* (Vienna, 1896), pp. 37ff.

[27] Cf. R. Stettiner, *Die illustrierten Prudentius-Handschriften* (Berlin, 1905), pls. 159–63 and O. Homburger, *Die illustrierten Handschriften der Burgerbibliothek Bern* (Bern, 1962), pp. 148ff.

[28] But cf. V. Elbern, *Der karolingische Goldaltar von Mailand* (Munich, 1952), pp. 41ff. and *idem*, "Der Ambrosiuszyklus am karolingischen Goldaltar von Mailand," *Mitteilungen des Kunsthistorischen Institutes in Florenz*, VII (1953), 1ff.

[29] Goldschmidt, *Elfenbeinskulpturen*, I, no. 57.

[30] K. Weitzmann, "Illustrations for the Chronicles of Sozomenos, Theodoret and Malalas," *Byzantion*, XVI (1942–43), 87ff. and *idem*, "Selection of Texts," pp. 84ff.

[31] Vienna, Nationalbibliothek, Cod. med. gr. 1, fol. 5[v].

[32] Vatican, Cod. Palat. lat. 1564, fols. 2[r] and 3[r].

[33] E. Zimmermann, *Vorkarolingische Miniaturen* (Berlin, 1916), II, pl. 88.

[34] W. Neumüller and K. Holter, *Der Codex Millenarius* (Linz, 1959), pp. 58ff.

the Bald (Fig. 134) and in a number of post-Carolingian manuscripts.[35] In several of these, he is shown writing or dictating to his scribes. He recalls in this way, the portrait of St. Augustine in the Egino Codex of 796–99 (Berlin, Staatsbliothek, Cod. Phill. 1676, fol. 18ᵛ, Fig. 136),[36] where much as in the fifth episode of the San Paolo frontispiece, the scholarly saint is shown dictating one of his treatises before four monks. These author frontispieces are single miniatures. They must be considered, therefore, as narratively enlivened portraits rather than as portrait narratives, and this distinguishes them from the sequences that form the Jerome frontispieces.[37]

Perhaps the Jerome frontispieces were inspired by the treatment of David in certain Psalter manuscripts. In the East and in the West, portraits of David composing the Psalms were often distributed over several prefatory miniatures in Books of Psalms. In the "Aristocratic" Psalter tradition, the subjects depicted were taken from David's biography in the Book of Kings.[38] In Western art, the themes were based on the Psalm prefaces and include David as musician and David as scribe.[39] It is quite possible, of course, that the inventor of the Jerome cycle had David in mind when he created the scenes. Jerome's role as reviver of the Psalms was often cited and in Carolingian art it was given pictorial expression on the Dagulph covers (Figs. 133 and 145) and in the Psalter of Charles the Bald. On the front cover of the Dagulph Psalter, David is depicted twice: dictating to his scribes and composing the Psalms with his co-psalmists. On the back cover, Jerome is similarly depicted: first receiving a rotulus from Bonifatius and then dictating to his scribes. The idea is clear. David composed the Psalms. Jerome revised them.[40] The same idea lies behind the inclusion of Jerome in the Psalter of Charles the Bald. With the possible exception of the Folchard Psalter (Fig. 170), specific pictorial parallels with David pictures cannot be adduced for the Jerome illustrations. If narrative author portraits of King David did inspire the invention of the Jerome cycles, therefore, their influence was only general.

The best parallels to the Jerome cycles occur in Byzantine manuscripts of the Octateuch. The Greek Old Testaments also begin with representations of the Bible being translated. These illustrate the Letter of Aristeas, a pseudepigraphic epistle written during the first or second century B.C. that recounts how the Septuagint came to be translated at the orders of Ptolemy Philadelphus.[41] Most of the extant examples are abbreviated; but in Vatican codex gr. 747, the most reliable reflection of the arche-

[35] Cf. Bloch and Schnitzler, op. cit., pp. 144ff. and Schnitzler, op. cit., pp. 11ff.

[36] H. Belting, "Probleme der Kunstgeschichte Italiens im Frühmittelalter," Frühmittelalterliche Studien, I (1967), 126ff.

[37] The Touronian frontispieces remained unique. Cf. P. Bloch, "Novem opus facere me cogis, Zum Hieronymusbild in Kölner Evangeliar der Ambrosiana," Festschrift für Hermann Usener (Marburg an der Lahn, 1967), pp. 119ff.

[38] K. Weitzmann, "Prolegomena to a Study of the Cyprus Plates," Metropolitan Museum Journal, III (1970), 97ff.

[39] Cf. Chapter VII.

[40] Cf. von Euw, op. cit., pp. 48ff.

[41] H. B. Swete, An Introduction to the Old Testament in Greek (Cambridge, 1914), pp. 499ff. I am grateful to Prof. Weitzmann for calling my attention to the Aristeas narratives.

type,[42] eight scenes are included within the columns of text: Ptolemy orders a Letter to be Written to the Jewish High Priest (fol. 2ᵛ); He Orders the Manufacture of Implements (fol. 3ᵛ); Andreas and Aristeas Present Ptolemy's Letter to Eleazar (fol. 6ʳ); They Bring the Priest's Reply to Ptolemy (fol. 6ʳ); Ptolemy Gives a Banquet for the Translators (fol. 6ᵛ); The Finished Translation is Brought to Ptolemy (fol. 10ᵛ); Ptolemy Gives a Letter to the Messenger (fol. 12ʳ); the Messenger Delivers the Letter to Eleazar (fol. 12ʳ).

Although no direct connection can be made between the Aristeas miniatures and the Carolingian Jerome pictures, the Greek Octateuch cycles do establish the existence of prefatory illustrations depicting the story of biblical translation. To be sure, the Greek cycles follow a specific text whereas no comparable source has been found for the Western miniatures. Nevertheless, the Jerome frontispieces can no longer be considered unique. Parallel translation pictures also exist in the Byzantine East.

THE PICTORIAL MODELS

The depictions of St. Jerome on the Dagulph cover introduce the issue of specific pictorial prototypes for the Touronian frontispieces. They suggest that the Jerome cycle may not have been invented at Tours and may, instead, have been based on a much earlier model.

Anton von Euw, who examined the Dagulph covers in considerable detail and who attempted to trace their sources, concluded that they are Carolingian compilations of disparate antique motifs.[43] He referred to the Vivian and San Paolo frontispieces, but could see no relationship between them and the ivories. Gaehde took exception to von Euw's findings. He pointed out the agreement that exists between the scribe, the man who looks over his shoulder, and Jerome in the lower panel of the Dagulph cover and the similar group in the San Paolo Bible. He concluded, however, that the San Paolo illuminator "with similar sources at hand might have elaborated on the repertoire of the Vivian page in order to emphasize the narrative and episodical aspect of the miniature."[44] If, however, as argued above, the San Paolo frontispiece is actually the more faithful reflection of the model, then the parallel with the Dagulph cover suggests strongly that this model or its prototype was invented prior to 795. The evidence is scanty. Comparisons can only be made with one scene and that one is highly conventional. Nevertheless, the Dagulph cover is an important indication that the Jerome cycle originated at an early date.

The most convincing evidence that the Jerome frontispieces were derived from a pre-Carolingian model is developed from an analysis of style. As Köhler first pointed out, a number of elements of the Vivian page find striking parallels in Early Christian

---

[42] Cf. K. Weitzmann, *The Joshua Roll* (Princeton, 1948), pp. 31ff.

[43] *Ibid.*, pp. 51ff.

[44] "Turonian Sources," p. 365.

art.[45] Köhler's examples from the Vatican Virgil (Cod. lat. 3225)[46] are especially compelling. The ships in Pictura 39 (Fig. 137) are virtually identical to those in the Carolingian Bibles and the architecture—in particular, the walled cities—is also similar. One feature of the Vatican Virgil that Köhler did not note also corresponds to the presumed model of the Jerome frontispieces. The Vatican Virgil contains a single page (Pictura 1, Fig. 138) that portrays six small narrative pictures arranged in two columns.[47] In the related fourth/fifth century Book of Kings in Berlin (Staatsbibliothek, Cod. Theol. lat. fol. 485)[48] similar full page miniatures composed of narrative scenes are found. Because of the similarities between these fifth-century Roman works and the ninth-century frontispieces, Gaehde's dismissal of the possibility of an Early Christian model seems too hasty.[49]

The presumed model of the Jerome pages should not be tied too closely to the Vatican Virgil. Many of the similarities that are apparent in the manuscripts result from conventions which must have been current for decades. For example, walled towns similar to those in the Vatican Virgil and the ninth-century frontispieces can be found in the Codex Agrimensores of c. 500 (Wolfenbüttel, Herzog-August Bibliothek, Cod. Guelf. 3623A, fol. 60^r);[50] and there exists in the same manuscript an interesting parallel to the personification of Rome in the Bibles (cf. fol. 74^v). The indications are, then, that whereas the pictorial prototypes of the Jerome pictures originated in Italy in the fifth century, they may have post-dated the saint's death by several decades.

Jerome's portrait features and costume seem to be characteristically Carolingian. In earlier art, for example, in the Leningrad and Vienna author portraits, Jerome is represented as a bearded old man. This portrait tradition persists in the Dagulph cover, in the Lothar Psalter (London, British Library, Cod. Add. 37768, fol. 6^r),[51] and in Ottonian art.[52] In the Psalter of Charles the Bald, however, in the Psalterium Aureum of St. Gall (Stiftsbibliothek, Cod. 22, fol. 14^r),[53] and in the Bibles, St. Jerome is beardless and tonsured. Also, the mantle and tunic of earlier depictions have been superseded in these manuscripts by the chasuble and tunic. Jerome's staff in the Vivian Bible seems surely to be a Touronian addition. The Vivian illuminators also provided the Creator (Fig. 3) and St. Paul (Fig. 174) with similar staffs. The Carolingian illuminators refashioned Jerome's aspect and costume to make them conform to contemporary monastic custom. The archbishop (fol. 1^v, Fig. 139) and St. Gregory (fol. 5^v, Fig. 135) in the Raganaldus Sacramentary are examples of the type of figure that seems to have been emulated.

[45] *Kar. Min.*, I$_2$, 215ff.

[46] J. de Wit, *Die Miniaturen des Vergilius Vaticanus* (Amsterdam, 1959), pl. 22.

[47] *Ibid.*, pl. 1.

[48] H. Degering and A. Boeckler, *Die Quedlinburg Italafragmente* (Berlin, 1952), pls. I, II, and IV. Cf. K. Weitzmann, "Book Illustration of the Fourth Century," *Studies*, pp. 104ff.

[49] "Turonian Sources," p. 362.

[50] *Corpus Agrimensorum Romanorum*, ed. H. Butsmann (Leiden, 1970).

[51] Köhler, *Kar. Min.*, IV, pl. IIb.

[52] Bloch and Schnitzler, *op. cit.*, pp. 144ff.

[53] J. R. Rahn, *Die Psalterium Aureum von Sanct Gall* (St. Gall, 1878), pl. VII. Bloch and Schnitzler, *op. cit.*, p. 145.

CONCLUSIONS

Numerous questions remain after the examination of the Jerome frontispieces in the Vivian and San Paolo Bibles. The date and nature of the prototype are still unclear, although the strongest indications are that the model was a fifth-century prefatory cycle.[54] The textual source of the depictions is also unknown. Apparently, the inventor of the cycle consulted some biographical work, but whether this was Jerome's own writings or a lost *Vita Hieronymi* is not certain.

The detailed investigation of the Vivian and San Paolo frontispieces does clarify certain aspects of the problem. It confirms that both pages were derived from the same model, apparently a frontispiece illustrating six episodes of Jerome's story. It also indicates that the San Paolo frontispiece reflects this model more faithfully than does the Vivian Bible. In the latter, several episodes were amalgamated to form monumental compositions that focus on Jerome. An author portrait, similar to that in the Psalter of Charles the Bald may have been used to transform the narrative source.

Although the ultimate prototype seems to have been a fifth-century Italian work, there are indications that the immediate model was Carolingian. Jerome's portraiture and costume appear to be modifications of the earlier iconography intended to give the saint the appearance of a contemporary bishop. It seems likely that the choice of subject was itself dictated by contemporary concerns. Jerome's activity as translator of the Vulgate was certainly considered an apt parallel for the undertaking at Tours to produce newly revised editions of the same text. Such episodes as Jerome leaving Rome, Jerome paying his Hebrew teacher, and Jerome disputing the Pelagians, however, are unrelated to ninth-century Tours. They constitute adequate proof that, whereas it may have been selected for its typological significance, the cycle was not invented for that purpose. It originated as a biographical sequence covering Jerome's activities as the translator of the Vulgate.

[54] This was proposed by C. Nordenfalk, "Beiträge zur Geschichte der Turonischen Buchmale- rei," *Acta Archaeologica*, V (1936), 297 and by Bloch and Schnitzler, *op. cit.*, p. 145.

VII. DAVID REX ET PROPHETA

AS frontispieces to the Book of Psalms, the Vivian and San Paolo Bibles represent David, flanked by guards and accompanied by four musicians, composing the Psalms on a triangular psaltery (Figs. 140 and 141).[1] In the Vivian Bible, David is semi-nude and he is shown dancing at the center of a large mandorla; half-length personifications of the four cardinal virtues occupy the corners of the page.[2] In the San Paolo Bible, a fully clothed king stands with his bodyguards in the upper register of the page and the musicians and three scribes are ranked beneath them. Evidently both illuminators based their compositions on the same model. That prototype must have featured David, bearded and crowned, glancing over his shoulder while playing the psaltery. It must also have included two soldiers and the musicians Asaph, Heman, Ethan, and Jeduthun. Both illuminators departed from this basic source, however, by rearranging its elements and adding new figures to the composition.

Depictions of David composing the Psalms with his musicians were frequently used as Psalter frontispieces during the Middle Ages.[3] Almost without exception, these frontispieces represent David enthroned or dancing and his co-psalmists standing. Only the ninth-century Bible frontispieces depict the king dancing amid seated musicians.[4] The traditional images have antecedents in late antique author portraits and may represent one of the earliest methods for decorating Psalters.[5] The Touronian compositions, on the other hand, combine features of the standard author page with narrative and allegorical elements. Like the sources of the *Majestas* frontispieces, the origins of these compositions are difficult to trace and their meanings are complicated to decipher.

THE PRINCIPAL MODEL

There is considerable evidence that the Touronian illuminators based their Bible illustrations on a composition closely related to the frontispiece miniature in the Psalter of Charles the Bald (Paris, Bibliothèque Nationale, Cod. lat. 1152, fol. 1ʳ,

[1] Vivian Bible, fol. 215ᵛ. Cf. Köhler, *Kar. Min.*, I₂, 217f.; San Paolo Bible, fol. 170ᵛ. Cf. Gaehde, "Bible Manuscript," I, 426ff. and "Turonian Sources," pp. 376ff. The soldiers in the Vivian Bible are labeled: CERETHI and PELETHI and the musicians are identified as ASAPH, AEMAN, AETHAN, and IDITHUN. In the San Paolo Bible, only ASAPH, EMAN, and IDITHUN are clearly labeled.

[2] They are identified: PRUDENTIA, IUSTITIA, FORTITUDO, and TEMPERANTIA.

[3] Cf. H. Steger, *David Rex et Propheta* (Nuremberg, 1961).

[4] Another exception is the twelfth-century Hamilton Psalter in Berlin (Kupferstichkabinett, MS. 78.A.5, fol. 1ʳ). Cf. P. Wescher, *Beschreibendes Verzeichnis der Miniaturen des Kupferstichkabinetts* (Leipzig, 1931), p. 21, Fig. 24.

[5] Cf. K. Weitzmann, "Book Illustration in the Fourth Century," *Studies*, pp. 113ff. The frontispieces showing David and his musicians appear to be unrelated to the depictions of the shepherd David composing Psalms found in the "Aristocratic Psalters." Cf. H. Buchthal, *The Miniatures of the Paris Psalter* (London, 1938), pp. 13ff.

Fig. 142).[6] Although the Psalter manuscript was produced two decades after the Vivian Bible, that is, shortly before the death of Charles' first wife Hermintrude in 869, the less complex composition of the Psalter frontispiece preserves several elements that must have been features of the model used at Tours. As in the two Bible pages, David dances and looks backward while he plays his psaltery. In the Psalter manuscript, however, Asaph, Heman, Ethan, and Jeduthun are also shown in motion.

Two details indicate that the prototype of the Bible frontispieces also depicted dancing musicians. One is the figure of Jeduthun in the San Paolo Bible. As Gaehde has already pointed out, the animated upper torso of this figure must certainly have been copied from a dancing cymbalist similar to the figure in the Psalter of Charles the Bald.[7] The instruments played by the musicians in both Bible frontispieces are another indication that the model resembled the Psalter page. In the latter, as in the Vivian Bible, Heman plays cymbals,[8] Ethan plucks a cythara,[9] and Jeduthun blows a long horn. Heman and Jeduthun have simply been switched in the San Paolo page. The Psalter frontispiece represents Asaph dancing with a billowing scarf but without instruments.[10] A model that depicted a similar dancing figure would account for a peculiar feature of the Bible pages. In the Vivian Bible, the first psalmist is shown with two instruments: he blows a horn and he holds cymbals. In the San Paolo Bible, Asaph has been given the same attributes as Heman, a horn and a book. Had the model available at Tours represented Asaph dancing without instruments as in Paris 1152, the illuminators would have had to improvise instruments for him when they converted him into a seated figure. It seems, they simply duplicated those played by the other musicians.

An eleventh-century Psalter in Munich (Bayerische Staatsbibliothek, Clm. 13067, fol. 18ʳ, Fig. 143)[11] is further evidence that the model used at Tours showed David with the four dancing musicians. The king in the Munich Psalter is virtually identical

---

[6] Because Queen Hermintrude is mentioned in the litanies, the Psalter of Charles the Bald is to be dated between 842 and 869. V. Leroquais, *Les psautiers* (Macon, 1940–41), II, 67ff. and P. E. Schramm and F. Mütherich, *Denkmale der deutschen Könige und Kaiser* (Munich, 1962), p. 131.

[7] "Turonian Sources," p. 379.

[8] In all three frontispieces, rattle-like crotala were substituted for true cymbals. In antiquity, crotala were employed in licentious dances. Cf. H. Stern, *Le calendrier de 354* (Paris, 1953), pp. 269ff. They also appear in place of cymbals on the Dagulph cover (Fig. 145), in the Utrecht Psalter (fol. 83ʳ), and in the Stuttgart Psalter (fols. 84ᵛ and 163ᵛ, Fig. 144). Cf. R. Hammerstein, "Instrumenta Hieronymi," *Archiv für Musikwissenschaft*, XVI (1959), 132 and T. Seebass,

Musikdarstellung und Psalterillustration im früheren Mittelalter (Bern, 1973), 28ff.

[9] Actually, a combination of a lyre and a lute. Cf. F. Behn, *Musikleben im Altertum und frühen Mittelalter* (Stuttgart, 1954), p. 55.

[10] H. Morgan, "The Motive of a Figure Holding in Both Hands a Piece of Drapery which Blows Out Behind or Over the Figure," *Art Studies*, VI (1928), 163ff.

[11] The Munich Psalter was apparently produced near Dinant during the third quarter of the eleventh century. Cf. *Catalogus codicum manuscriptorum Bibliothecae Regiae Monacensis*, II, pt. 2 (Wiesbaden, 1968), pp. 98f.; K. H. Usener, "Das Breviar Clm 2361 der Bayerischen Staatsbibliothek, *Münchner Jahrbuch der bildende Kunst*, III (1950), 89ff.; Steger, *op. cit.*, pp. 190f. and Fig. 12b.

to the central figure in the Vivian Bible. Half-naked, he dances forward with his triangular psaltery while glancing back over his shoulder. Four musicians accompany David as in the Psalter of Charles the Bald; and here too, only three kinds of instruments are depicted; the cythara is played by two of the co-psalmists. The interlace borders with decorative bosses strongly indicate that the Munich frontispiece was based on a Carolingian model. Similar ornamental frames appear in manuscripts of the Franco-Saxon group, for example, in the Sacramentary of Hermintrude in the Pierpont Morgan Library (Glazier MS. 57).[12] It seems likely, therefore, that the Munich composition was based on a ninth-century model. If so, then that model must have been derived from the same prototype that served the illuminators of the Touronian Bibles.

Its relationship to the textual source of these compositions supports the conclusion that the frontispiece in the Psalter of Charles the Bald is closest to the model. This literary source is not the Bible text. Elements of the illustrations can ultimately be traced to the Books of Kings and Chronicles,[13] but the immediate source of the illustrations was a preface to Psalms known as the *Origo Psalmorum*.[14] Anton Springer had noted the relationship of the *Origo* to these frontispieces almost a century ago[15] and subsequent scholars have verified the correspondence.[16] The preface accompanies the illustrations in all three ninth-century manuscripts[17] and there can be no doubt that it was the basis of the pictures,

Origo psalmoru(m) david prophet(i). David, filius jesse, cum e(ss)et in regno suo, quattuor elegit, qui psalmos facerent, id est asaph eman, ethan, et idithun. LXXX ergo octo dicebant psalmos et ducenti subpsalma et cythara(m) percuoiebat abiuth. Cu(m) david reduxisset arca(m) in hierusalem post annos XX revocata(m) ab azotis et mansit in domo aminadab, hanc imposuit subiugali novo et adduxit in hierusale(m), electis viris ex omni genere filioru(m) israhel LXX viros de tribu aute(m) levi ducentos septuaginta milia octo viros, ex quibus quattuor principes praee(ss)e cantionibus constituit asaph, eman, ethan, et idithun, uni-

[12] J. Plummer, *The Glazier Collection* (New York, 1968), pp. 10f. Interlace frames decorated with four or six large square or circular bosses are found in most Franco-Saxon manuscripts. Folio 4ʳ of Glazier 57 is representative. The ornament of the boss in the lower right is virtually identical to that in the Munich Psalter.

[13] David's dance is described in II Sam., VI, 15–20 and I Chron., XV, 25ff. The Kerethite and Pelethite guards are mentioned in II Sam., VIII, 18; XV; XX, 7 and I Chron., XVIII, 17. The Musicians are referred to in various passages of Chronicles and in the superscriptions of the Psalms. Asaph: I Chron., XV, 19; XVI, 5–7; XXV, 6; Ps., XLIX. Heman: I Chron., XV, 19; XVI, 42; XXV, 6. Ethan: I Chron., XV, 19. And Jedithun: I Chron., XVI, 42; XXV 6; and Ps. XXXVIII.

[14] D. De Bruyne, *Les préfaces de la Bible latine* (Namur, 1920), p. 43.

[15] *Die Psalter-Illustration im frühen Mittelalter* (Leipzig, 1880), pp. 207ff.

[16] F. Landsberger, *Der St. Galler Folchard Psalter* (St. Gall, 1912), pp. 45ff.; Steger, *op. cit.*, pp. 113ff.; D. Wright, review of Steger, *Speculum*, XXXIX (1964), 753; *idem, The Vespasian Psalter* (Early English Manuscripts in Facsimile) Copenhagen-London-Baltimore, 1967, pp. 71ff.; A. von Euw, "Studien zu den Elfenbeinarbeiten der Hofschule Karls des Grossen," *Aachener Kunstblätter*, XXXIV (1967), 42ff.; Gaehde, "Turonian Sources," pp. 377f. Wright observes correctly that Paris lat. 1152 "reflects the Origo Psalmorum most accurately" and that the Vivian page "is related but more complicated."

[17] Paris lat. 1, fol. 216ʳ; Paris lat. 1152, fols. 2ʳ–2ᵛ; San Paolo Bible, fol. 169ʳ.

cuique eoru(m) dividens septuaginta duos, viros succlamante laude(m) cantio-
nu(m) d(omi)no. Et unus quide(m) eoru(m) feriebat cymbalum, alius cith-
ara(m), alius tuba cornea exultans; in medio aute(m) eorum stabat david tenens
et ipse psalteriu(m). Arca aute(m) antecedebat choros septe(m) et sacri-
ficiu(m) vitulus, populus aute(m) universus subsequebatur retro arca(m). Sunt
ergo omnes psalmi dav(id) numero CL, quoru(m) omniu(m) quidem novem
fecit ipse david, triginta et duo non sunt suprascripti, LXXII in david, XII in asaph,
XII in idithun, VIIII filiis chore, I moysi, II in salomonem, II in aggaeu(m) et zacha-
ria(m). Fiunt aute(m) omnes psalmi david numero CL, dyapsalmo numero
LXXV, canticu(m) graduum numero XV. Psalm(us) primus nulli assignatus est,
q(uonia)m omnium est deinde quis alius intelligitur in primo nisi primogenitus?
ut merito suprascriptio non fuit necessaria; deinde quia ipse psalmus Xpi men-
tionem facit ut adversus Xpm tuu(m) exponendo ipsius inducit personam inscri-
bendi causa(m) omnino non habe(n)t tituli inscriptionem.[18]

The ninth-century miniatures correspond, not to the parent text of the *Origo Psalmorum*, but to a Carolingian variant of it. This variant, which first appeared in the
Dagulph Psalter of c. 795 (Vienna, Nationalbibliothek, Cod. 1861)[19] and which is
repeated in the later Bibles and in the Psalter of Charles the Bald, differs from the
original version in that it omits the fourth instrument, the cinyra (ten-string lyre) in the
list of instruments played by the co-psalmists.[20] The parent text reads, "Et unus quidem
eorum feriebat cymbalum, alius cynaram, alius citharam, alius tuba cornea exultans.
In medio autem stabat david rex tenens ipse psalterium."[21] The representation of a
cymbalum, cythara, and tuba cornea—but not a cinyra—in the ninth-century frontispieces indicates that the model of these pages was based on the Carolingian reading of
the *Origo* text. It follows from this that the prototype was a Carolingian creation.

ANTECEDENTS OF THE PSALTER MODEL

David dancing with musicians had appeared in Carolingian art before the theme
was used as a Psalter frontispiece in the Vivian Bible. For example, to illustrate
Psalm 150, the illuminator of the Stuttgart Psalter (Württembergische Landesbibliothek, fol. 23, fol. 163ᵛ, Fig. 144)[22] represented David playing the psaltery in the company of other musicians. The Stuttgart Psalter illustration, which was based on II Sam.,
VI, contains many of the elements depicted in the frontispiece compositions. One
woman plays the crotala, a man blows the horn, and at the bottom of the miniature
there is a tiny nude man dancing with a scarf. David's dance was also illustrated in
later ninth-century Psalters. In the Golden Psalter of St. Gall (Stiftsbibliothek, Cod.

[18] Transcribed from Paris lat. 1152. Prof. Ali-
son Stones kindly prepared this transcription. The
last lines of the *Origo* text are missing in the Psalter of Charles the Bald.
[19] Köhler, *Kar. Min.*, II, 42ff.

[20] Cf. De Bruyne, *op. cit.*, p. 43 and D. Wright,
Vespasian Psalter, p. 49.
[21] De Bruyne, *op. cit.*, p. 43.
[22] B. Bischoff *et al.*, *Der Stuttgarter Bilderpsalter* (Stuttgart, 1968), II, 149.

22, fol. 66ʳ),[23] the theme was used to illustrate Ps. XXIX; however, the illustration has no resemblance to the Touronian composition. In the Folchard Psalter (St. Gall, Stiftsbibliothek, Cod. 23, fol. 12ʳ)[24] David is shown being handed his psaltery and the blasphemer Uzzah is represented dancing behind the oxcart that transports the Ark of the Covenant.

Despite the coincidence of several figures and certain details, narrative depictions such as those in the Stuttgart and Folchard Psalters seem not to have been the principal source of the frontispieces in the manuscripts of Charles the Bald. From the very beginning of the Carolingian period, representations of David and his musicians had been incorporated as independent author portraits in Books of Psalms, and it was evidently from this tradition that the Touronian illuminators developed their compositions.

The earliest Carolingian portrait of David appears on the ivory book cover that once adorned Charlemagne's Dagulph Psalter (Paris, Louvre, Fig. 145).[25] In the lower of the two scenes on the cover, David is represented enthroned and playing his psaltery amid soldiers and musicians. The musician to David's left plays the cythara while he dances; the man to David's right plays the crotala.

A similar representation occupies a two-page opening in the early ninth-century Psalter in Angers (Bibliothèque Municipale, MS. 18(14), fols. 13ᵛ and 14ʳ, Figs. 146 and 147).[26] On the left hand page, David is enthroned and holds a lyre and one of his companions plays the pan-pipes. On the facing page, three other musicians are depicted playing the organum, crotala, and horn. Two scribes are also represented. Because of its provincial style, it is difficult to determine whether the Angers illustration was meant to illustrate dancing musicians. This point is not clarified by the Vallicelliana Psalter in Rome (Cod. E.24, fols. 26ᵛ and 27ʳ, Figs. 148 and 149),[27] a later Umbro-Roman copy of the same prototype.

The Golden Psalter of St. Gall also contains an illustration of David and his musicians. On folio 2ʳ (Fig. 150), David is shown enthroned and playing his psaltery amid four young men. Two of the men vigorously clap their crotala and two dance gracefully with scarves billowing above their heads.

There can be no doubt that the inventor of the prototype used at Tours drew on this frontispiece tradition. The crotalists, the Dagulph cytharist, and the dancers in the St. Gall manuscript are especially close to the figures in the Psalter of Charles the Bald; and David's guards on the Dagulph cover parallel the soldiers on the Bible pages. Only the dancing David finds no counterpart in the frontispiece portraits.

[23] Cf. J. Rahn, *Das Psalterium Aureum von Sanct Gallen* (St. Gall, 1878), pp. 30f. and pl. XIV.

[24] Landsberger, *op. cit.*, p. 47.

[25] Goldschmidt, *Elfenbeinskulpturen*, I, 9 and pl. III, Fig. 3 and von Euw, *op. cit.*, pp. 36ff.

[26] Leroquais, *op. cit.*, pp. 19ff. and pls. VIII

and IX; von Euw, *op. cit.*, pp. 43ff. and Gaehde, "Turonian Sources," pp. 379f. and Fig. 81.

[27] E. Garrison, *Studies in Medieval Italian Painting*, II (1955), 86ff. and Wright, *review*, p. 752. Wright asserts that the Valicelliana miniatures are the most accurate witnesses of the prototype of the Angers manuscript.

David and his musicians had been the subject of Psalter frontispieces produced before the Carolingian period. A full-page miniature was devoted to them, for example, in the eighth-century Vespasian Psalter in London (British Library, Cod. Cotton Vespasian, A. I., fol. 30ᵛ, Fig. 151).[28] David is depicted between two scribes playing his harp in the company of dancers and horn blowers. Despite such analogies as the arched frame, however, the Vespasian miniature seems not to be directly related to the Carolingian compositions.[29]

Considerable evidence, including the Vespasian Psalter page, itself, indicates that the theme of David and his musicians had also been popular in the East during the Early Christian period. The earliest extant Byzantine example appears in the Khludov Psalter (Moscow, Public Library, Cod. gr. 129), a Constantinopolitan manuscript produced shortly after the end of Iconoclasm in 843 or perhaps even earlier, during the interim period between the two Iconoclastic phases (787–815).[30] Folio 1ᵛ (Fig. 152) of the Khludov Psalter represents David playing the psaltery in the company of four musicians. The frontispiece has been repainted[31] and consequently, it is impossible to identify the original instruments. In its present state, the miniature depicts musicians playing a drum, a horn, cymbals, and a lute.[32] There is reason to believe that the Khludov composition reflects a pre-Iconoclastic model. The same Greek prototype may have served as the ultimate model of the Vespasian page which, according to David Wright, was copied from a Justinianic Psalter;[33] and it may also have been the source of a related composition in the ninth-century Cosmas Indicopleustes manuscript in the Vatican (Cod. gr. 699, fol. 63ʳ, Fig. 153) which evidently was copied from a sixth-century model.[34] As in the Khludov page, in the Cosmas miniature David is enthroned playing his harp. In the latter, however, he is surrounded by six choirs and two dancers. Even though they post-date the earliest Western examples, these Greek frontispieces may reflect the same archetype that was used by the Carolingian artists to illustrate their Psalters.

Early models may also be reflected in a number of later Byzantine Psalters. Wright has already called attention to the eleventh-century Barberini Psalter (Vatican, Cod.

[28] Wright, *Vespasian Psalter*, pp. 73ff.

[29] *Ibid.*, p. 71.

[30] N. P. Kondakov, *Miniatures du manuscrit grec du Psautier du IXᵉ siècle de la Collection A.I. Chloudow à Moscou* (Moscow, 1878) and K. Weitzmann, *Die byzantinische Buchmalerei des 9. und 10. Jahrhunderts* (Berlin, 1935), p. 55.

[31] V. Lasarev, "Einige kritische Bemerkungen zum Chludov-Psalter," *Byzantinische Zeitschrift*, xxix (1929–30), 279ff.

[32] Wright, *Vespasian Psalter*, p. 72, identified the instruments as a drum (?), horn, writing tablet and scroll. The excellent photograph supplied to me by Prof. Weitzmann, however, clearly

shows four musical instruments. These instruments are also listed in the Princeton Index of Christian Art. Wright's suggestion that the drum was an addition of the restorer to a dancing figure is open to question. Whereas dancers appear in later frontispieces, so do drummers: in Vatican, gr. 342; Vatican Barb. gr. 372 (Fig. 154); and London, Additional MS 40731, it is unlikely that originally only one musician, the horn-blower was represented in the Khludov composition.

[33] *Vespasian Psalter*, p. 74.

[34] J. Stornajolo, *Le miniature della Topografia cristiana di Cosma Indicopleuste* (Milan, 1908) pl. 26.

Barb. gr. 372, fol. 5ᵛ, Fig. 154).³⁵ As in the ninth-century manuscripts, David is represented in the Barberini Psalter wearing imperial regalia and playing the psaltery in the presence of musicians, dancers, and, in this case, scribes. Wright has pointed out how the figure directly below David raises his arms in much the same manner as does the drummer in the Khludov Psalter. There are also other parallels in the two compositions. The man shown in profile to the right of the Barberini dancer recalls the Khludov castanet player and the harpist and horn-blower in the Vatican Psalter are akin to the figures in the Moscow manuscript.

Another reflection of an early frontispiece composition may be preserved in a second eleventh-century Psalter in the Vatican, Cod. gr. 752 (fol. 5ʳ, Fig. 155).³⁶ David, playing a viol, is enthroned amid dancers and musicians, including a flutist, cymbalist, drummer, and players of various stringed instruments. A manuscript in Istanbul (Seraglio, Cod. 13, fol. 2ʳ)³⁷ attests to the popularity of the theme as late as the thirteenth century. The frontispiece shows David seated between a flutist, a lute player, and a dancing cymbalist.

A number of variations on the composition exist. In the Vatican Psalter grec. 752, for instance, a second representation serves as the frontispiece to the text of Psalms (fol. 18ᵛ, Fig. 156).³⁸ The placement of musicians around David is not unlike that in the depiction on fol. 5ʳ (Fig. 155), but in this portrayal David stands beneath a baldachin and does not play an instrument. He is also accompanied by two prophet-like figures (labelled Asaph and Heman) as well as by the musicians—a drummer, a horn-blower (Jeduthun), a flutist and a harpist. The prophets and horn-blower, as well as the figure of Christ enthroned above David, are not paralleled in the preceding miniature but they do appear in the Barberini Psalter (Fig. 154). There are also clear similarities with the Khludov composition which suggests that the Vatican depictions were derived from an early model. David standing amid his musicians is also represented in the thirteenth-century Spencer Psalter (New York, Public Library, Spencer Cod. gr. 1, fol. 1ᵛ, Fig. 157);³⁹ while in the eleventh-century Bristol Psalter (London, British Library, Cod. Add. 40731), a frontispiece presents David enthroned holding an open book and flanked by four musicians (fol. 7ᵛ).⁴⁰

Another type of Byzantine Psalter frontispiece portrays David with large groups of musicians. This version, which may find an early reflection in the Vatican Cosmas

³⁵ *Vespasian Psalter*, p. 72 and *Il libro della Bibbia* (catalogue of an exhibition, Vatican, 1972), pp. 21f. and pl. XX.

³⁶ E. T. Dewald, *The Illustrations in the Manuscripts of the Septuaginta* (Princeton, 1942), III, pt. 2.

³⁷ A. Muñoz, "Tre codici miniati della biblioteca del Seraglio a Costantinopoli," *Studi bisantini*, I (1924), 202ff.; R. Hamann-MacLean, "Der Berliner Codex Graecus Quarto 66," *Studien zur Buchmalerei und Goldschmiedekunst des Mittelalters. Festschrift K. H. Usener* (Marburg an der Lahn, 1967), pp. 237ff.

³⁸ Dewald, *op. cit.*, pp. 7f.

³⁹ *Illuminated Greek Manuscripts from American Collections: An Exhibition in Honor of Kurt Weitzmann* (Princeton, 1973), no. 47; A. Cutler, "The Spencer Psalter: A Thirteenth Century Byzantine Manuscript in the New York Public Library," *Cahiers Archéologiques*, XXIII (1974), 129ff.

⁴⁰ S. Dufrenne, *L'illustration des Psautiers grecs du Moyen-Age* (Paris, 1966), pl. 47.

manuscript (Fig. 153), is also depicted in Vatican gr. 752 (fol. 7ᵛ, Fig. 158).[41] The latter representation has more of a narrative character than the other frontispieces. David stands behind the Ark of the Covenant and Uzzah dances before him. In other examples, however, such as Vatican Cod. gr. 342 (fol. 24ᵛ)[42] and the Serbian Psalter in Munich (Bayerische Staatsbibliothek, Cod. Slav. 4, fols. 4ᵛ and 5ʳ)[43] the composition is more hieratic.

Three basic types can be discerned among the depictions of David and his musicians in Greek Psalters. The most common represents David playing his psaltery; the second shows him standing and holding a book; and the third presents the king with four choirs.

The overall similarity of these three types as well as certain differences among them are to be explained by the texts on which they were based. These texts are the commentaries on the Book of Psalms by Eusebius,[44] Theodoret,[45] the pseudo-Chrysostom,[46] and Hesychius,[47] which serve as prefaces in many Greek Psalters. The fact that these prologues were all derived from the Homily on the Book of Psalms by Hippolytus[48] explains the fundamental agreement among the texts and, in turn, among the illustrations based on them. Hippolytus' homily and the other commentaries all describe King David composing the Psalms with his musicians. It is not surprising, therefore, that it is so difficult to pinpoint the specific textual source of any one illustration. There are reasons to believe, however, that the prologue of the pseudo-Chrysostom was the literary basis for the type of frontispiece that shows David enthroned. The pseudo-Chrysostom text is found most frequently in Psalters containing that form of the composition and it is paraphrased in the section on David in the *Christian Topography* of Cosmas Indicopleustes.[49] Whereas the other prefaces clearly state that David *stood* among the musicians, the opening lines of the pseudo-Chrysostom text emphasize David's regal aspect and his position as a predecessor of Christ. The musicians listed in the preface: a cymbalist, flutist, drummer, horn-blower, singer, and players of the psaltery and cythara[50] also conform to the miniatures. Theodoret's preface may have been the source of the compositions showing David standing and David with his choirs. Although the homily of Hippolytus could also have been the source, it is the Theodoret text that accompanies the miniatures in Vatican gr. 752.[51]

To decorate their own Psalters, Carolingian artists seem to have drawn extensively

[41] Dewald, *op. cit.*, pp. 5f.

[42] K. Lake, *Dated Greek Minuscule Manuscripts to the Year 1200* (Boston, 1934–39), VIII, pl. 545a. Cf. also Mt. Athos, Vatopedi MS. 761, fol. 14ᵛ.

[43] J. Strzygowski, *Die Miniaturen des Serbischen Psalter* (Vienna, 1906).

[44] *PG*, XXIII, cols. 73ff.

[45] *PG*, LXXXIV, col. 24.

[46] *PG*, LV, col. 531.

[47] G. Mercati, "Il commentario d'Esichio Gerosolimitano sui psalmi," *Studi e Testi*, V (1901), 145ff.

[48] P. Nautin, *Le Dossier d'Hippolyte et de Méliton* (Paris, 1953), pp. 99ff. and G. Mercati, "Osservazioni a proemi de Salterio," *Studi e Testi*, CXLII (1948), 1ff.

[49] *PG*, LXXXVIII, col. 248.

[50] Hippolytus mentions cymbals, psaltery, harp, cythara, and horn.

[51] Dewald, *op. cit.*, pp. 5f.

on the rich tradition of Byzantine Psalter frontispieces that is known in the East only in later examples. King David on the Dagulph cover (Fig. 145)[52] and in the Angers and St. Gall miniatures (Figs. 146 and 150) resembles the enthroned king in the Greek manuscripts and there are specific parallels among the musicians and dancers. The cytharist on the Dagulph cover and the horn-blower in the Angers Psalter, for example, compare well with the figures on the Khludov page (Fig. 152); and there are close parallels between the dancing men in the Golden Psalter of St. Gall and those in the Vatican Cosmas (Fig. 153). The only Carolingian figure with no Byzantine counterpart is the "cymbalist" who, in the Western examples, is always represented playing the crotala.

Because the *Origo Psalmorum* was, itself, derived from the homily of Hippolytus,[53] the Carolingian artists found the Byzantine compositions well suited to serve as illustrations for their Latin preface. The conformity of the borrowed images to the *Origo* text was, however, imperfect. The Greek frontispieces include as many as nine companions to David and sometimes four large groups; and the musicians play a variety of instruments in addition to the cymbals, cythara, and horn that are described in the Carolingian variant of the prologue.

It is not surprising, therefore, that the Western artists sought to bring their Greek models into closer accord with the *Origo* preface by abbreviating the compositions and modifying the instruments. The Dagulph cover and the Angers and St. Gall miniatures are three intelligent revisions of the source compositions. The most significant modification of the Greek prototypes, however, seems to have been accomplished by the creator of the model of the Psalter of Charles the Bald and the Touronian Bibles. Not only did he reduce the number of co-psalmists to four, but he provided them with the three instruments specified in the *Origo Psalmorum*. The result was an essentially new illustration compiled from Byzantine elements.

The originator of the Tours model made another emendation. He substituted a dancing figure for the more majestic enthroned David in his prototype.[54] David's backward glance and animated pose in the three frontispieces produced for Charles the Bald indicates that the source of this change was a narrative illustration of David's dance before the ark (II Sam., VI, 1ff.). David's dance is depicted in two miniatures of the eleventh-century Greek Book of Kings in the Vatican (Cod. gr. 333).[55] Fol. 45ᵛ (Fig. 159) shows David following the ark which is transported on an oxcart and fol. 46ʳ (Fig. 160) represents the king dancing wildly with two musicians before the ark. David's backward glance and the poses of his companions in the latter scene recall the

---

[52] Von Euw, *op. cit.*, pp. 48ff., has argued that the Dagulph panel was composed by the Carolingian artist. He seems not to know the Byzantine frontispieces other than the page in the Vatican Cosmas.

[53] J. Gribomont is investigating the Greek sources of the *Origo* prologue. Cf. Wright, *Vespasian Psalter*, p. 49 and *review*, p. 753.

[54] Cf. H. Schade, "Zum Bild des tanzenden David in frühen Mittelalters," *Stimmen der Zeit*, CLXXII (1962/63), 1ff.

[55] J. Lassus, "Les miniatures byzantines du 'Livre des Rois,'" *Mélanges d'Archéologie et d'Histoire*, XLV (1928), 67f. and *idem*, *L'illustration byzantine du Livre des Rois* (Paris, 1973).

figures of the Psalter of Charles the Bald. Even closer to the Carolingian figures is King David in the ninth-century *Sacra Parallela* in Paris (Bibliothèque Nationale, Cod. gr. 923, fol. 369ʳ, Fig. 161).[56] The *Sacra Parallela* illustration, which shows David in much the same pose adopted in the Carolingian frontispieces, was certainly copied from a illustrated Book of Kings. A narrative Kings manuscript, related to the Vatican and Paris illustrations, was known in the West during the ninth century when it served as the source for certain illustrations in the Stuttgart Psalter[57] and for three frontispieces in the San Paolo Bible.[58] It may also have provided the figure of the dancing David for the model of the Psalter frontispiece.

The scene of David's dance may, however, have been available in a Byzantine Psalter. In Vatican gr. 752, for example, the episode is depicted twice: on fol. 7ᵛ (Fig. 158) and on the facing page (fol. 8ʳ, Fig. 162). In the latter, David is shown alone, playing the psaltery and castanets. His pose is remarkably like that in the Carolingian frontispieces, especially the Vivian Bible page.

David's bodyguards in the two Bible manuscripts may also have been depicted in the basic model. Although they are not illustrated in the Psalter of Charles the Bald or in the Munich Psalter (Fig. 143), flanking soldiers are represented on the Dagulph cover. The imperial formula of an enthroned ruler attended by armsbearers had been adopted in Early Christian representations of biblical monarchs[59] and they appear frequently in Byzantine and Western depictions of King David. For example, bodyguards are represented throughout the Vatican Kings manuscript, and they are included in at least one Byzantine Psalter frontispiece.[60] They are also represented throughout the Utrecht Psalter[61] and on two ninth-century ivories, one in the Louvre (Fig. 163) and the other in Florence (Museo Nazionale, Fig. 164).[62]

Guards similar to those of the Psalter frontispieces were also associated with other rulers in Carolingian art. In the Utrecht Psalter, the formula was applied to Saul (fol. 91ᵛ, Fig. 165);[63] and in the San Paolo Bible, it was used for Pharaoh (fol. 21ᵛ),[64] for Saul (fol. 83ᵛ),[65] for Solomon (fol. 188ᵛ, Fig. 166),[66] and for Holofernes (fol. 234ᵛ).[67] The closest parallels to the guards on the Psalter frontispieces, however, appear beside Charles the Bald on the Dedication pages of the Vivian (fol. 423ʳ, Fig. 196) and San

[56] Weitzmann, *Byzantinische Buchmalerei*, p. 80.

[57] Bischoff *et al.*, *op. cit.*, pp. 167f.

[58] Gaehde, "Bible Manuscript," I, 490f. and *idem*, "The Pictorial Sources of the Illustrations to the Books of Kings, Proverbs, Judith and Maccabees in the Carolingian Bible of San Paolo Fuori Le Mura in Rome," *Frühmittelalterliche Studien*, IX (1975), 360ff.

[59] Cf. Chapter IX.

[60] Jerusalem, Patriarchal Library, Taphou, 53, fol. 16ᵛ.

[61] Fol. 91ᵛ, cf. E. T. Dewald, *The Illustrations in the Utrecht Psalter* (Princeton, 1933), pl. CXLIV.

[62] Goldschmidt, *Elfenbeinskulpturen*, I, 113, 141.

[63] Dewald, *Utrecht Psalter*, pl. CXLIV.

[64] Gaehde, "Bible Manuscript," I, 161ff. and *idem*, "Carolingian Interpretations of an Early Christian Picture Cycle to the Octateuch in the Bible of San Paolo Fuori Le Mura in Rome," *Frühmittelalterliche Studien*, VIII (1974), 351ff.

[65] *Ibid.*, I, 279ff. and "Pictorial Sources," pp. 360ff.

[66] *Ibid.*, I, 330ff. and "Pictorial Sources," pp. 372ff.

[67] *Ibid.*, I, 352ff. and "Pictorial Sources," pp. 379ff.

Paolo Bibles (fol. 334ᵛ, Fig. 197).[68] In costume and pose, Charles' guards are virtually identical to King David's; and there can be little doubt, therefore, that they were copied from the same model. Because the armsbearers also appear on the Dagulph cover, it seems likelier that this model was a Psalter frontispiece than that it was a secular portrait.[69] There is, however, no way to establish the precise source.

TOURONIAN ALTERATIONS OF THE MODEL

The illuminators of the Vivian and San Paolo Bibles modified their Psalter prototype in a number of significant ways. Both converted the dancing musicians into seated figures. The Vivian master also organized his composition within a large mandorla and added personifications of the four virtues in the corners. The illustrator of the San Paolo Bible, on the other hand, represented three scribes in addition to the four musicians.

By depicting seated musicians, the Touronian artists sought to stress the association of David and his co-psalmists with Christ and the evangelists.[70] This association is implied in the *Origo Psalmorum*, and it is suggested on the Dagulph cover by the evangelist symbols, Lamb of God, and angels depicted in the frame of the David leaf. The Touronian illuminators made the connection by depicting the musicians in the manner commonly employed to represent evangelists. The parallels with the figures in the San Paolo Bible are especially striking. The type of Asaph, seen in three-quarter view, seated with his left leg drawn back and his right arm extended, appears as Luke in the Weingarten Gospels (Stuttgart, Württembergische Landesbibliothek, Cod. H.B. II, 40, fol. 95ᵛ, Fig. 167)[71] and in the Prüm Gospels (Berlin, Staatsbibliothek, Cod., Theol. lat. fol. 733, fol. 116ᵛ)[72] and by Mark in the Nevers Gospels (London, British Library, Cod., Add. 11848, fol. 74ᵛ).[73] Heman is basically a mirror image of the same type. He has a somewhat fuller chest, however, and his manner of holding the codex recalls Luke in the Vivian Bible *Majestas* page (Fig. 49)[74] and St. John in the Prüm Gospels (fol. 178ᵛ).[75] Ethan, seated frontally and turning to the left, parallels Mark in the Vivian *Majestas* and St. Matthew in the Prüm (fol. 22ʳ, Fig. 168), Le Mans (fol. 17ᵛ), and Nevers Gospels (fol. 18ᵛ).[76] Jeduthun, in turn, whose upper torso still betrays its dancer model, was refashioned after an evangelist such as the Prüm Gospels St. Mark (fol. 79ʳ, Fig. 83),[77] St. Mark in the Weingarten Gospels (fol. 63ᵛ),[78] or the Nevers Gospels St. Luke (fol. 166ᵛ).[79] The stone benches of the two lower figures were also derived from evangelists portraits (cf. Figs. 79, 81, and 82)[80] while Asaph's and Heman's chairs may have been adapted from a model similar to the evangelist portraits of the

---

[68] See Chapter IX.
[69] See Chapter IX.
[70] Steger, *op. cit.*, pp. 113ff.
[71] Köhler, *Kar. Min.*, I₂, 262.
[72] *Ibid.*; I₂, 263f.   [73] *Ibid.*, I₂, 262.
[74] See Chapter III.

[75] Köhler, *Kar. Min.*, I₂, 270f.
[76] *Ibid.*, I₂, 268ff.
[77] *Ibid.*, I₂, 255ff.
[78] *Ibid.*, I₂, 261f.
[79] *Ibid.*, I₂, 269f.
[80] *Ibid.*, I₂, 94f.

Nancy Gospels (Cathedral Treasury), although it is likelier that they were simply invented by the Touronian illuminators.

A single type of figure was adjusted to serve for the four psalmists in the Vivian Bible. Seated in three-quarter view facing the center of the page, these figures are similar to Asaph and Heman in the San Paolo Bible and differ from one another only in the placement of their legs and in their instruments. Even the chairs are of a single variety. The closer conformity of the San Paolo Bible figures to Touronian evangelist portraits suggests that the lost Touronian prototype of the later manuscript was less homogeneous and hence probably pre-dated the Vivian manuscript. In the latter, the illuminator unified the series and rearranged the composition to focus on David.

The association of David with Christ, implied pictorially in the Bible frontispieces, is explicitly stated in the *titulus* of the San Paolo manuscript:

SPS ACCELERANS DAVID COREGIS ADURIT

INFLAMMANSQ: IUBET PSALMOS CONSCRIBERE CUNCTOS

QUATTUOR INSCRIBUNT PROCERES ORACULA VATIS.

ATQ: CHORI CYTHARAEQ: SONITUSQ: TUBARUM MODI

ORGANA DAVICIS PULSATIS ORDINE FIBRIS

SCI EVANGELLI. XPI MISTERIA SIGNANT.[81]

The allusion is obscured in the portrayal, however, by the inclusion of three scribes in addition to the four musicians. These scribes may also have been adapted from Touronian author portraits. The profile figures seated on curved-back thrones and the type of scribe who pauses with pen upraised and looks upward appear in the Vivian Bible *Majestas Domini* and in the Lothar Gospels (Paris, Bibliothèque Nationale, Cod. lat. 266, fols. 75ᵛ and 112ᵛ, Figs. 80 and 81).[82] Only the scribe at the bottom of the page has no parallel among the Touronian evangelist portraits. A similar figure, holding a tablet and raising his foot on a pedestal appears in the upper panel of the Dagulph Psalter cover (Fig. 145).

The parallel on the Dagulph cover suggests that the ultimate source of the San Paolo Bible scribes may not have been a set of evangelist portraits but, instead, a representation of David with his scribes similar to the upper panel of the ivory leaf. David and the scribes was a popular theme in Carolingian art. In addition to the Dagulph scene, it survives in fragmentary form in the early ninth-century Wolfcoz Psalter (St. Gall, Stiftsbibliothek, Cod. 20, p. 1, Fig. 169)[83] where two young men are shown sitting at their lecterns waiting to hear David's words and two others are depicted writing in their books. David certainly occupied the facing page in this manuscript but his portrait has been lost. The second half of the *Origo Psalmorum* is transcribed on the verso of the Wolfcoz leaf and the first half of the preface must originally have been written on the recto of the leaf with the depiction of David. David and the scribes was also

[81] Gaehde, "Bible Manuscript," II, 141.
[82] See Chapter III.
[83] Von Euw, *op. cit.*, pp. 44ff.

depicted in the Folchard Psalter (p. 9, Fig. 170).[84] Again, active and contemplative scribes respond to David's poetry. One scribe, who with his back to David is shown writing on a scroll which he supports on his knee, may be an ancestor of the figure in the San Paolo Bible. He has a counterpart in the Angers Psalter (Fig. 147) where two scribes are included in the scene of David and his musicians. David and his scribes is also the theme of the late Metz school ivory in Paris (Fig. 163) and it is the subject of a number of post-Carolingian Psalter manuscripts.[85] In Byzantine Psalters, scribes were often included in frontispieces representing David with his musicians (cf. Figs. 154 and 156) and occasionally, as in Vatican cod. gr. 752, scribes were depicted separately. On folio 4ʳ (Fig. 171), Moses is shown writing in a codex which he holds on his knee in much the same fashion as the scribes do in the Folchard Psalter and the San Paolo Bible.

A full-page composition portraying David and his scribes is unknown in the East. In the West, however, it appears both as an alternative theme in Books of Psalms, and as a complementary miniature with David and his musicians. The two scenes are presented on the Dagulph Psalter ivory; and judging from the Vallicelliana manuscript (Figs. 148 and 149), they were also depicted separately in the model of the Angers Psalter. Like the scene of David and his musicians, the representations of David and his scribes were based on the *Origo Psalmorum*. The depictions were strongly influenced by representations of the evangelists.

It appears, then, that the San Paolo Bible frontispiece is an amalgamation of two compositions from a Carolingian Psalter the appearance of which is suggested by the Dagulph cover and the Angers/Vallicelliana manuscripts. Although the illuminator refashioned the seated scribes after Touronian evangelist portraits, the inclusion of seven assistants weakened the pictorial allusion to Christ and his evangelists.

The Vivian master clarified the reference to Christ by integrating the two source compositions more fully. The *titulus* states:

PSALMIFICUS DAVID RESPLENDET ET ORDO PERITUS
EIUS OPUS CANERE MUSICA AB ARTE BENE.[86]

It makes no reference to Christian typology. The allusion is conveyed entirely by the picture which makes clear reference to the *Majestas Domini*.[87] David, at the center of an enormous blue mandorla, is overtly the counterpart of Christ; and the four seated musicians occupy the places of the evangelists.

By introducing personifications of the four cardinal virtues into the corners of the page, the Vivian illuminator may have been alluding to another aspect of King David. Virtues appear in no other Psalter frontispiece;[88] and although cowled female figures

---

[84] Landsberger, *op. cit.*, pp. 47ff.; Steger, *op. cit.*, pp. 171f.; and von Euw, *op. cit.*, p. 45.

[85] Steger, *op. cit., passim.*

[86] Köhler, *Kar. Min.*, I₂, 217.

[87] See Chapter III.

[88] The *locus classicus* of the four cardinal virtues is Cicero, *De Officiis*, I, 15–17. Personifications of the four Virtues are unknown in ancient art. Virtues are associated with scenes from the life of David on the twelfth-century ivory cover

personifying "truth, meekness, and justice" are depicted behind David in the Utrecht Psalter (fol. 26ʳ, Fig. 172),[89] in Carolingian art the cardinal virtues were more often associated with secular rulers than with biblical figures. They were represented, for example, in three portraits of Charles the Bald (Figs. 78, 196, and 197) and they were depicted in the portrait of Abbot Raganaldus in the Tours Sacramentary (Autun, Bibliothèque de la Ville, MS. 19bis, fol. 173ᵛ, Fig. 208).[90] The illuminator could have found his model for these figures close at hand. In the portrait of Charles the Bald in the Vivian Bible itself (Fig. 196),[91] two half-length female figures are represented holding palms and offering crowns to the king. Although they are not identified, analogies with other portraits suggest that these two women are Virtues.[92] The palms, extended arms, and costumes of the personification at the top of the Psalter page indicate that they were copied from the portrait miniature. This conclusion seems to be confirmed by the two lower figures which, because they had no direct models on the Dedication page, were freely but awkwardly adapted from the upper figures.

The visual parallel between David and the secular ruler was further sustained by imparting to the Old Testament king the facial features of Charles the Bald and by giving him a Carolingian crown.[93] The illuminator clearly intended to link the two monarchs to each other. Ever since Pepin I, Carolingian rulers had identified themselves with Old Testament kings and had considered their realm as the continuation of the "regnum Davidicum."[94] In the Vivian Bible itself, Charles the Bald is compared to David three times.[95] The modification of the Psalter model through references to the Dedication miniatures is another manifestation of this political pretension.

No association with the contemporary ruler seems to have been intended by the illuminator of the Psalter page in the San Paolo Bible. The frontispiece does not include the Virtues, and neither David's facial features nor his guards resemble the Dedication miniature in the same manuscript (Fig. 197). In fact, the armsmen are closer to the guards in the portrait miniature of the Vivian Bible, but this similarity seems to be due to the dependence of both miniatures on the same Psalter model. The arched frame of the San Paolo page may also reflect the Psalter source. Although

---

of the Melisende Psalter. Cf. A. Goldschmidt and K. Weitzmann, *Die byzantinischen Elfenbeinskulpturen* (Berlin, 1934), II, no. 224.

[89] Dewald, *Utrecht Psalter*, pl. XLI. See Chapter IX.

[90] Köhler, *Kar. Min.*, I₂, 96ff. and Chapter IX.

[91] See Chapter IX.

[92] See Chapter IX.

[93] Lothar wears a virtually identical crown in the portrait in his Gospelbook (Paris, Bibliothèque Nationale, Cod. lat. 266, fol. 1ᵛ, Fig. 198). Cf. P. E. Schramm, "Die Kronen der Karolinger," *Festschrift für Karl Gottfried Hugelmann* (Aalen, 1959), pp. 561ff. (reprinted in *Kaiser, Könige, und Päpste* [Stuttgart, 1968], II, 99ff.).

[94] E. Kantorowicz, *The King's Two Bodies* (Princeton, 1957), p. 81 *et passim*; Steger, *op. cit.*, pp. 126ff.; H. H. Anton, *Fürstenspiegel und Herrscherethos in der Karolingerzeit* (Bonn, 1968), pp. 419ff.; Schramm, "Das alte und neue Testament in der Staatslehre und Staatssymbolik des Mittelalters," *Settimane di studio del Centro Italiano di Studi sull'alto medioevo*, X (1962), 229ff. (reprinted in *Kaiser, Könige, und Päpste*, III, 123ff.); idem, "Kaiser Karl der Kahle der Stifter des Thrones in St. Peter," *La cattedra lignea di S. Pietro in Vaticano* (Memorie, vol. X, *Atti della Pontificia Accademia Romana di Archeologia*), pp. 277ff.

[95] See Chapter IX.

frames appear in ruler portraits and in representations of the evangelists, parallels also exist in the Vespasian, Khludov, and St. Gall Psalters (Figs. 151, 152, and 150).[96] Like the allusions to Christ, if they were intended at all in the San Paolo Bible frontispiece, the references to the contemporary ruler are only vaguely suggested.

CONCLUSIONS

The creation of the Psalter frontispiece in the Touronian pandects closely resembled the development of the *Majestas* compositions at Tours. In both instances, the illuminators illustrated exegetic prologues contained in the manuscripts by creatively drawing upon an established pictorial tradition; and in both, they fashioned complex new images from a variety of diverse images.

Their basic inspiration for the Psalter frontispieces was the *Origo Psalmorum*. Following this Latin prologue to the Book of Psalms, the illuminators portrayed King David composing poems on his psaltery while accompanied by several co-psalmists. The basic pictorial model for the depictions seems to have been a pair of miniatures in which David was shown with musicians and then, again, with his scribes. Although the model can be linked to pre-Carolingian representations and ultimately can be traced to Byzantine art, it appears to have been a ninth-century revision of the popular tradition. This revision, which is also reflected in the Psalter of Charles the Bald, was made to correlate the illustrations with the peculiar, Carolingian variant of the *Origo* prologue. The revised image included a depiction of David dancing with Asaph, Heman, Ethan, and Jeduthun in which the king and only three of the musicians were shown playing instruments.

To create frontispieces for their pandects, the Touronian illuminators combined the two miniatures of their model. They depicted David and his guards in a single scene; they reduced the number of co-psalmists; and they represented the musicians seated, not dancing. The merger was less adept in the San Paolo Bible than in the Vivian manuscript and this suggests that the Touronian prototype of the former predated the latter. In the Vivian Bible, the illuminator went far beyond the source pictures and several steps further than the San Paolo artist. He stressed the association of David with Christ by representing only four co-psalmists surrounding the king in a large mandorla; and he linked David with Charles the Bald by depicting a Carolingian crown, recognizable facial features, and four Virtues in the portrait of the Old Testament ruler. In so doing, he succeeded in connecting the Psalter page with other pictures in the Bible and he emphasized the dual aspects of David as *Rex et Propheta*.

[96] See Chapter IX.

VIII. CONVERSION OF ST. PAUL

THE Pauline Epistles in the Vivian and San Paolo Bibles are preceded by frontispieces illustrating the conversion of St. Paul. Both pages are composed of narrative sequences arranged along three horizontal registers. The Vivian frontispiece (Fig. 173)[1] represents six episodes: the Blinding of Saul, Saul Fallen to the Ground, Saul Led to Damascus, the Dream of Ananias, the Healing of Saul, and St. Paul Preaching in the Synagogue. The San Paolo page (Fig. 174)[2] depicts eight scenes: Saul Receiving the Letters, the Blinding, Saul Led to Damascus, the Dream of Ananias, the Healing of Saul, Paul Preaching, Paul Lowered Over the Wall, and Paul Fleeing the City. Despite the difference in the number of events represented, it is immediately apparent that the two frontispieces are closely related to each other. Of the events depicted in both, only the Blinding scenes differ appreciably in the two manuscripts. The illustrations of the Blinding, therefore, deserve special attention as do the three additional scenes in the San Paolo Bible.

Either of two circumstances could account for the general concordance of the two frontispieces and at the same time explain the differences. Both explanations have been suggested in recent studies. According to the first, argued by Hugo Buchthal,[3] the San Paolo illuminator copied a model similar to the Vivian page and supplemented it with borrowings from a second source. Buchthal proposed that the first model originated in Early Christian Rome, while the second was a post-Iconoclastic Byzantine product. A second hypothesis, advanced by Joachim Gaehde[4] and independently by this author,[5] rejects Buchthal's idea that two traditions were amalgamated in the San Paolo Bible. It proposes, instead, that each frontispiece is simply a somewhat different selection from the same source.[6]

The examination of the Genesis and Exodus frontispieces affirms the *a priori* reasonableness of both theories. Only a careful study of the individual scenes and of their textual basis will resolve the issue.

THE COMMON MODEL

Of the five episodes depicted in both Carolingian manuscripts, the Blinding of Saul presents the most complicated problems. In the Vivian Bible, two distinct moments

---

[1] Fol. 386ᵛ, Köhler, *Kar. Min.*, I₂, 219ff.

[2] Fol. 310ᵛ, Gaehde, "Bible Manuscript," I, 425ff.; and "Turonian Sources," pp. 386ff.

[3] "Some Representations from the Life of St. Paul in Byzantine Art," *Tortulae: Studien zu altchristlichen und byzantinischen Monumenten* (Rome, 1966), pp. 43ff.

[4] "Turonian Sources," pp. 386ff. In this article, Gaehde modified his earlier hypothesis ("Bible Manuscript," I, 425ff.) that both pages were derived from a lost Turonian model.

[5] "The Conversion of St. Paul in the Carolingian Bibles" (address delivered at the symposium, "Current Work in Medieval and Byzantine Studies," Dumbarton Oaks Center for Byzantine Studies, Washington, D.C., May 5, 1972), cf. *Dumbarton Oaks Papers*, XXVII (1973), p. 328.

[6] Although she is critical of aspects of Buchthal's thesis, L. Eleen presents no new and comprehensive explanation, "The Illustration of the Pauline Epistles" (unpublished Ph.D. dissertation. University of Toronto, 1972), pp. 23ff.

are represented. First, Saul, accompanied by an armed attendant and carrying a roll of letters, emerges from Jerusalem. He is struck in the face by the "light from heaven" that emanates in five gold rays from the fingers of God's hand; and then he is shown lying on his side upon the ground, his right arm awkwardly raised over his head and his staff thrown before him. Two companions express their astonishment by raising their arms toward the hand of God in the previous scene. Like the other episodes illustrated on the frontispieces, the Blinding is narrated in the ninth chapter of the Books of Acts:

> While he was still on the road and nearing Damascus, suddenly a light flashed from the sky all around him. He fell to the ground and heard a voice saying, "Saul, Saul, why do you persecute me?" "Tell me, Lord," he said, "who are you?" The voice answered, "I am Jesus, whom you are persecuting. But get up and go into the city, and you will be told what you have to do." Meanwhile, the men who were travelling with him stood speechless; they heard the voice but could see no one (3–7).

In the San Paolo Bible, the Blinding of Saul is a single, complex action. Saul falls backward and shields his eyes from the light as his companions react in surprise.

Although the action is different in the two manuscripts, several elements of the Blinding scenes are the same: the portrayal of Saul, the hands of God, and the pairs of gesticulating companions. Gaehde has concluded that the San Paolo representation is an abbreviated and dramatically heightened version of the same model that is reflected in the Vivian Bible.[7] Certainly, however, the Vivian frontispiece is also not an accurate copy of the prototype. The narrative flow is disjunctive and confused. In the first scene, Saul seems unaffected by the sudden apparition that startles the attendants in the second depiction. In the next episode, the fallen figure is rendered awkwardly; Saul seems to float on his side above the ground and the gesture of his right arm is difficult to read as an attempt to cushion his fall. In fact, the figure is more plausible when rotated into an upright position as in the reconstruction (Fig. 175). In this position, Saul's gesture makes sense as a shield against the light. The same gesture is echoed in the San Paolo Bible.

The model used by the Carolingian illuminators seems to have depicted two episodes: Saul's Departure from Jerusalem and the Blinding. The Vivian Master copied both representations; the illuminator of the San Paolo Bible focused on the second. Both artists, however, transformed the Blinding into scenes of Saul's Fall—one by rotating the figure ninety degrees, the other, somewhat more ambitiously, by combining the standing and prone postures in a single, awkward figure.

The subsequent episodes are more alike in the two manuscripts and, hence, it is easier to reconstruct their model. In accord with the text of Acts, IX, 8, ". . . and when

---

[7] "Turonian Sources," p. 390.

his eyes were opened, he could see nothing; so they led him by the hand and brought him to Damascus," both frontispieces show Saul being led by the hand toward the open city-gate. The forward motion and backward glance of Saul's guide in the San Paolo Bible better conveys the action and the inclusion of more than one attendant corresponds more precisely to the Acts text and to the Blinding scenes where two companions are depicted. We may conclude, with Gaehde, that the later manuscript reflects the model more accurately than does the Vivian Bible.[8]

The next event, the Vision of Ananias, is properly disposed in the Vivian sequence but is out of place in the San Paolo page. The story is recounted in Acts, IX, 10–16:

> There was a disciple in Damascus named Ananias. He had a vision in which he heard the voice of the Lord: "Ananias!" "Here I am Lord," he answered. The Lord said to him, "Go at once to Straight Street, to the house of Judas, and ask for a man from Tarsus named Saul. You will find him at prayer; he has had a vision of a man named Ananias coming in and laying his hands on him to restore his sight." Ananias answered, "Lord, I have often heard about this man and all the harm he has done to thy people in Jerusalem. And he is here with authority from the chief priests to arrest all who invoke thy name." But the Lord said to him, "You must go, for this man is my chosen instrument to bring my name before the nations and their kings, and before the people of Israel. I myself will show him all that he must go through for my name's sake."

The iconography is essentially the same in the two manuscripts. Ananias, lying on a mattress and resting his head on his right arm, is summoned by God (in the form of a hand issuing from a cloud). Gaehde was undoubtedly correct to propose that Ananias' awkwardly raised left arm in the San Paolo Bible represents a change in the model.[9] It may even be the vestige of a second phase of the vision which showed Ananias' response to God's command. The long biblical description of the conversation between God and Ananias may have inspired a second picture in the model. In this case, then, the Vivian Bible seems to be more reliable than the San Paolo Bible.

The Healing of Saul is represented in the two manuscripts with essentially identical, though reversed, compositions. The illustrations follow Acts, IX, 17–19:

> So Ananias went. He entered the house, laid his hands on him and said, "Saul, my brother, the Lord Jesus who appeared to you on your way here, has sent me to you so that you may recover your sight, and be filled with the Holy Spirit." And immediately it seemed that scales fell from his eyes, and he regained his sight. Thereupon he was baptized and afterwards he took food and his strength returned.

Both manuscripts show Ananias approaching the seated Saul and touching his eyes. In the Vivian Bible, even the scales dropping from Saul's eyes are represented. Be-

---

[8] *Ibid.*, p. 390.   [9] *Ibid.*, p. 391.

cause of his desire to focus the second register on this event—with Saul led into the city at the left and Ananias at the right—the San Paolo illuminator reversed the composition. There is little difficulty, however, reconstructing the model.

Paul disputing in the Synagogue, the convert's first mission, is described in Acts, IX, 20–22:

> He stayed some time with the disciples in Damascus. Soon he was proclaiming Jesus publicly in the synagogues: "This," he said, "is the Son of God." All who heard were astonished. "Is this not the man," they said, "who was in Jerusalem trying to destroy those who invoke this name? Did he not come here for the sole purpose of arresting them and taking them to the chief priests?" But Saul grew more and more forceful, and silenced the Jews of Damascus with his cogent proofs that Jesus was the Messiah.

The illustrations are basically the same in the two manuscripts. St. Paul stands between two groups of men and addresses his sermon to an astounded audience. In the Vivian Bible the Jews hold lances and Paul clutches a scroll in his right hand as he directs his lecture to the three men at the right. In the San Paolo Bible, Saul speaks to both groups simultaneously. Dramatic heightening is characteristic of the San Paolo master;[10] the Vivian composition, therefore, is probably more faithful to the basic model.

The same source was used by both Carolingian illuminators to construct the core of their St. Paul pages. In certain details, the Vivian Bible is more reliable; in others, the San Paolo frontispiece followed the model more faithfully.

Developing the observation of Kurt Weitzmann,[11] Buchthal,[12] Gaehde,[13] and Eleen[14] have accepted the affiliation of the Carolingian Bibles with the Conversion of St. Paul represented in the eleventh-century manuscript of the *Christian Topography* of Cosmas Indicopleustes on Mt. Sinai (St. Catherine's, Cod. 1186, fol. 128v, Fig. 176).[15] The Sinai illustration is richer than the Conversion sequences in its sister manuscripts, the ninth-century Cosmas in the Vatican (Cod. gr. 699, fol. 83v, Fig. 177)[16] and the eleventh-century codex in Florence (Biblioteca Medicea-Laurenziana, Plut., IX, 28, fol. 171v, Fig. 178).[17] The affinities between all three Cosmas manuscripts and the reconstructed model of the Carolingian Bibles are particularly striking. In the scene of the Blinding, the Byzantine manuscripts show Saul raising his right arm to shield his eyes as in the reconstruction; and two of the Cosmas illustrations also include the

[10] *Ibid., passim.*
[11] *Roll and Codex*, p. 194.
[12] *Op. cit.*, p. 44.
[13] "Turonian Sources," p. 387.
[14] *Op. cit.*, pp. 25f.
[15] Cf. K. Weitzmann, *Die byzantinische Buchmalerei des IX. und X. Jahrhunderts* (Berlin, 1935), pp. 58f. For an examination of the Old Testament illustrations in the Cosmas manuscripts, cf. D. Mouriki-Charalambous, "The Octateuch Miniatures of the Byzantine Manuscripts of Cosmas Indicopeustes" (unpublished dissertation, Princeton University, 1970).
[16] C. Stornajolo, *Le Miniature della Topographia Cristiana di Cosma Indicopleuste* (Milan, 1908), pl. 48.
[17] *Byzantine Art, An European Art* (catalogue of an exhibition) Athens, 1964, no. 366, pp. 346ff. Cf. H. Kessler, "Paris. Gr. 102: A Rare Illustrated Acts of the Apostles," *Dumbarton Oaks Papers*, XXVII (1973), 211ff.

gesticulating companions. For the Fall, the Vatican and Sinai manuscripts represent Saul in the attitude of *proskynesis*; and they include a nimbed Saul standing with a codex.[18] Neither of these figures seems to have been present in the model of the Carolingian pages. The Byzantine scenes of Saul Led to Damascus do recall the Carolingian depictions. Curiously, however, in the Cosmas manuscripts, Saul leads Ananias. Only the Florence Cosmas shows the men entering the walled city.[19] The Greek representations depict Saul with only one attendant and, hence, are closer to the Vivian scene. They may, however, also be abbreviations of the model. On the basis of the Blinding scene and the depiction of Saul Led to Damascus, one may conclude that the Cosmas illustrations share a common ancestry with those in the ninth-century Bibles.

The second cycle discussed by Buchthal, Gaehde, and Eleen in connection with the Carolingian frontispiece is the fresco cycle of San Paolo fuori le mura in Rome. Painted perhaps as early as the fifth century, the San Paolo frescoes were restored at least once (by Cavallini between 1277 and 1279) before they were destroyed in 1823. They are known today from a set of watercolor copies made in the seventeenth century when the paintings were already badly damaged.[20] The identification and sequence of scenes is not certain[21] and, in general, the copies of the frescoes can be used only with caution. There do seem to be affinities between the depictions of Saul Led to Damascus (Fig. 179) and St. Paul Preaching (Fig. 180) in the San Paolo frescoes and those in the Carolingian Bibles. No conclusion about the nature of the connections, however, can be drawn.

Two other monuments, hitherto largely ignored, must be introduced into the discussion of the Pauline frontispieces in the Vivian and San Paolo Bibles. The first is a volume of the Pauline Epistles, transcribed and illustrated during the ninth century in the Rheinhessen region (Munich, Bayerische Staatsbibliothek, lat. 14345).[22] In addition to the Stoning of St. Stephen (fol. 1ᵛ), the Munich Epistles contains two full-page illustrations. Fol. 7ʳ (Fig. 181) depicts the Fall and Saul Led to Damascus and fol. 7ᵛ (Fig. 182) illustrates St. Paul Preaching. In the Fall, the blinded Saul has fallen to the ground in the attitude of *proskynesis* much as in the San Paolo frescoes and the Byzantine manuscripts.[23] The scene of Saul Led to Damascus also recalls the Roman and Cosmas scenes.[24] The Munich Epistles establishes the presence of a Greek prototype in the Carolingian sphere before the end of Iconoclasm.

The relationship of the Munich illustrations to the Bible frontispieces is partly ob-

[18] The single figure was probably taken from an author portrait of the type found throughout the Vatican and Sinai Cosmas manuscripts.

[19] Cf. Buchthal, *op. cit.*, p. 47. In other aspects, also, the Florence manuscript is more reliable than are its sister books. Cf. Kessler, "Paris. Gr. 102," p. 215.

[20] Cf. S. Waetzoldt, *Die Kopien des 17. Jahrhunderts nach Mosaiken und Wandmalereien in Rom* (Wien/München, 1964), pp. 55ff.

[21] Buchthal, *op. cit.*, p. 36 reidentified one scene.

[22] A. Goldschmidt, *German Book Illumination* (Florence, 1928), pl. 53. and B. Bischoff, *Die südostdeutschen Schreibschulen und Bibliotheken in der Karolingerzeit* (Wiesbaden, 1960), p. 239.

[23] Cf. also the Homilies of Gregory Nazianzenus in Paris (Bibliothèque Nationale, Cod. gr. 510, fol. 264ᵛ).

[24] Cf. also Saul Led to Damascus in the Rockefeller-McCormick New Testament (University of Chicago Library, fol. 115ʳ). H. Willoughby, *The Rockefeller-McCormick New Testament* (Chicago, 1932).

scured by the absence of an unaltered scene of the Fall in the latter. The depictions of Saul Led to Damascus, however, are very similar. As in the Vivian Bible, the Munich Epistles manuscript depicts the blind Saul carrying a staff and being led by a youth who grasps Saul's wrist. The San Paolo Bible omits the blind man's staff and includes the two additional companions. The basic composition is the same, however, and even the costumes recall the Munich illustration. In the Munich codex, St. Paul Preaching is a simple confrontation between the preacher and three men. The correspondence of the Munich scene to the core of the Vivian composition cannot be ignored easily. Perhaps the ultimate model also represented a simple confrontation which the Touronian artists transformed into a symmetrical composition. In any case, the Munich illustrations appear to be related to the Bible frontispieces and help to refine the reconstruction of the model.

The second cycle, unstudied in connection with the Carolingian Bibles, is the thirteenth-century rotulus in Vercelli (Biblioteca Capitolare, Figs. 183 and 184).[25] The Vercelli Rotulus was intended to serve as an aid for the restoration of the frescoes in the local church of S. Eusebio. The date of the frescoes and, hence, the date of the iconography can no longer be established;[26] but the paintings may have post-dated the Carolingian depictions by as many as four hundred years. Nevertheless, there can be little doubt that the Bible frontispieces and the Vercelli Rotulus were ultimately derived from the same prototype. The Vercelli Roll shows the bald Saul leaving Jerusalem after he has received the letters. Then, it shows him struck in the face by the light from heaven while a companion tries to break his fall. As in the Bible frontispieces, the Vercelli Rotulus combines the Fall and Blinding scenes. The depiction of Ananias' Vision in the Vercelli Roll is similar to that in the Vivian Bible and the Healing scenes also are strikingly alike. The Vercelli Roll represents Saul's Baptism—a notable lacuna in the Bibles—and continues with Paul Preaching. Paul holds a book and instructs a single group of men in short tunics. The Vercelli Preaching scene is closer to the Munich Epistles than to the later Carolingian representations; and it adds evidence to the hypothesis that the model depicted Paul Preaching as a simple confrontation.

A SECOND MODEL?

The question of those scenes in the San Paolo Bible that are not portrayed on the Vivian page remains. These scenes are very significant, for in the origin of Saul Receiving the Letters, Paul Being Lowered Over the Wall, and Paul Fleeing Damascus, lies the nature of the model or models available in ninth-century France. Were the scenes that bracket the core illustration of the San Paolo page taken from a second, post-Iconoclastic model as Buchthal postulated? Or was the entire sequence derived

[25] C. Cipolla, "La Pergamena della Basilica di S. Eusebio in Vercelli," *Miscellanea di Storia Italiana*, XXXVII (1901), 3ff.; R. Scheller, *Medieval Model Books* (Haarlem, 1963), pp. 95ff.; Eleen, *op. cit.*, pp. 68ff.

[26] Cf. Eleen, *op. cit.*, pp. 68f.

from a single narrative model that the Vivian Master exploited to a lesser extent? Gaehde has already pointed to the inconsistency in Buchthal's argument which supposed that the first scene but not the final depictions is a Byzantine intrusion.[27] Now, with a more complete body of related material, the problem can be solved.

Again, following Weitzmann,[28] Buchthal and Gaehde have accepted the correspondence of Saul Receiving the Letters to the illustration in the Sinai Cosmas (Fig. 176). The text is Acts, IX, 1–3, "Meanwhile, Saul was still breathing murderous threats against the disciples of the Lord. He went to the High Priest and applied for letters to the synagogues at Damascus authorizing him to arrest anyone he found, men or women, who followed the new way, and bring them to Jerusalem." In both compositions, Saul, slightly bent down, approaches the seated priests and accepts the letter. The number of attendants differs. The remarkable agreement in details, however, extends even to the gesture of the second priest. The relationship between the San Paolo and Sinai representations, therefore, is certain.

It is not clear whether or not this event was depicted on the walls of San Paolo f.l.m. The two figures at the right of fol. 91 of the Barberini copy (Fig. 179), however, seem best explained as fragments of the Letter scene.[29] Saul Receiving the Letters was depicted in S. Eusebio. The Conversion series on the Vercelli Rotulus (Fig. 183) begins with a reduced version of the San Paolo Bible/Sinai Cosmas composition. Even the arched building resembles the background architecture in the San Paolo illustration.[30] The parallel between the initial scene in the San Paolo series and the illustrations in the Sinai Cosmas and Vercelli Rotulus leaves little doubt that the San Paolo master turned to the same model for Saul Receiving the Letters that he had used for the other illustrations.

Neither the Sinai Cosmas nor the Vercelli Rotulus extends to the scenes of Paul Lowered Over the Wall and Paul Fleeing Damascus which are illustrated at the end of the San Paolo Bible sequence. The escape is recounted in Acts, IX, 25–26, "They kept watch on the city gates day and night so that they might murder him; but his converts took him one night and let him down by the wall, lowering him in a basket." The San Paolo Bible represents St. Paul stuffed into a basket being lowered by two young men. Apparently through neglect, the artist omitted the requisite ropes. The flight was depicted in San Paolo f.l.m. (Fig. 185).[31] Although the copy of the fresco shows the full figure of St. Paul in the basket, it is clear that, as Buchthal proposed, both scenes ultimately depended on the same prototype. Remarkable is the similarity between the Carolingian composition and the illustration of Paul's Flight in the eleventh-century Prüm Lectionary (Manchester, John Rylands Library, Cod. 7, fols. 133ʳ–134ᵛ, Fig. 186).[32] Not only does the Prüm manuscript show Paul in a basket

[27] "Turonian Sources," p. 388.

[28] *Roll and Codex*, p. 187.

[29] Waetzoldt, *op. cit.*, p. 60, Fig. 370.

[30] This similarity has been emphasized by Eleen, *op. cit.*, p. 71.

[31] Waetzoldt, *op. cit.*, p. 60 and Buchthal, *op. cit.*, p. 48.

[32] Manchester, John Rylands Library, MS. 7, fols. 133ᵛ–134ʳ. Cf. R. Schilling, "Das Ruotpertus-Evangelistar aus Prüm, MS. 7 der John Rylands

held by two men, but the accomplices lean their heads toward one another and are framed by the arch of a towered structure as in the San Paolo Bible. The Prüm illustration follows a depiction of the Blind Saul Led to Damascus. This scene, too, appears to be a simple modification of the Carolingian composition. In the Prüm depiction, the companion who, in the San Paolo composition stands behind Saul, has merely been incorporated into the main action. The illuminator of the Prüm Lectionary seems to have excerpted two scenes from a Book of Acts to illustrate a passage from the Gospel of Mark. The same Acts cycle must have been available during the Carolingian period when it was used to construct the frontispiece of the San Paolo Bible. Apparently, it included the scene of Paul Lowered Over the Wall.

There is no direct indication that the cyclic model also included the single figure of Paul fleeing the city. The event is illustrated in the San Paolo Bible but in no other member of the pictorial family and it could have been an *ad hoc* invention. Gaehde has rightly questioned the idea of Dinkler-v. Schubert that the figure was added as a reference to the contemporary quarrel between Hincmar of Reims and Hincmar of Laon.[33] Indirect evidence exists, however, that even the fleeing Paul may have been found in the model. To illustrate the title of Psalm 58, "To the chief Musician, Altaschith, Michtam of David: when Saul sent, and they watched the house to kill him," Byzantine Psalters frequently represent David's Flight from Saul, an event described in I Samuel, XIX, 12, "So Michal let David down through a window and he slipped away and escaped." It is Dinkler-v. Schubert's hypothesis that these Old Testament representations were actually based on depictions of Paul's flight,[34] because several show David being lowered over the wall in a basket, a detail not specified in the Samuel text.[35] Many of these scenes also represent David fleeing the city after he has been lowered to the ground.[36] They establish a tradition of showing the figure escaping after he has been let down in a basket. The tenth-century Byzantine ivory casket in the Palazzo Venezia (Fig. 187),[37] which is decorated with scenes from the Book of Kings, is an example that shows David being lowered over the wall in a basket and then David escaping on foot. It provides circumstantial evidence, at least, that the figure of the fleeing Paul was represented in the model of the San Paolo Bible.

Evidently, then, the additional scenes in the San Paolo Bible were also copied from the model that served as the source for the other scenes in the Vivian and San Paolo

Library in Manchester," *Studien zur Buchmalerei und Goldschmiedekunst des Mittelalters. Festschrift für Karl Hermann Usener* (Marburg an der Lahn, 1967), pp. 143ff. and E. Dinkler-v. Schubert, " 'Per Murum Dimiserunt Eum,' zur Ikonographie von Acta IX, 35 und 2 Cor. XI, 33," *Usener Festschrift*, pp. 79ff.

[33] Dinkler-v. Schubert, *op. cit.*, p. 85 and Gaehde, "Turonian Sources," p. 389.

[34] *Op. cit.*, p. 88.

[35] E.g., Paris gr. 923, fol. 107. Cf. Dinkler-v. Schubert, Fig. 12.

[36] London, British Library, Add. Cod. 40731, fol. 93^r and Vatican, Barb. gr. 372, fol. 9^v. Cf. Dinkler-v. Schubert, *op. cit.*, Figs. 10–11.

[37] Dinkler-v. Schubert, *op. cit.*, p. 86 and Fig. 13. A. Goldschmidt and K. Weitzmann, *Die byzantinischen Elfenbeinskulpturen*, I (Berlin, 1930), pl. LXXI and Weitzmann, *Roll and Codex*, pp. 152ff.

frontispieces. The model apparently illustrated the ninth chapter of Acts with nine scenes. These seem to have been basically identical to the cycle in the San Paolo Bible except that the model must also have included a depiction of Saul Departing Jerusalem. This conclusion is at variance with that of Buchthal which proposed two models, one Western and the other post-Iconoclastic Byzantine; and it expands Gaehde's proposal by defining aspects of the model more precisely.

THE MODEL

The model of the Carolingian Conversion pages must have been a Byzantine cycle that may have been known in the West as early as the fifth century—if it was used as a source of the San Paolo frescoes. The same archetype was also the model of the Munich Epistles, the Rylands Lectionary, the Greek Cosmas manuscripts, and the Vercelli Rotulus. Apparently it was a Book of Acts. Except for the Carolingian Bibles and the eleventh-century Lectionary, all other members of this pictorial family extend beyond the ninth chapter and illustrate other stories in Acts. The Munich Epistles shows the Stoning of St. Stephen (Acts, VIII, 59–60); the Cosmas manuscripts depict the Stoning and Laying of Coats Before Saul;[38] and the Vercelli Rotulus presents eighteen compositions with scenes based on Acts, II–XXI. The frescoes in San Paolo f.l.m. originally illustrated Acts, VI–XXVIII in forty-two panels. Illustrated manuscripts of the Acts of the Apostles are extremely rare. But three Greek manuscripts[39] and one Latin book,[40] containing narrative illustrations and the Acts text, survive. The situation is similar to the history of Kings illustration. Only one Kings manuscript (Vatican gr. 333)[41] is known; but numerous scenes derived from Kings cycles are preserved in other contexts, principally in Psalters.[42]

The same Acts cycle was still current in the Byzantine world as late as the fourteenth century when it was used as the model for the scenes of St. Paul's life in the church at Decani.[43] Saul Receiving the Letters, the Blinding, and Saul Led to Damascus conform well to the Carolingian depictions; while the preaching scene is the simple confrontation composition.

[38] Kessler, "Paris. Gr. 102," pp. 214f.

[39] Rockefeller-McCormick New Testament (University of Chicago Library). Cf. Willoughby, op. cit., pp. 233ff. It originally contained sixteen miniatures in the Acts section. The Rockefeller-McCormick New Testament has been redated to the twelfth century. Cf. Illustrated Greek Manuscripts from American Collections: An Exhibition in Honor of Kurt Weitzmann (Princeton, 1973), no. 45. Acts and Epistles, London, Robinson Trust. Cf. Buchthal, op. cit. It contains three scenes of Paul's Conversion and Martyrdom. Paris grec. 102. Cf. Kessler, "Paris. Gr. 102." It contains four Acts scenes. All three manuscripts belong to the same pictorial recension and may be tied to the conversion cycle of the Carolingian Bibles.

[40] Vat. lat. 433. Cf. Eleen, op. cit, pp. 72ff.

[41] J. Lassus, "Les miniatures byzantines du 'Livre des Rois,'" Mélanges d'Archéologie et d'Histoire, XLV (1928), 38ff. and idem, L'illustration byzantine du Livre des Rois (Paris, 1973).

[42] Weitzmann, Roll and Codex, et passim and idem, "Selection of Texts," p. 74.

[43] V. Petkovic, Decani (Belgrad, 1941).

One of the most complete reflections of the cycle appeared not in the East, at all, however, but among the twelfth-century mosaics in Norman Sicily.[44] Fourteen scenes based on the Acts narrative are represented on the walls of the Capella Palatina in Palermo and eighteen appear in the nearby cathedral of Monreale. Both cycles include sequences of the Conversion of St. Paul. Even though the mosaicists had to adjust their borrowed compositions to the lunettes and unusually shaped spaces of the church walls, they clearly worked from a model closely related to the prototype of the Carolingian Bibles.[45]

In Palermo (Fig. 188), the series begins with Saul Receiving the Letters from the High Priests. The composition is crowded and the priests are shown standing. As Kitzinger has pointed out,[46] however, the mosaicist made modifications to accommodate the model to his restricted space. Even in Monreale (Fig. 189), however, where an entire lunette is devoted to Saul Receiving the Letters, the priests are shown standing. Clearly, the later mosaicist referred to the nearby cycle in Palermo as a source for his composition. He must also have turned to the basic model. In Monreale, the gestures of the two priests and Saul's pose are closer to the San Paolo Bible and Sinai Cosmas than are the Palermo figures.

The mosaics do not include the scene of Saul Departing Jerusalem which is represented only in the Vivian Bible and in the Vercelli Rotulus. The next scene in both cycles is the Blinding. Palermo (Fig. 190) shows Saul falling forward, a kind of reversal of the curious pose in the San Paolo Bible. He is hit by the light on the back of the head which suggests that the mosaicist may have adapted the figure from an upright type. The gesticulating companions resemble those in the Carolingian Bibles and the Cosmas manuscripts. The greater agitation of the attendants in Monreale (Fig. 191) is closer to the reconstructed prototype of the ninth-century frontispieces and is another indication that the later mosaic cycle was dependent on the basic model. Saul falls in an attitude recalling the figures in San Paolo f.l.m., the Munich Epistles, and the Cosmas manuscripts; but the light again strikes the back of his head. It is highly probable, therefore, that the composition represents an amalgamation of the two moments that are separately depicted in the Cosmas illustrations: the Blinding and the Fall.

Saul Led to Damascus is abbreviated in Palermo (Fig. 190). A single, togate man leads Saul by the hand. Thus, the composition more closely resembles the Vivian Bible, the Munich Epistles, and the Cosmas manuscripts. Monreale (Fig. 192), however, may again be more faithful to the model. As in the San Paolo Bible, the vigorous companions lead Saul toward the open city gate.

Perhaps the most compelling evidence that the artists at Monreale returned to the original model and did not depend exclusively on the Palermo cycle is the scene of Healing. This event is not represented in Palermo at all but is depicted in Monreale

[44] Cf. O. Demus, *The Mosaics of Norman Sicily* (London, 1948), pp. 294ff. and E. Kitzinger, *The Mosaics of Monreale* (Palermo, 1960), pp. 33ff.

[45] That the model was a Byzantine Acts cycle has been suggested by Kessler, "Paris. Gr. 102," pp. 211ff.

[46] *Op. cit.*, p. 42.

(Fig. 193). The Carolingian Bibles and the Vercelli Rotulus adequately disprove Kitzinger's assertion that "this is not the event usually depicted at this point" in the narrative.[47] Furthermore, the Monreale scene corresponds well to these depictions. Ananias approaches from the left and points toward the seated Saul who raises his right arm in response. The intervening window forced the mosaicist to separate the two figures and to eliminate the enclosing architecture. The similarity of the scene to the other depictions, however, leaves no doubt that Kitzinger was wrong to conclude that the Healing "is made up entirely of conventional elements . . . (and) was invented *ad hoc* to fill the space."[48] It proves that the Monreale artist had access, not only to Palermo but to its model as well.

Palermo[49] and Monreale (Fig. 194) both illustrate Paul's Baptism as the next scene. The Baptism must have been represented in the densely illustrated archetype; but inexplicably it appears only in the Vercelli Rotulus and at Decani. Following the Baptism, the mosaics show Paul disputing the elders in the synagogue (Figs. 195 and 194). The two compositions are essentially the same, although again Palermo is more reduced. Paul addresses the elders who are seated. The simple confrontation composition resembles the Munich Epistles, Decani, and the Vercelli Rotulus more than the Carolingian Bibles, but all the representations may have been derived from the same archetype.

If there still is a question that the mosaics were derived from a model closely related to that on which the ninth-century frontispieces were based, it is dispelled by the scenes of Paul Lowered over the Wall. Both mosaic cycles show Paul huddled in a basket which is being lowered by two men. The compositions are remarkably like the scene in the San Paolo Bible which was produced in France three centuries earlier. In turn, the Sicilian cycles provide additional proof that Paul Lowered Over the Wall was illustrated in the basic cyclic model used to construct the Carolingian pages.

It is very likely that the ultimate source of these Conversion illustrations was a Greek Book of Acts. Though surviving examples of the Acts text containing narrative scenes are rare, the extant manuscripts do relate to the several monuments identified in connection with the ninth-century Bibles.[50] The model must have been very richly illustrated: at least eleven scenes based on the ninth chapter alone are known. Of these, nine were copied in the Carolingian frontispieces.

THE RELATIONSHIP OF THE *TITULI* TO THE ILLUSTRATIONS

The Vivian master seems to have followed the *tituli* in selecting scenes from his narrative model. These *tituli* conform to the Acts text but are less detailed than the biblical story and, hence, could not have served as the literary source of the repre-

---

[47] *Op. cit.*, p. 42. The Healing may also have been represented in the San Paolo frescoes. Cf. Waetzoldt, *op. cit.*, p. 60 and Buchthal, *op. cit.*, p. 46.

[48] *Op. cit.*, p. 42.

[49] Demus, *op. cit.*, pl. 40B.

[50] Cf. Buchthal, *op. cit.*, pp. 47ff. and Kessler, "Paris. Gr. 102," pp. 211ff.

sentations. For example, the first caption: HIC SAULUM DOMINUS CAECAT, HINC FUNDIT IN IMAM, explains why the Blinding of Saul is represented in two phases. It does not account for Saul's letters or for the men that accompany him. These derive from the Bible. The same is true of the other *tituli*:

> TERRAM POST TRAHITUR CAECOS UT IRE QUEAT.
>
> ALLOQUITUR SABAOTH ANNANIAM QUAERERE SAULUM,
>
> REDDIT ET EN OLLI LUMINA ADEMPTA SIBI.
>
> QUAM BENE, SANCTE, DOCES VITALIA DOGMATA, PAULE,
>
> EX SERIE PRISCA CAELITUS ATQUE NOVA.[51]

They outline the action but do not specify the details. The relation of caption to picture, then, is the same as that in the Genesis pages. The Vivian illuminator used the *tituli* as guidelines for choosing the scenes from a rich, narrative cycle.

The *tituli* on fol. 310ʳ of the San Paolo Bible are less directly connected to the illustrations:

> PRICIPIS ACCIPIENS OLIM PORISMATA SAULUS.
>
> CORRUIT IN FACIEM SUBITO DE NUBE VOCATUS
>
> ANNANIAEQ: MANU SACRO BAPTISMATE TINCTUS
>
> CORDA REPLET FRATRUM VERUM DN̄MQUE FATETUR.
>
> TURRIEUS IS SEPTUS. SAXIS ATQ: UNDIQ: MAGNIS
>
> SUMISSUS SPORTA MANIBUS SIC FUGIS INIQUIS.
>
> AD GENTES PERGENS LARGITUR SEMINA VITAE.
>
> ROBORAT ET SCRIPTIS. TRIBUIT QUIS VERBA SALUTIS.[52]

The brief sentence, "Annaniaeq: Manu sacro baptismate tinctus," is an inadequate explanation for the three scenes in the middle register; while the last two lines are illustrated by the single, fleeing figure. The selection of scenes in the San Paolo Bible does not correspond to the Vivian *tituli* either. This is not surprising. From the other frontispieces, too, it is evident that the lost Touronian model of the San Paolo Bible was based on a different set of captions that was replaced in the San Paolo Bible by *tituli* which relate only generally to the illustrations.

SEVERAL PROBLEMS

A number of questions remain: (1) why were the important episodes of the Fall and Baptism not illustrated in the model? (2) what was the original form of Paul Preaching in the Synagogue? and (3) what was the appearance of the costumes and architecture in the prototype?

One can only speculate about the Fall and Baptism scenes. The Munich Epistles proves that the scene of Saul upon the ground in the attitude of *proskynesis* was avail-

---

[51] Köhler, *Kar. Min.*, I₂, 219.　　　　　[52] Gaehde, "Bible Manuscript," II, 145f.

able during the Carolingian period. The fact that the Vivian and San Paolo illustrators had such difficulty creating the scene of the Fall from elements of the Blinding, however, is compelling proof that they did not have a ready model for this event. As for the Baptism, the Touronian *tituli* did not call for this scene, so it may have been available in the model and simply not copied.

The uniformity of the Preaching compositions in the two Bibles suggests that the model represented Paul between two groups of men. The composition is somewhat confusing, however, because it has Paul doing two things at once. With the possible exception of the San Paolo frescoes (Fig. 180), the symmetrical scene appears in no other member of this Acts family. The simpler confrontation composition was known during the Carolingian period and the Munich representation (Fig. 182) is remarkably like the Vivian scene, except that it does not include two men behind Paul. It is reasonable to conclude, therefore, that the model did present the normal composition and that the illuminators at Tours modified the scene.

In the upper register of the Vivian Bible, Saul wears the garb of a Roman field soldier. The costume consists of a diadem, strip armor (*pteryges*), and a paludamentum tied by a clasp at the shoulder. In the lower two registers (following his conversion), Paul wears a long toga. In the San Paolo Bible, Paul wears the same short tunic and red paludamentum throughout. Which manuscript best reflects the original? The Byzantine manuscripts, Decani, the Vercelli Rotulus, and the Sicilian mosaics all show Paul in a long toga. This costume, which suits the dignity of the saint, is traditional. The depiction of the Stoning of St. Stephen in the Munich Epistles and the Saul picture in the Prüm Lectionary (Fig. 186) show Saul in a cape, short tunic, and leggings much as in the San Paolo Bible. In the Conversion pictures of the Munich manuscript, however, he wears a long toga. It is possible, therefore, that in the model Saul's costume changed to indicate his status before and after his conversion. The Munich and Manchester manuscripts indicate that the tunic of the San Paolo Bible illustrations was the first type of costume. After the conversion, the dress became a long toga. The Vivian master could have classicized his model by copying armor from an ancient diptych.[53] More likely, he copied the costume from one of the bodyguards in the Vivian David Miniature (Fig. 140) or Dedication Page (Fig. 196). It should be noted that the bodyguards in the David and Dedication miniatures of the San Paolo Bible (Figs. 141 and 197) do not wear armor but, like Paul, are clothed in short tunics and red capes. It would seem, then, that the Vivian master preserved the change of costume from his model but introduced the armor and that the San Paolo master retained the details of one type of dress but unified the costume.

Good parallels for the architecture appear in other miniatures of the Vivian and San Paolo Bibles. As Köhler noted,[54] the colonnade in the Vivian Preaching scene could have been copied from the Exodus miniature (Fig. 88) in the same manuscript.

---

[53] Cf. the Barberini diptych. R. Delbrueck, *Die Consulardiptychen* (Berlin, 1929), pp. 41ff. and pl. I, 48, 66.

[54] *Kar. Min.*, I₂, 219f.

Similarly, the baldachinos in several scenes of the San Paolo page recur in other miniatures in that Bible.[55] Parallels to the city wall that encloses the Healing scenes in both frontispieces are also found in the San Paolo Bible and in earlier Carolingian art.[56] This suggests that the ninth-century illuminators supplemented the Acts model with conventional elements from their artistic vocabulary. The biblical account of Paul's conversion, however, specifies several architectural settings: Saul is led into the city of Damascus; Ananias heals Saul in a house; Paul proclaims Jesus in the synagogues; and he is lowered over the wall of the city. The pictorial model must have illustrated these settings, and it is likely that the Carolingian artists were influenced by the architectural representations in the prototype.

The other members of the Acts family confirm the hypothesis that the settings in the Vivian and San Paolo frontispieces are not entirely ninth-century inventions. In the Vercelli Rotulus and in Decani, the priests are seated within an architectural enclosure in the scene of Saul Receiving the Letters. The schematic representation of Jerusalem in the Vivian Bible could have been based on conventional walled-city formulae such as those in the Cosmas manuscripts. The gate to Damascus is represented in the Vercelli Rotulus, in Monreale, and in Decani and even the turrets, copied only in the San Paolo Bible, are indicated. Ananias' house with its arched opening has a very close parallel in the Vercelli Rotulus; and crenellated, turreted walls similar to the one over which Paul is lowered in the final scene of the San Paolo Bible, are represented in Palermo, Monreale, and in the Rylands Lectionary. Only the settings of the Blinding and Preaching scenes have no close correspondence in other Acts illustrations. It is not surprising that these find the best parallels in ninth-century art.

CONCLUSIONS

In contrast to Köhler who considered the Vivian Epistles page to be a ninth-century creation composed of various conventional elements, it can be shown that it, and the related frontispiece in the San Paolo Bible, were constructed from a pre-existent model, namely from an illustrated Acts of the Apostles. This hypothesis is in basic agreement with the proposals of Weitzmann, Buchthal, and Gaehde. In suggesting that both ninth-century cycles were derived independently from the same model, however, it differs somewhat from Buchthal's thesis. This investigation goes beyond all previous studies to identify other monuments derived from the same archetype as the Carolingian frontispieces. Of these, the most important are the Munich Epistles and the Vercelli Rotulus. Together with other members of the family, they lead to the conclusion that the Conversion of St. Paul cycles were excerpted from a Byzantine manuscript of the Acts of the Apostles that may have been known in the West as early as the fifth century.

[55] Fols. 234ᵛ and 243ᵛ.

[56] For example, in the Utrecht Psalter, fols. 5ʳ, 9ʳ, 16ʳ, 27ᵛ, and 63ᵛ.

IX. KAROLUS REX

FULL-PAGE portraits of Charles the Bald are included in the Vivian Bible (Fig. 196)[1] and in the San Paolo manuscript (Fig. 197).[2] This is not surprising. Charles the Bald favored portraits of himself; and, whereas likenesses of his predecessors are surprisingly rare,[3] as many as eight representations of Charles survive.[4] Among these, the dedication miniatures in his two great Bible manuscripts are the most complex and most difficult to understand. The elaborate verses that accompany both depictions contribute to the interpretation of the pictures. Nevertheless, the identification of a number of figures, the significance of the assemblies, and the origins of the pictorial motifs in both portraits are still subjects for debate.

THE DEDICATION MINIATURE IN THE VIVIAN BIBLE

Within a great arched frame, the dedication miniature of the Vivian Bible presents the king, in the presence of court figures and clergy, receiving his new manuscript. Charles, the largest figure in the composition, sits between two princely men and two royal bodyguards at the back of the circle of men. Before him are eleven clerics. Three of them carry the magnificent volume in veiled hands and the others hail the king. At the right, a laymen joins these religious figures in saluting the ruler.

Three references to Karolus Rex in the Paris Bible[5] and the naming of Count Vivian in the dedicatory verses, secure the identification of the king as Charles the Bald. Vivian, who died in 851, had served as the lay abbot of the monasteries of St. Martin at Tours and of Marmoutier during the first decade of Charles' reign. There can be

---

[1] Fol. 423ʳ. Köhler, *Kar. Min.*, I₁, 238 and 398ff.; I₂, 60ff. and 220ff.

[2] Fol. 334ᵛ. Gaehde, "Bible Manuscript," I, 453ff.

[3] Excluding coins, no contemporary portrait of Charlemagne survives. Several later copies are reproduced in P. E. Schramm, *Die deutschen Kaiser und Könige in Bildern ihrer Zeit* (Leipzig, 1928). Conventional images of Louis the Pious are included in manuscripts of Hrabanus Maurus' *Liber de laudibus sanctae crucis* (cf. Schramm, *op. cit.*, pl. 15) and a portrait of his wife Judith is found in the Geneva manuscript of Hrabanus' *Commentary on the Books of Judith, Esther, and Maccabees* (cf. Schramm, *op. cit.*, pl. 16). A greater number of portraits of Lothar are known (cf. Schramm, *op. cit.*, pls. 17–19).

[4] In addition to the dedication pages in the Vivian and San Paolo Bibles these are: Prayerbook of Charles the Bald (Munich, Schatzkammer der Residenz, fol. 38ᵛ); Psalter of Charles the Bald (Paris, Bibliothèque Nationale, lat. 1152, fol. 3ᵛ); Sacramentary of Charles the Bald (Paris, Bibliothèque Nationale, lat. 1141, fol. 2ᵛ); Codex Aureus of St. Emmeram (Munich, Bayerische Staatsbibliothek, Cod. clm 14000, fol. 5ᵛ); Cambrai Gospels (Bibliothèque Communale, Cod. 327, fol. 16ᵛ) questioned; Coronation Throne of Charles the Bald (Cathedra Petri), Vatican; Ellwangen Casket (Collegiate Church of St. Vitus); Equestrian Statuette (Paris, Louvre). The identification of the Paris equestrian is still disputed. For the most recent discussion of these portraits, cf. P. E. Schramm, "Kaiser Karl der Kahle der Stifter des Thrones in St. Peter," *La cattedra lignea di S. Pietro in Vaticano (Atti della Pontificia Accademia Romana di Archeologia*, serie II, vol. X, 277ff); F. Mütherich, "Die Reiterstatuette aus der Metzer Kathedrale," *Studien zur Geschichte der europäischen Plastik, Festschrift Theodor Müller* (Munich, 1965), 9ff.; idem, *Sakramentar von Metz* (Graz, 1972).

[5] Fols. 1ᵛ, 422ᵛ, and 423ʳ.

no doubt, therefore, about the identity of the king or about the approximate date of the manuscript. Because the charter (*praeceptum*) referred to in the dedication was granted by Charles to the monastery of St. Martin at the very end of 845, the period 846–51 can be established for the manuscript.[6]

The dedicatory verses state that Vivian and four monastic dignitaries (*primi*) are represented with Charles the Bald in miniature:

> HAEC ETIAM PICTURA RECLUDIT, QUALITER HEROS
> OFFERT VIVIANUS CUM GREGE NUNC HOC OPUS.
> ANTE UBI POST PATREM PRIMITES, MUNDUS AMANDUS,
> SIGUALDUS JUSTUS, SUMMUS AREGARIUS:
> QUIS TRIBUS EST PROBITAS, PIETAS VERUMQUE FIDESQUE,
> CETERA HONESTA QUOQUE CONSOCIATA SIMUL;
> QUARTUS HIS JUNCTUS HAERET, SANCTISSIME DAVID,
> QUI TE VI TOTA MENTIS AMORE COLIT.
> HI PRONI TIBIMET DOMINO DE PARTE BEATI
> MARTINI AC FRATRUM ECCE LIBRUM TRIBUUNT.
> CUIUS HONORE ROGANT: PLACEAT LAUDETUR AMETUR
> SCRUTETUR PROSIT AUXILIETUR ALAT.
> IN QUO NIL ALIUD QUAM FRATRUM SOLA VOLUNTAS
> EX, TUA QUAS, VILLIS, IUSSIO REDDIDERAT.
> REDDIS EAS, CAESAR, MARTINI PRO VENERATU,
> DOMNI CEU PRECIBUS SEMPER AMABILIBUS
> PERPETUI NEC NON BRICCII TUTAMINE SANCTI
> PROQUE ALIIS RELIQUIS, O PARADISE, TUIS,
> IMMO MAGIS PRO TE, JESU SALVATOR AMATE,
> SIS UT EI VITA DENIQUE PERPETUA,
> PRO FAMULIS NOBIS ETIAM ORATORIBUS APTIS,
> QUOS SITIS OBRUERAT, FRIGUS ET ATRA FAMES
> O REX, O REVERENDE, FIET RENOVATIO FIXA
> A MERCEDE DATA SIVE SALUTE TUA.
> PRAEVALEAT REGALE DECUS SUPERETQUE POTESTAS
> REGUM DE MORE, QUI COLUERE BONUM.
> PRAECEPTUM GENITORIS, AVI, PROAVI RENOVASTI:
> HOC STET, HOC MANEAT, HOC NEC OBIRE QUEAT.
> QUOD TUA SANCTA MANUS NUPER FIRMAVIT HONESTE
> PRAECEPTI SERIE, PRORSUS EAT STABILE. . . .[7]

The identification of the men in the portrayal is not obvious. Köhler maintained that Vivian was the layman at the right of the miniature who looks toward the king while pointing at the book, and he recognized the dignitaries in the group of four clerics be-

---

[6] Köhler, *Kar. Min.*, I,, 339f. Köhler favored a date of 846.

[7] *Ibid.*, I,, 398f.

low the lay abbot.[8] P. Lauer, on the other hand, contended that Köhler's arguments are inconclusive.[9] Specifically, he argued, they are at variance with the verse, "Ante ubi, post patrem, primi," because the group of four clerics stands before, not behind, the layman. Lauer proposed that Vivian is the cleric who faces Charles at the center of the page.

It seems unlikely in a composition which is so clearly ordered according to the principles of hierarchical ranking, that Count Vivian would be the smallest figure, shown from the rear at the very bottom of the page. Certainly, the composition was intended to be viewed as a circular assembly of men facing the king. Either to maintain the hierarchy or to avoid depicting dignitaries with their backs turned, the artist turned the figures to face forward. Within the circle, the layman precedes the group of four clerics. Köhler was certainly correct, therefore, that he is Count Vivian leading the dignitaries named in the verses.

A convincing identification of the princely figures who stand beside Charles' throne has not yet been offered. Despite the importance suggested by their positions, their diadems, and their costumes, the fact that they are not named in the dedication tends to support Köhler's proposal that they are the *ostiarius* and *sacellarius* of Charles' palace.[10] There are no grounds for identifying other figures on the page, Köhler's ingenious proposal, notwithstanding, that the three monks who carry the Bible manuscript are its illuminators.[11]

In a general sense at least, the dedication miniature in the Vivian Bible represents a contemporary event—the presentation sometime between 846 and 851—of the sumptuous manuscript to the bibliophilic king by Count Vivian and the monks of St. Martin's. The fact that it stands apart from its predecessors and from most subsequent dedication miniatures in its elaborateness and specificity confirms the contemporary aspect of the page.[12] The dedication frontispiece in the Vivian Bible was not, however, an *ad hoc* creation, a free and genuine rendering of a real event in the modern sense. Its overall format and many of its details have Carolingian antecedents and many of these elements, in turn, are rooted in deep antiquity.

THE SOURCES

Ruler portraits with flanking attendants are common in early medieval art. In a Gospel Book (Paris, Bibliothèque Nationale, Cod. lat. 266), produced at Tours between 849 and 851, Lothar is depicted between two bodyguards, nearly identical to

[8] *Ibid.*, I₂, 227f.

[9] "Iconographie Carolingienne: Vivien et Charlemagne," *Mélanges en hommage à la Mémoire de Fr. Martroye* (Paris, 1940), pp. 191ff.

[10] Köhler, *Kar. Min.*, I₂, 226. See also Lauer, *op. cit.*, pp. 196ff. Lauer preferred to identify these figures as members of the royal family or as officers of the court. Comparable anonymous "princes" are represented beside Otto III in the

Aachen Gospels of c. 1000. Cf. K. Hoffmann, *Taufsymbolik im Mittelalterlichen Herrscherbild* (Düsseldorf, 1968), p. 37.

[11] *Kar. Min.*, I₂, 228f.

[12] Cf. K. Weitzmann, "Book Illustration in the Fourth Century: Tradition and Innovation," *Studies*, pp. 96ff. and J. Prochno, *Das Schreiber und Dedikationsbild in der deutschen Buchmalerei* (Leipzig, 1929).

those in the Vivian miniature (fol. 1ᵛ, Fig. 198).[13] The Lothar portrait is more faithful to the formula for ruler portraits well-known in ancient and medieval art than is the representation of Charles the Bald. A similar convention was used, for example, in the ninth-century illustrations of Prudentius' *Passio Romani martyris* in Bern (Burgerbibliothek, Cod. 264, p. 131).[14] It also was employed in the early ninth-century volume of canon law in Vercelli (Biblioteca Capitolare, MS. CLXV)[15] and on the gilt bronze plaque of King Agilulf of c. 600 (Florence, Museo Nazionale).[16]

The popularity of this motif was due, at least in part, to its frequent use in ancient imperial works. The formula was employed, for example, on the medallions of Constantine where the emperor is shown seated on a high-backed throne between two bodyguards (Fig. 199).[17] A variation on this composition, which shows Constantine with four rather than two attendants (Fig. 200),[18] is particularly close to the portrait of Charles the Bald. Were it not for the banality of the convention, one would be tempted to consider the Touronian representations of Charles and Lothar as meaningful imitations of the Constantinian images.[19]

The imperial formula of the enthroned ruler flanked by armsbearers had been adopted in Early Christian representations of biblical monarchs. In the Vienna Genesis, for example, Pharaoh is shown with two bodyguards (Vienna, Nationalbibliothek, Cod. gr. 31, p. 35. Fig. 201);[20] and he is represented in a similar fashion in the Byzantine Octateuchs (e.g., Vat. gr. 747, fol. 80ʳ).[21] King David was also provided with bodyguards. On the ivory cover of the Dagulph Psalter, produced at Aachen c. 795 (Paris, Louvre, Fig. 145),[22] David is flanked by armsbearers in both scenes; and in the Utrecht Psalter, he is shown repeatedly with bodyguards.[23] David with bodyguards

---

[13] Köhler, *Kar. Min.*, I₁, 241ff. and 403ff.; I₂, 81ff.

[14] R. Stettiner, *Die illustrierten Prudentius-Handschriften* (Berlin, 1905) and O. Homburger, *Die illustrierten Handschriften der Burgerbibliothek Bern* (Bern, 1962), Fig. 118, pp. 136ff. The Bern *Prudentius*, which postdates the Vivian Bible, was based on pre-Carolingian sources.

[15] C. Walter, "Les dessins carolingiens dans un manuscrit de Verceil," *Cahiers Archéologiques*, XVIII (1968), 99ff.

[16] J. Hubert *et al.*, *L'Europe des Invasions* (Paris, 1967), Fig. 271.

[17] M. Alföldi, *Die Constantinische Goldprägung* (Mainz, 1963), pls. 16 and 17.

[18] *Ibid.*, pl. 20.

[19] Gaehde, "Bible Manuscript," I, 469, suggested that the facial features of Charles the Bald were based on a late antique emperor portrait such as the head of Constantine in the Palazzo Conservatori in Rome. The portrait of Charles the Bald in his Psalter (Paris, Bibl. Nat. lat. 1152) may have been derived from a depiction of Constantine

similar to the one in the Pseudo-Apuleius Herbal in Kassel (Landesbibliothek, Cod. Phys. fol. 10, fol. 1ᵛ, Fig. 212). Cf. K. Weitzmann, "Fourth Century," pp. 118f. and Fig. 98.

[20] W. von Hartel and F. Wickoff, *Die Wiener Genesis* (Vienna, 1895), pl. 35.

[21] A Creek Octateuch manuscript was used c. 870 for certain frontispieces in the San Paolo Bible, including fol. 21ᵛ, which depicts the miracle of the rod and serpent before Pharaoh (cf. Gaehde, "Bible Manuscript," I, 161ff. and *idem*, "Carolingian Interpretations of an Early Christian Picture Cycle to the Octateuch in the Bible of San Paolo Fuori Le Mura in Rome," *Frühmittelalterliche Studien*, VIII [1974], 351ff.). It is worth noting that Pharaoh's bodyguards on that page are nearly identical to those in the dedication miniature in the Vivian Bible.

[22] Goldschmidt, *Elfenbeinskulpturen*, I, no. 3. See above Chapter VIII.

[23] E. Dewald, *The Illustrations of the Utrecht Psalter* (Princeton, 1933), fols. 1ᵛ, 30ʳ, 51ᵛ.

also appears on two later Carolingian ivories, one in Paris (Fig. 163)[24] and another in Florence (Museo Nazionale, Fig. 164).[25] In the Utrecht Psalter, the formula was also applied to Saul (fol. 91^v, Fig. 165); and in the San Paolo Bible, it was used for Pharaoh (fol. 20^v), David (fol. 170^v, Fig. 141), Solomon (fol. 188^v, Fig. 166), and Holofernes (fol. 234^v).[26]

The dedication miniature in the Vivian Bible was probably based on a representation of one of these Old Testament monarchs, most likely on a depiction of King David, rather than directly on a classical ruler portrait. This dependence is clearly indicated by the Psalter frontispiece of the Vivian Bible itself (Fig. 140) where David is accompanied by soldiers virtually identical to those that stand beside Charles in the dedication miniature. It is possible, of course, that the portrait of the secular king influenced the David page rather than vice versa. The relationship of the Psalter miniature to the Dagulf cover,[27] however, suggests strongly that the guards were features of the David model. This conclusion is supported by the Psalter Page in the San Paolo Bible (Fig. 141). It, too, shows David between two bodyguards who closely resemble the figures in the Vivian Bible. Because the frontispiece in the San Paolo Bible may have been copied from a lost Touronian manuscript that predated the Vivian Bible, the Psalter frontispiece constitutes evidence that the armsbearers were depicted with David before they entered the secular context. There is, however, some evidence that the lost Touronian Bible also had a portrait of Charles which included the bodyguards and so the original context of the guards is impossible to specify with precision. Charles the Bald frequently was likened to David;[28] and in the dedicatory inscription of the Vivian Bible itself he is addressed as "splendide David."[29] This association may have motivated the Touronian illuminator to include aspects of the David depiction in his portrait of King Charles.

The two courtly men, who grasp either side of the throne, may also have been derived from conventional ruler images. Non-military attendants do appear in earlier portraits. They are depicted on consular diptychs such as the Asturius plaque in Darmstadt;[30] and they exist in the fresco at Dura Europos where Pharaoh is enthroned between a courtier and a scribe.[31] In the Rossano Gospels, Pilate is attended by two

[24] Goldschmidt, *Elfenbeinskulpturen*, I, no. 141.

[25] *Ibid*, no. 113.

[26] Gaehde, "Bible Manuscript," I, 161ff.; 317ff.; 330ff.; and 352ff.; "Carolingian Interpretations," pp. 352ff., and *idem*, "The Pictorial Sources of the Illustrations to the Books of Kings, Proverbs, Judith and Maccabees in the Carolingian Bible of San Paolo Fuori Le Mura in Rome," *Frühmittelalterliche Studien*, IX (1975), 372ff.

[27] Cf. Chapter VII.

[28] Cf. Chapter VII and E. Kantorowicz, *The King's Two Bodies* (Princeton, 1957), p. 81; H.

H. Anton, *Fürstenspiegel und Herrscherethos in der Karolingerzeit* (Bonn, 1968); K. Weitzmann, "The Iconography of the Carolingian Ivories of the Throne," *Cattedra Lignea*, p. 225ff.; Schramm, "Stifter des Thrones," pp. 392ff.

[29] Köhler, *Kar. Min.*, I,, 398.

[30] R. Delbrück, *Die Consulardiptychen* (Berlin, 1929), nos. 4 and 37.

[31] C. Kraeling, *The Synagogue* ("The Excavations at Dura Europos. Final Report," 8, part I, New Haven, 1956), pl. LXVIII.

young men.[32] David is flanked by two scribes in the eighth-century Vespasian Psalter (London, British Library, Cod. Cotton Vespasian A.I., fol. 30[v], Fig. 151);[33] and in the ninth-century manuscript of the *Christian Topography* of Cosmas Indicopleustes (Vatican gr. 699, fol. 63, Fig. 153),[34] Solomon stands to David's left. It is possible, therefore, that Charles' companions were also based on a David picture or similar representation. Charlemagne may also have been portrayed with members of his court. An eleventh-century portrait of Charlemagne in Gotha (Bibliothek, Cod. 84, fol. 2[v])[35] and a seventeenth-century engraving,[36] both presumably copies of ninth-century originals, show the emperor with members of his court. Unfortunately, these iconographic precedents do not help in the identification of the princely men in the Vivian Bible.

Specific models for the features and costumes of the secular figures are difficult to pinpoint. Charles' heavy, rectangular face, his moustache, his long nose, and his cleft chin also are features of the portraits in the San Paolo Bible, the Codex Aureus of St. Emmeram, the Vatican throne, and the Paris Equestrian statue.[37] Charles' costume, a long-sleeve tunic and golden mantle fastened with a circular fibula at the right shoulder, may have been copied from an ancient monument. Theodosius, for example, is shown in similar garb on the Madrid missorium.[38] The dress of the attendants is also antique. The short, belted tunics, red palliums, long stockings, and fillets worn by the two "princes" are similar to those on the Stilicho diptych.[39] The Roman field dress (breastplates, skirts of overlapping *pteryges*, and stockings) of the bodyguards is like that worn by the emperor on the Barberini Diptych;[40] and similar helmets are depicted in the frescoes of Dura Europos.[41]

Charles' elaborate hoop crown is one feature of the dedication miniature that certainly reflects contemporary usage.[42] Hoop crowns are also depicted in the San Paolo Bible, the Codex Aureus of St. Emmeram, and in the Psalter of St. Gall (Figs. 197, 210, and 150). Even the aspects of the dedication miniature that can be traced to ancient sources, however, had entered the Carolingian illustrative vocabulary before the middle of the ninth century, Charles' dress, for example, recalls the robes worn by Charlemagne in the tenth-century Paris drawing (Bibliothèque Nationale, lat. 9654 fol. A[v]).[43] It is basically the same dress worn by David and Saul in the Utrecht Psalter (cf. Figs. 165 and 172). The costume of Charles' companions also has precedents in the Utrecht Psalter[44] and is similar to the dress worn by the donor in the early ninth-century

[32] A. Muñoz, *Il codice purpureo di Rossano* (Rome, 1907), pls. XIII–XIV.

[33] Fol. 30[v]. D. Wright, *The Vespasian Psalter* ("Early English Manuscripts in Facsimile," vol. XIV, Copenhagen-London-Baltimore, 1967).

[34] Chapter VII, above.

[35] Schramm, *Kaiser*, pl. 9b.

[36] *Ibid.*, pl. 10c.

[37] See note 4, above.

[38] Delbrück, *op. cit.*, no. 62.

[39] *Ibid.*, pl. 63.

[40] *Ibid.*, pl. 48.

[41] Kraeling, *op. cit.*, pp. 169ff. and pl. 72.

[42] Cf. P. E. Schramm, "Die Bügelkrone, ein karolingisches Herrschaftszeichen," *Festschrift für K. G. Hugelmann* (Aalen, 1959), pp. 569ff. (reprinted in *Kaiser, Könige, und Päpste* [Stuttgart, 1968ff.], II, 98ff.). The leaf-like superstructure may be a misunderstanding.

[43] Schramm, *Kaiser*, pl. 9a.

[44] Fols. 26[r] and 91[v].

frescoes at Malles.[45] The Roman field dress of the bodyguards is not unlike that depicted on an Ada ivory in Florence (Museo Nazionale),[46] on the Einhard Arch,[47] and in the Bern Prudentius.[48]

Because of the popularity of the imperial motif and of specific details, it is impossible to determine with certainty whether the Touronian artist consulted one model or several or whether his sources were secular or biblical. The evidence that the immediate model of the bodyguards was a Psalter frontispiece is the only firm indication of the kind of prototype that was used.

Count Vivian is similar in pose and costume to the court attendants on either side of Charles' throne and may have been patterned after the same model.

Precedents also exist for the arrangement in a semi-circle of the group of monks before King Charles. Köhler cited the scene of the council presided over by Ascanius in the Vatican Virgil (Cod. lat. 3225, fol. 73^v) and the depiction of the Council of 382 in the Paris *Homilies of Gregory* (Bibliothèque Nationale, Cod. gr. 510, fol. 355^r).[49] The latter, which is not truly a circular assembly, is an unconvincing parallel and, in fact, better examples can be adduced. Folio 1^r of the Rabbula Gospels (Florence, Biblioteca Medicea-Laurenziana, Cod. Plut., I, 56, Fig. 202),[50] for instance, represents the Election of Matthias as a circular assembly. The arched frame with hanging lanterns and the man shown in three-fourths rear view in the foreground recall the Vivian miniature. Similar late antique compositions must have been known in Carolingian times when they were used for two miniatures in the ninth-century Corpus Agrimensorum in the Vatican (Cod. Palat. lat. 1564, fols. 2^r and 3^r, Fig. 203).[51] The authors are all seated, but like the clerics on the Vivian frontispiece, they display a variety of activities focused toward the top of the page. The illustrator of the Vatican Agrimensores, like the Touronian illuminator, had difficulty with foreshortening and, in the case of the bearded man at the right, he broke the circle and turned a figure forward.

Closest to the composition of the Vivian Bible dedication picture is the Judges frontispiece in the tenth-century Leo Bible (Vatican, Biblioteca, Cod. Reg. gr. 1, fol. 206^r, Fig. 204).[52] Samson, Gideon, Barac, and Jepthe are seated on a great semi-circular throne, engaged in a lively discussion. Behind them is a group of young Israelites and before them twelve men stand in a semi-circle facing the judges. Not only is the hierarchically ordered circular assembly of the Byzantine page remarkably close to that in the Vivian Bible, specific parallels also can be noted. These include the men at the middle

[45] J. Hubert *et al.*, *L'empire carolingien* (Paris, 1968), Fig. 18.

[46] Goldschmidt, *Elfenbeinskulpturen*, I, no. 10 and J. Déer, "Ein Doppelbildnis Karls des Grossen," *Forschungen zur Kunstgeschichte und christliche Archäologie* (Baden-Baden, 1953), II, 103ff.

[47] Cf. H. Belting, "Der Einhardsbogen," *Zeitschrift für Kunstgeschichte*, XXXVI (1973), 93ff.

[48] Homburger, *op. cit.*, pls. 9, 110, and 111.

[49] *Kar. Min.*, I₂, 229f. A centralized composi-

tion was also incorporated into the frontispiece to Acts in the San Paolo Bible. Cf. Gaehde, "Bible Manuscript," I, 408ff.

[50] M. Salmi *et al.*, *The Rabbula Gospels* (Olten, 1959). See also M. Koch, *Die Rückenfigur im Bild* (Recklinghausen, 1965).

[51] M. Salmi, *op. cit.*, p. 46 and A. Goldschmidt, *German Illumination* (Florence, 1929), pl. 16b.

[52] *Miniature della Bibbia cod. Vat. Regin. Greco 1* (Milan, 1905), p. 11.

left of the Leo Bible frontispiece who lean forward toward the central group, the man with arms raised, the figure seen from the rear at the bottom of the page, and the men at the right who raise their hands in acclamation.

Together with the compositions in the Rabbula Gospels and in the Vatican *Agrimensores*, the Judges miniature is compelling evidence that the form of the Vivian Dedication page was derived from a pre-existent model. It must be noted, however, that in none of the other representations does the composition focus on a single figure as in the Vivian manuscript. There are precedents also for that aspect of the Carolingian composition. The circular composition in the Vienna Genesis (Fig. 201) is dominated by a single man albeit not at the center; and an even closer parallel to the Vivian page is the representation of Christ and the Apostles on an Early Christian ivory plaque in Dijon (Musée des Beaux-Arts, Fig. 205).[53] Like Charles the Bald, Christ is enthroned at the top of the composition, slightly in front of the assembly which is arranged in a hierarchically graded circle before him. A similar antique composition was known during the ninth century when it served as the model for one scene carved on the Flabellum of Tournus (Florence, Museo Nazionale).[54]

During the early part of the Carolingian period, the same compositional device was employed in a miniature representing the Ancestors of Christ in the Lorsch Gospels (Alba Julia, Batthyaneum Library, fol. 14ʳ, Fig. 206).[55] At the center, thirteen young men are shown saluting a portrait of King David. Their gestures and poses recall the Vivian Bible dedication miniature; and it is particularly interesting that the figures at the lower right face forward, interrupting the circle as in the Vivian composition.

The fact that the Lorsch miniature features David raises the question once again of whether the model of the dedication page may not have been a portrait of the Old Testament king. In his discussion of the frontispiece miniature in the Vespasian Psalter (Fig. 151), David Wright concluded that the eighth-century frontispiece and the portrait of Charles the Bald must have been derived from similar, late antique compositions;[56] and he adduced the Dijon plaque as an example of the type of format he envisioned. The Vespasian Psalter frontispiece which, like the miniature in the Vivian Bible shows the enthroned king beneath an arch surrounded by figures heirarchically arranged in a circle on a receding plane, indicates that the entire Vivian composition may have been derived from an Early Christian representation of King David.

The poses of individual clerics could, to some extent, reflect the basic model, but they must have been modified. For the men who actually carry the book, the illuminator may have consulted a presentation miniature such as the one in Hrabanus Maurus' *De laudibus sanctae crucis* (Vienna, Nationalbibliothek, Cod. 652, fol. 1ʳ, Fig. 132).[57]

[53] W. F. Volbach, "Fruhmittelalterliche Elfenbeinarbeiten aus Gallien," *Festschrift des Römisch-Germanischen Zentralmuseum in Mainz*, I (1952), 49f.

[54] L. Eitner, *The Flabellum of Tournus* (New York, 1944).

[55] W. Braunfels, *Das Lorscher Evangeliar* (Munich, 1965).

[56] *Op. cit.*, pp. 73ff.

[57] Prochno, *op. cit.*, no. 11; P. Bloch, "Zum Dedikationsbild im Lob des Kreuzes des Hrabanus Maurus," *Das erste Jahrtausend*, ed. V. Elbern

The clerics all wear ivory-colored dalmatics over pale blue albs and they all carry maniples. Their chasubles are of various colors. The vestments appear to reflect contemporary liturgical dress.[58]

The meaning and specific origin of the framing arch, the Hand of God, and the two female figures who hold palm branches and extend crowns from the upper corners of the miniature are difficult to trace.

Arched frames were employed in a wide variety of contexts prior to the middle of the ninth century. They occur in secular portraits,[59] in depictions of David,[60] in portraits of the evangelists,[61] and even in miniatures of large assemblies.[62] The draped arch on spiral columns is closest to the frame of the San Paolo Bible Psalter frontispiece (Fig. 141) which suggests that the source of the frame was a David picture, a suggestion that is supported by the St. Gall Psalter (Fig. 150) in which the portrait of David is framed in a similar manner.[63]

The St. Gall Psalter also includes the Hand of God above David's head. This emblem of divine providence is common in portraits of the Old Testament king. It is depicted throughout the Utrecht Psalter (e.g., fol. 72[r], Fig. 207)[64] and it is shown in the Bodleian Psalter (Cod. Douce 59, fol. 51[v]),[65] on the Florence Ivory plaque (Fig. 164), and later in a Vatican manuscript, Cod. lat. 83, fol. 12[v].[66] The Hand of God is less common in secular portraits. During the first half of the ninth century, however, it was included in the portrait of the Empress Judith in the Fulda manuscript of c. 831 (Geneva, Bibliothèque, Cod. 22, fol. 3[v]).[67] It became a normal feature in portraits of Charles the Bald.[68]

Cowled female figures similar to those that offer crowns to King Charles personify the four cardinal virtues on the Psalter frontispiece in the Vivian Bible. It is likely, therefore, that the figures of the dedication miniature also personify kingly virtues. Women personify "truth, meekness, and justice," in the Utrecht Psalter (fol. 26[r], Fig. 172);[69] and virtues were depicted at Tours in the portrait of Abbot Raganaldus (Autun, Bibliothèque Municipale, Cod. 19bis, fol. 173[v], Fig. 208).[70] Furthermore, personifications of the four virtues are represented in three other portraits of Charles the Bald himself: in the San Paolo Bible (Fig. 197), in the Codex Aureus of St. Emmeram

(Düsseldorf, 1962), I, pp. 471ff.; *Codex Vindobonensis 652* (Graz, 1972).

[58] J. Braun, *Die liturgische Gewandung* (Freiburg im Breisgau, 1907).

[59] E.g., Apuleius in the Kassel Herbal (Fig. 213).

[60] E.g., Khludov Psalter in Moscow (cf. Fig. 152) and Vespasian Psalter (Fig. 151). Cf. H. Steger, *David Rex et Propheta* (Nurenberg, 1961), pls. 3, 19, 23, 31.

[61] Numerous examples are known. Cf. A. M. Friend, Jr., "The Portraits of the Evangelists in Greek and Latin Manuscripts," *Art Studies* (1927 and 1929).

[62] Rabbula Gospels, fol. 1[r] (Fig. 202).

[63] H. Rahn, *Das Psalterium Aureum von Sankt Gallen* (St. Gall, 1878). Cf. Chapter VII.

[64] Dewald, *op. cit.*, pl. CIX.

[65] S. Dufrenne, "Deux psautiers carolingiens à Oxford et à Troyes," *Synthronon*, II (1968), 167ff.

[66] Steger, *op. cit.*, pl. 9.

[67] Schramm, *Kaiser*, pl. 66.

[68] Cf. Figs. 196, 197, 209–11.

[69] Dewald, *op. cit.*, pl. XLI. Cf. Weitzmann, "Carolingian Ivories," pp. 226f.

[70] Köhler, *Kar. Min.*, I₂, 96ff.

(Fig. 210), and in the Cambrai Gospels (Fig. 78).[71] There can be little doubt, therefore, that the women of the Vivian miniature also are Virtues.

Though they were also occasionally portrayed in depictions of David,[72] Virtues were commonly depicted in secular portraiture; and they were attributed to the mundane ruler by Alcuin who may have known Cicero's *De Officiis*.[73] It seems probable, therefore, that the Virtues in the Vivian Bible originated in the Dedication picture rather than in the Psalter frontispiece. This conclusion is sustained by the awkward rendering of the personifications at the bottom of the David page (Fig. 140)[74] and by the absence of Virtues in the Psalter frontispiece of the San Paolo page (Fig. 141).

The crowns seem to be additions to the personifications. It is true that in the Byzantine Paris Psalter (Bibliothèque Nationale, Cod. gr. 139, fol. 6^v)[75] a female figure crowns David and that on ancient coins, nikes are shown offering crowns to the triumphant emperor.[76] In Carolingian art, however, angels usually offer crowns to the ruler. Angels proffering crowns appear in the Utrecht Psalter and are depicted on the ivory throne of Charles the Bald (Fig. 209).[77] Angels may have been depicted in the model and may have been merged with personifications of the Virtues. Angels appear in approximately the same position as the Vivian Bible personifications in the Codex Aureus of St. Emmeram (Fig. 210), and in the San Paolo Bible (Fig. 197). It should be noted, however, that in the Metz Sacramentary (Paris, Bibliothèque Nationale, Cod. lat. 1141, fol. 5^v)[78] both angels and women are depicted offering crowns to Christ.

Parallels to individual elements and to the overall composition of the Vivian Bible dedication miniature can be traced to earlier art. Associations with depictions of King David are especially clear; the enthroned ruler flanked by soldiers, the encircling group of men, and even the arch, the Hand of God, and the personifications all appear in representations of the Old Testament monarch. The question naturally arises, therefore, was the portrait of Charles the Bald patterned on a single model—presumably a frontispiece miniature of David and his entourage? It is entirely possible that a frontispiece, similar to the one in the Vespasian Psalter, served the Touronian illuminator. Such a frontispiece would have represented David enthroned between attendants within a circle of musicians, dancers, and scribes. Even the arched frame and the Hand of God (though presumably not the personifications), may have been features of this model. If such a model was known at Tours, it is curious that it had so little impact on the Psalter frontispieces themselves.[79] The likelier hypothesis is that the creator of the Dedication miniatures copied no single David picture but freely composed his representations from various sources including Psalter frontispieces. A desire to draw a

---

[71] P. E. Schramm, *Sphaira. Globus. Reichsapfel* (Stuttgart, 1958), p. 59 and Hoffmann, *op. cit.*, p. 18.

[72] Déer, *op. cit.*, pp. 129ff.

[73] Cf. Chapter VII.

[74] Cf. Chapter VII.

[75] H. Buchthal, *The Miniatures of the Paris Psalter* (London, 1938), pp. 24f.

[76] Cf. Alföldi, *op. cit.*, pl. 70.

[77] Weitzmann, "Carolingian Ivories," pp. 225f.

[78] Mütherich, *Sakramentar*.

[79] Cf. Chapter VII.

parallel between Charles the Bald and King David may have dictated the choice of models.[80] This desire apparently was the Vivian master's alone, for it is not evident in the San Paolo manuscript.

THE SAN PAOLO BIBLE

Like the portrait in the Vivian Bible, the dedication page in the San Paolo Bible poses difficult problems of identification, origin, and meaning. The frontispiece depicts a disproportionately large king seated on an enormous circular throne. To his right are the king's bodyguards—as in the Vivian Bible, young men carrying a lance and shield and a sword; to his left are his consort and her attendant. Above the king, seen through the arches of his throne, are female personifications of the four cardinal virtues flanked by two angels.

The dedicatory verses refer explicitly to many of these elements:

REX CAELI DNS SOLITA PIETATE REDUNDANS.

HUNC KAROLUM REGEM TERRAE DILEXIT HERILEM

TANTI ERGO OFFICII UT COMPOS VALUISSET HABERI.

TETRANTI IMPLEVIT VERTUTUM QUATTUOR ALMO

IMMINENT HIC CAPITI DE VERTICE CUNCTA REFUNDENS.

DENIQ: SE PRIMUM TUNC OMNIA RITE GUBERNAT

PRUDENTER IUSTE MODERATE FORTITER ATQUE.

HINC INDE ANGELICO SEPTUS TUTAMINE SACRO

HOSTIBUS UT CUNCTIS EXULTET PACE REPULSIS

AD DEXTRAM ARMIGERI PRAETENDUNT ARMA MINISTRI

ECCLESIAM CHRISTI INVICTUS DEFENSOR IN AEVUM

ARMIPOTENS MAGNIS QUIS ORNET SAEPE TRIUMPHIS

NOBILIS AD LEVAM CONIUNX DE MORE VENUSTAT.

QUA INSIGNIS PROLES IN REGNUM RITE PARETUR.[81]

Unfortunately, however, the verses do not identify King Karolus specifically and do not name his consort. This has led to considerable discussion concerning the origin and date of the Bible.

Since the mid-nineteen fifties when, in independent studies, E. Kantorowicz[82] and H. Schade[83] came to the same conclusion, there has been general agreement that the king portrayed in the San Paolo Bible is Charles the Bald. This identification of the ruler is completely convincing. The arguments that Charles' consort in the miniature is his

---

[80] Cf. Chapter VII.

[81] Gaehde, "Bible Manuscript," II, 146.

[82] "The Carolingian King in the Bible of San Paolo fuori le mura," *Late Classical and Mediaeval Studies in Honor of Albert Mathias Friend, Jr.* (Princeton, 1955), pp. 287ff.

[83] "Studien zu der Karolingischen Bilderbibel aus St. Paul vor den Mauern zu Rom," *Wallraf-Richartz Jahrbuch*, XXI (1959), 12ff. and XXII (1960), 20ff.

second queen, Richildis, whom he married in 870 after the death of Hermintrude a year before, has, however, been questioned by Gaehde.[84] Gaehde argued that the San Paolo Bible served as the model for the portrait of Charles the Bald in the Codex Aureus of St. Emmeram (fol. 5ᵛ, Fig. 210)[85] and must, therefore, predate 870. Gaehde reasoned that Charles' consort must be Queen Hermintrude and that the volume must be dated between 866 and 870.

Gaehde's conclusion is based principally on three points: (1) the relationship in pose and costume of the portraits of Charles the Bald in the two miniatures; (2) the similarity of the angels; and (3) the relationship of the baldachin and armsbearers in the Codex Aureus with those features in the Solomon miniature of the San Paolo Bible (fol. 188ᵛ, Fig. 166).[86] These similarities are obvious. They do not prove, however, the direct dependence of one miniature on the other. In fact, Gaehde's proposal that the Codex Aureus dedication miniature was derived from two frontispieces in the San Paolo Bible is *a priori* unlikely. Is it not more reasonable to suppose that the similarities evident in these depictions are due to their dependence on another, lost, model?

Charles' pose and costume in the Codex Aureus of St. Emmeram are not compelling indications of its dependence on the San Paolo Bible. Charles is shown wearing similar garb in the Psalter manuscript in Paris (fol. 3ᵛ, Fig. 211) which predates 869.[87] Furthermore, the turn of his head, his crown, and his throne, and the hand of God are features of the Psalter portrait which are repeated in the Codex Aureus but are not in the San Paolo Bible.

The angels are very similar in the two manuscripts. On the basis of internal evidence, however, it is impossible to decide which pair has precedence. If anything, their superior articulation, stouter bodies, and down-turned wings suggest the priority of the Codex Aureus figures. These are more like the angels on the throne of Charles the Bald (Fig. 209).[88] Also, like the angels in the Utrecht Psalter[89] and in the Golden Altar of Milan,[90] they carry staffs. The angels in the San Paolo Bible appear to be variations on a common type squeezed to fit the space.

The bodyguards in the San Paolo Bible are also departures from the standard formula. To make room for the two men, the illuminator of the San Paolo Bible depicted both armsbearers at Charles' right. This led Gaehde to conclude that the artist of the Codex Aureus page, who represented the bodyguards in the usual fashion, had turned to the Solomon miniature (Fig. 166) for these figures. Again, is it not likelier that the illuminator of the Codex Aureus consulted a single source that showed Charles flanked by two guards than that he compiled the portrait from two models?

[84] "Bible Manuscript," I, 453ff. and "The Bible of San Paolo fuori le mura in Rome: Its Date and Its Relation to Charles the Bald," *Gesta*, V (1966), 9ff.

[85] G. Leidinger, *Der Codex Aureus der Bayerischen Staatsbibliothek in München* (Munich, 1921–25), pl. 10 and Hoffmann, *op. cit.*, pp. 51ff.

[86] Gaehde, "Bible Manuscript," I, 329ff. and

"Pictorial Sources," pp. 372ff.

[87] V. Leroquais, *Les psautiers* (Macon, 1940–41), II, 67ff.

[88] *Cattedra Lignea*, pls. XXXVI–XXXVII.

[89] Dewald, *op. cit.*, pls. VII, XVIII, LXII, LXV, LXXV, LXXVIII.

[90] V. Elbern, *Der Karolingische Goldaltar von Mailand* (Bonn, 1952).

Gaehde's best evidence that the Codex Aureus was derived from the San Paolo Bible is the baldachin. The structure above King Charles' head is indeed close to that in the Solomon miniature. There is reason to believe, however, that the illuminator of the Codex Aureus did not depend directly on the Old Testament frontispiece. The baldachin in the Codex Aureus, but not the one in the Solomon miniature, is draped with a cloth that functions as a kind of halo behind Charles' head. A similar cloth hangs from the baldachin in the depiction of Abraham and Melchizedek in the Vienna Genesis;[91] and it is a feature of the baldachin that frames the portrait of Apuleius in the Carolingian Herbal in Kassel (Landesbibliothek, Cod. Phys. Fol. 10, fol. 2[r], Fig. 213).[92] It is unlikely that the illuminator of the Codex Aureus restored this traditional element to the baldachin of the Solomon miniature. More probably, it was a feature of his model.

Both the San Paolo Bible and the Codex Aureus of St. Emmeram seem to have been copied from the same portrait of Charles the Bald. The latter is more traditional; the former seems to be a radical refashioning undertaken for a special occasion. The model probably showed King Charles enthroned between his bodyguards and saluted by two angels. It may also have included the baldachin, the Hand of God, the Virtues, and the provinces (transformed into the consort and her attendant in the San Paolo Bible).

If such a model did serve the illustrators of the Codex Aureus and the San Paolo Bible, the date of the latter remains an open question. Gaehde's arguments are no more and no less convincing than those of Kantorowicz and Schade.

What was the origin of this hypothetical model? Could it have been a Touronian creation, in fact part of the same manuscript that served as the pattern for seven other frontispieces in the San Paolo Bible and for the *Majestas* picture in the Codex Aureus?[93] This is difficult to decide. Charles' facial features recall those in the Vivian Bible; his bodyguards are similar types; and the massive, curving throne of the San Paolo page recalls that in the Touronian portrait of Lothar. The angels and baldachin seem not to have been known in Tours; but the personifications of the Virtues are found, not only in the dedication and Psalter frontispieces of the Vivian Bible, but also in the Portrait of Abbot Raganaldus in the Marmoutier Sacramentary (Fig. 208). The nimbed female figures of the Tours Sacramentary are almost identical to those in the San Paolo Bible. Except for Temperance, they face the same direction and hold identical attributes.[94] It is conceivable, therefore, that the lost Touronian manuscript that was used by the illuminators of the San Paolo Bible and the Codex Aureus for other frontis-

[91] P. 7. Hartel, *op. cit.*, pl. 7.

[92] Weitzmann, "Fourth Century," pp. 118ff. has proposed that the Apuleius miniature was based on a late antique ruler portrait.

[93] Cf. Gaehde, "Turonian Sources."

[94] Similar personifications appear in the portrait of a ruler, perhaps Charles the Bald, in the Cambrai Gospels. Cf. Schramm, *Kaiser*, pl. 32. The association of the ruler and virtues goes back to

late antiquity (Cicero, *De Officiis*, I, 15–17). Cf. Déer, *op. cit.*, pp. 103ff. The special role of the four cardinal virtues, however, may be Carolingian. The letter of Alcuin is especially interesting in this respect. Cf. Chapter III. The Cambrai portrait (Fig. 78) is virtually an illustration of these verses. The lozenge is *mundus* at the center of which is the *homo*, the ruler, and the Virtues occupy the positions of the four elements.

pieces, also contained a portrait of Charles the Bald that served as the model for their dedication miniatures.

The superstructure of Charles' throne in the San Paolo Bible apparently was an original feature, perhaps patterned after the ivory throne made for the king between c. 870 and 875.[95] Charles' orb, although ultimately derived from ancient sources, may also be a late addition.[96] If Schade's reading of the monogram is correct, it contains a reference to Charles' descent from Solomon and from the rulers of ancient Rome.[97]

CONCLUSIONS

With the Psalter frontispieces and the *Majestas* pictures, the dedication miniatures are the most innovative and complex of the Bible pages. Like the others, they are ingenious elaborations of traditional ideas designed to convey contemporary concepts.

The San Paolo Bible frontispiece (and also its presumed Touronian model) was intended to express three aspects of Charles' kingship: his earthly might (armsbearers), his personal goodness (Virtues), and his divine appointment (angels). No single pictorial prototype is known that combines these qualities in a portrait of a secular ruler. The four cardinal virtues seem to be a popular Carolingian concept. They were identified as kingly attributes by Alcuin; they were depicted at Tours in the portrait of Abbot Raganaldus; and they were included in the Cambrai portrait of Charles the Bald. Putti and angels had been incorporated in the imperial portraits on consular diptychs; but, again, the closest parallels to the angels in the San Paolo Bible and the Codex Aureus are found in Carolingian art. The same is true of Charles' bodyguards. Thus, the San Paolo Bible dedication miniature—or its model—appears to have been a ninth-century creation inspired, perhaps, by antique ruler portraits.

The frontispiece in the Vivian Bible is more ambitious. It, too, may have been inspired by earlier ruler portraits, but its principal model seems to have been a depiction of David in a Psalter manuscript. From this model, the Touronian illuminator apparently derived the overall format and such details as the arch and the Hand of God. The use of a representation of David as the basis of a portrait of Charles the Bald was certainly not incidental. It was a manifestation of the political pretension, often repeated during the ninth century, that the secular king was the successor of the great Old Testament monarch.[98]

---

[95] Schramm, "Stifter des Thrones," pp. 277ff. and K. Weitzmann, "The Heracles Plaques of St. Peter's Cathedra," *Art Bulletin*, IV (1973), 33ff.

[96] Gaehde, "Bible Manuscript," I, 330.

[97] *Op. cit.*, XXI, 14.

[98] Schramm, "Stifter des Thrones," pp. 292ff.

X. THE CONSTRUCTION OF THE
TOURONIAN BIBLES

THE Touronian Bibles were derived from no single model. They were created at Tours during the ninth century from diverse sources and are the products of several projects undertaken at different times to illustrate the full Bible as a single unit.

To provide their one-volume Bibles with coherent sets of illustrations, the Touronian artists developed sequences of frontispieces. The most rudimentary of these programs is preserved in the Bamberg Bible and comprises only two pages: a frontispiece devoted to the life of Adam and Eve affixed at the head of Genesis and another representing the *Majestas Agni* placed before the Gospels.[1] A second Old Testament miniature and a complementary New Testament picture are included with this basic pair in the Grandval Bible; while in the Vivian Bible, two additional biblical pictures, as well as translation and dedication miniatures, raise the number of frontispieces to eight. The Touronian system was incorporated into the San Paolo Bible where it was expanded to include twenty-four full-page miniatures.

No pre-existent model included the entire range of Old and New Testament subjects depicted in the ninth-century pandects;[2] and as a consequence, the Touronian illuminators had to compile their frontispieces from various sources. They drew freely on the rich heritage of late antique, Byzantine, and earlier Carolingian art. Their models included a Greek Genesis manuscript, Western and Byzantine *Majestas* compositions, a Latin Pentateuch and Apocalypse, a biographical sequence, a ninth-century frontispiece Psalter, a Greek Acts of the Apostles, and a number of secular portraits. Several of these models contained full-page pictures that the Touronian illuminators easily adapted to the new context. Others, however, were illustrated with sequences of pictures interspersed throughout the text. Those required selection or abbreviation and arrangement on a single leaf to suit a system that permitted no more than one illustration for any book of the Bible.

The Bible illustrations created from these models are not altogether homogeneous. Whereas the distribution of illustrations within the manuscripts is generally balanced, considerable variation exists from page to page. The Jerome, Genesis, and Epistles frontispieces consist of narrative scenes arranged on three or four horizontal registers; the Exodus and Apocalypse pages comprise two representations each; and the *Majestas*, David, and Dedication pictures are single, unified compositions. To a certain extent, this variety corresponds to the different purposes the Touronian frontispieces

---

[1] C. Nordenfalk ("Noch eine turonische Bilderbibel," *Festschrift Bernhard Bischoff* [Stuttgart 1971], pp. 153ff.) has postulated the existence of a still more elementary pandect illustrated with a single, Genesis page.

[2] The Touronian system was adumbrated in the Codex Amiatinus (Florence, Biblioteca Medicea-Laurenziana, Cod. Am. 1) which contains a portrait of the Scribe Ezra before the Old Testament and a *Majestas Domini* (Fig. 71) as a Gospels frontispiece. Cf. Chapter I.

were designed to serve; to a greater degree, it reflects the diversity of models from which the pages were composed.

THE NARRATIVE FRONTISPIECES

The narrative pages provide the clearest insight into the procedures employed at Tours to construct full-page miniatures. The detail and number of episodes, the general adherence of the illustrations to well-known texts, and the precise comparative materials constitute informative evidence of Touronian practices.

Of the five narrative frontispieces, those for Genesis are certainly the most important in an investigation of ninth-century procedures. They survive in the greatest number of replicas—four Carolingian examples and an eleventh-century copy; and they can be compared to the richest body of well-studied material, the pictorial family of the Cotton Genesis. It is evident from a study of this material that the Touronian pages were compiled, independently of one another, from a rich sequence of narrative depictions. The model must have contained at least nineteen scenes representing events from chapter II through IV. Although it is conceivable that all these episodes were represented on a single page, numerous aspects of the Touronian frontispieces indicate that the immediate model consisted of independent pictures interspersed through the text. Had they all been copied from a single, full-page frontispiece, the Touronian pages would certainly be more consistent in the placement and sequence of individual scenes. Instead, they exhibit the variety and randomness that resulted from an independent selection of scenes from a model that contained unassociated miniatures, a manuscript similar to the Cotton Genesis or the Millstatt paraphrase. Furthermore, whereas it is not impossible that nineteen scenes were illustrated on one leaf, it is difficult to imagine a single frontispiece containing that many episodes rendered in the elaborate detail that must have characterized the prototype known at Tours. The richest sequence in the San Paolo Bible, for example, the Kings frontispiece (fol. 83v),[3] comprises ten scenes; and the densest series in the Paris *Homilies of Gregory Nazianzenus* (Bibliothèque Nationale, Cod. gr. 510, fol. 69v) depicts only thirteen episodes from the life of Joseph.[4]

Despite the attempts to unify each register with landscape features, the episodes in the Grandval and Bamberg Bibles preserve the character of individual column pictures. The narrative flows more smoothly in the Vivian Bible where redundant elements have been merged with one another; while in the San Paolo Bible, the episodic quality of the model is even less evident. In the initial five scenes, the narrative traits of the prototype are preserved: the story of the creation of Adam and Eve is traced in

---

[3] Gaehde, "Bible Manuscript," I, 289ff. and *idem*, "The Pictorial Sources of Illustrations to the Books of Kings, Proverbs, Judith and Maccabees in the Carolingian Bible of San Paolo Fuori Le Mura

in Rome," *Frühmittelalterliche Studien*, IX (1975), 360ff.

[4] H. Omont, *Miniatures des plus anciens manuscrits grecs de la Bibliothèque Nationale* (2nd ed. Paris, 1929), pl. XXVI.

five separate scenes. The Temptation and Fall, on the other hand, are illustrated in a most summary fashion. It is as if the illuminator, having failed to plan the entire page before starting, began copying the dense cycle from his model scene by scene until he realized he was running out of space. Only then did he begin to abbreviate and condense the series.

The Epistles frontispieces in the Vivian and San Paolo Bibles are analogous to the Genesis pictures. The two pages were constructed independently of one another from the same narrative source, in this case from an illustrated Byzantine Book of Acts. For the kernel of the story, the illuminators copied the same episodes; but at the beginning and end, the artist of the San Paolo Bible also included scenes that the Vivian master had omitted. Those three scenes were also derived from the basic model which must have consisted, not of a single frontispiece, but of a series of unassociated miniatures.

It seems likely that the Jerome pages were also compiled from a narrative cycle. In the absence of a text and of comparative pictorial material, one must base that conclusion on internal evidence and on analogies with the Genesis and Epistles frontispieces. The two Jerome pictures seem to have been constructed from a prefatory cycle that traced the saint's scholarly activities in a regularly paced succession of pictures. Because the San Paolo Bible preserves the narrative structure more clearly, it is certainly closer to the prototype than is the Vivian Bible. In a manner that must be considered characteristic of him, the Vivian master merged several scenes and in other ways adjusted his prototype to the full-page format.

To construct narrative frontispieces, the Touronian illuminators followed a simple procedure. They selected scenes from rich cycles and copied them onto pages divided into three or four horizontal registers. Because the Bibles were constructed at different times, more or less independently of one another, they exhibit considerable variety. Because the illuminators followed established procedures, however, and because they utilized the same sources, their frontispieces are generally alike. In certain instances, the use of the same *tituli* ensured uniformity.

Although the sources of the Genesis, Epistles, and Jerome pages were not single-page frontispieces, the Touronian illuminators may have been guided by earlier models in developing their layouts.[5] Full-page miniatures comprising separate narrative episodes are found in the earliest extant illustrated codices: the Vatican Virgil (Biblioteca, Cod. lat. 3225, pictura 1, Fig. 138),[6] the Quedlinburg Itala (Berlin, Staatsbibliothek, Cod. theol. lat. fol. 485)[7] and the Ashburnham Pentateuch (Paris, Bibliothèque Nationale, Cod, nouv. acq. lat. 2334, fols. 6ᵛ, 44ʳ, 50ʳ, 56ʳ, 58ʳ, & 65ᵛ).[8] The latter manuscript contains the closest parallels to the Touronian frontispieces; and because

[5] Cf. Weitzmann, *Roll and Codex*, pp. 104ff. *et passim* and *idem*, "Book Illustration of the Fourth Century," *Studies*, pp. 96ff.

[6] J. de Wit, *Die Miniaturen des Vergilius Vaticanus* (Amsterdam, 1959), pl. I.

[7] H. Degering and A. Boeckler, *Die Quedlinburg Italafragmente* (Berlin, 1952).

[8] O. van Gebhardt, *Miniatures of the Ashburnham Pentateuch* (London, 1883).

it seems to have been at Tours during the ninth century, the Ashburnham Pentateuch is especially interesting.[9] The layout of fol. 6ᵛ in the Ashburnham Pentateuch (Fig. 34) resembles the Touronian frontispieces most closely. Eight scenes from the third and fourth chapters of Genesis are arranged along three horizontal bands, distinguished from one another by color. The narrative does not progress consistently from left to right. It is conceivable, nonetheless, that the Ashburnham Pentateuch provided the inspiration and example for the Touronian artists when they began to convert text narrative into frontispiece illustration.

Full-page compositions in Middle Byzantine manuscripts offer even closer analogies to the ninth-century Bibles and suggest that the Touronian illuminators may have relied on other models. In the luxury edition of the Homilies of Gregory Nazianzenus (Paris, Bibliothèque Nationale, Cod. gr. 510) produced in Constantinople toward the end of the ninth century many pages comprise narrative sequences arranged along horizontal registers.[10] These registers are divided from each other by colored bands and, in a number of cases, the bands contain explanatory legends. Fol. 52ᵛ is especially close to the Touronian pages. The upper and middle registers present several episodes from the life of Adam and Eve which, like the Touronian pictures, were copied from a cyclic model. The lower register, however, which contains depictions of Moses Receiving the Laws and the Schismatic Monks Returning to Orthodoxy, is not part of the narrative series. It is associated with the Adam and Eve registers through Gregory's sixth homily rather than by a narrative source. Other pages of the Paris *Homilies* present more consistent cycles. Fol. 69ᵛ, for example, depicts thirteen scenes from the life of Joseph arranged on five registers and fol. 104ᵛ contains eight episodes from the Life of St. Basil arranged along four bands.[11] The similarity of these pages to the Touronian frontispieces is striking and suggests that the ninth-century illuminators in the West and the East may have been perpetuating an early tradition of creating single-page pictures from narrative cycles.

The tenth-century Regina Bible in the Vatican (Cod. Reg. gr. 1) also contains full-page frontispieces constructed from diverse narrative sources.[12] Fol. 11ʳ for example, presents, on three registers, scenes from the life of Adam and Eve. The similarities with the Carolingian frontispieces are apparent. What gives the Vatican manuscript special significance, however, is that it is a full Bible, albeit a three volume edition. It shows that, faced with the same problem that had confronted Western illustrators, Byzantine

---

[9] Cf. B. Narkiss, "Towards a Further Study of the Ashburnham Pentateuch (Pentateuque de Tours)," *Cahiers Archéologiques*, XIX (1969), 46ff.

[10] Omont, *op. cit.*; Weitzmann, *Roll and Codex*, pp. 196ff. *et passim*; S. Der Nersessian, "The Illustrations of the Homilies of Gregory of Nazianzenus," *Dumbarton Oaks Papers*, XVI (1962), 197ff.

[11] Omont, *op. cit.*, pls. XXVI, XXXI.

[12] *Miniature della Bibbia cod. Vat. Regina Gr. 1.* (Milan, 1905); K. Weitzmann, *Die byzantinische Buchmalerei des IX. und X. Jahrhunderts* (Berlin, 1935), p. 40 *et passim; idem, Roll and Codex*, p. 195 and "The Illustration of the Septuagint," *Studies*, pp. 49ff.; *Il libro della Bibbia* (catalogue of an exhibition, Vatican, 1972), p. 22.

artists developed similar solutions. They, too, constructed frontispieces from diverse narrative sequences to provide the full Bible with an appropriate series of illustrations.

The Paris Gregory and the Regina Bible were certainly created after the end of Iconoclasm. They are witnesses, nevertheless, of procedures that may go back to late antiquity. Those procedures are obvious ones and could have been developed independently at different times; but the parallels between the Byzantine narrative pages and the frontispieces in the Touronian pandects raise the possibility that the later illuminators adhered to methods already established during the Early Christian period. Full-page narrative pictures do survive, after all, from the fourth century on.

Bipartite pages, analogous to the Exodus and Apocalypse frontispieces, also appear in the Paris Gregory (fols. 67^v, 71^v, 78^r, 196^v, 215^v, 226^v, 239^r, 310^v, 316^r, 332^v and 360^r),[13] the Regina Bible (fol. 302^v),[14] and the Ashburnham Pentateuch (fols. 76^v and 127^v, Figs. 92 and 95).[15] The superimposition of two scenes was a simple and common method for adapting horizontal text pictures to a vertical, full-page layout. It is not surprising, therefore, that the themes of the Touronian frontispieces appear elsewhere on bipartite pages. The Ashburnham Pentateuch, for example, contains a page that illustrates Moses Receiving the Commandments and Moses Addressing the Israelites in the upper half and the Tabernacle below (fol. 76^r, Fig. 95). Even closer to the Carolingian frontispieces are certain pictures in Byzantine Psalters. The twelfth-century Psalter in Berlin (Universität)[16] is one example. In the upper frame of folio 118^v, Moses is shown removing his sandals and receiving the laws; in the lower register he is represented delivering the laws to the Israelites. The Psalter frontispiece was compiled from a Greek Octateuch and its similarity to the Touronian pictures, though striking, is only coincidental. The three Carolingian frontispieces, after all, were constructed from a Western Pentateuch manuscript, the iconography and layout of which appear to have been akin to the Aelfric Paraphrase.

Two-part pages are also common in the illustrated Carolingian Apocalypse manuscripts (cf. Figs. 65, 121, 124); and the consistency of the three Touronian pages suggests that the two major images in the Revelation pictures may have been linked to each other in the model. Were that the case, then the use of bipartite layouts for the Exodus pictures, as well, may have been inspired by the desire to connect the Old Testament pictures visually to the Apocalypse pages.

If the Touronian illuminators did follow earlier models when they created the layouts of the narrative frontispieces, they used those models only for the general compositions. For the specific iconography of their illustrations, they turned to various manuscripts illustrated with separate miniatures distributed through their texts.

[13] Omont, *op. cit.*, pls. XXV, XXVII, XXIX, XXXVIII, XXXIX, XL, XLII, XLV, XLVI, XLVII, LI and Der Nersessian, *op. cit.*

[14] *Miniature*, pl. 14.

[15] van Gebhardt, *op. cit.*, pl. XVIII.

[16] G. Stuhlfauth, "A Greek Psalter with Byzantine Miniatures," *Art Bulletin*, XV (1933), pp. 331ff.

THE EFFIGIES

In certain aspects, the Touronian effigy frontispieces are more traditional than the narrative pages. Portrait miniatures had been introduced into codices from a very early time;[17] and sources for the *Majestas Domini*, Psalter, and Dedication pictures can be traced in earlier, full-page compositions.

Depictions of Christ were common Gospels frontispieces. A *Majestas Domini* (Fig. 71) precedes the New Testament section in the most important precursor of the Touronian pandects, the Codex Amiatinus; and portraits of Christ appear in many pre-Touronian Gospelbooks. In the Gundhonius Gospels, the text is preceded by a *Majestas* page (Fig. 53); in the Godescalc Evangeliary, the portrait of Christ is one of six full-page depictions, including the four evangelists and the *fons vitae*; and in the Lorsch Gospels, a true *Majestas Domini* is part of an enlarged complement of illustrations. A page in the Xanten Gospels (Fig. 54) represents Christ enthroned on a blue orb above depictions of the four evangelists and their symbols.

The theme was also popular at Tours. *Christ in Majesty* appears in the early Weingarten Gospels (Fig. 51) and is represented in several other Touronian Gospelbooks (Figs. 52, 61, 62, 63). A variant of the theme, the *Majestas Agni*, also appeared at Tours (Fig. 64) and it, too, seems to have been derived from pre-Carolingian prototypes.

The New Testament pages in the Touronian pandects are direct descendents from the earlier Gospel frontispieces. The composition in the Bamberg Bible is virtually identical to the *Majestas Agni* of the Nancy manuscript; and the frontispieces in the Grandval, Vivian, and San Paolo Bibles are directly related to the *Majestas Domini* pages of the other Touronian Gospelbooks.

The Bible illustrators did not simply transfer the traditional Gospel themes to their pandects. They merged the *Majestas Agni* with the *Majestas Domini*; and, in the later Bibles, they added seated evangelists. With the depiction of the major prophets and a schema of the *fons vitae* they also extended the harmony idea, inherent in the *Majestas* theme, to the Old Testament. In a sense, what they did was to merge into a single composition, images that had occupied five or six pages in earlier manuscripts and, in so doing, they created frontispieces suitable not only to the Gospels but also to volumes containing the New and Old Testaments.

The Psalter frontispieces were also created by merging and embellishing older full-page compositions. Portraits of David and his co-psalmists are preserved in many Byzantine and Western Psalters and were particularly popular during the Carolingian period. Often these representations occupy more than one page, but the Touronian illuminators restricted their portraits to single folios. They also modified their prototypes in order to strengthen the parallel between David and Christ and between David and Charles the Bald. In imitation of evangelist portraits, they depicted Asaph, Heman,

---

[17] Weitzmann, "Fourth Century," pp. 113ff.

Ethan, and Jeduthun as seated figures; and the Vivian master—obviously with a *Majestas Domini* in mind—enclosed the group in a large blue mandorla. They gave the great Old Testament monarch the facial features and attributes of the contemporary ruler and represented him flanked by two soldiers. The intention is clear. As in the *Majestas* frontispieces, the idea was to extend the references of the pictures beyond the single biblical book and, thereby, to integrate the frontispiece more fully into the pandect.

Although the portraits of Charles the Bald are tied to contemporary circumstances, they, too, were based on late antique models. Portraits of patrons had been included in Early Christian manuscripts, and several features of the ninth-century compositions— the ruler flanked by armsbearers, the circular organization, and the hierarchical ranking—are ultimately of late antique derivation. The Touronian illuminators also introduced a number of new elements. Personifications were added to symbolize Charles the Bald's virtuous governance of the Carolingian realm and angels or the Hand of God were included to signify his divine authority. Those elements distinguish the Touronian portraits from the known antecedents and mark them as truly medieval creations.

The arrangement of the narrative sequences along horizontal registers on full-page frontispieces represents a radical change in the layouts of the models of those pages. The specific iconography of those sequences, the depiction of the individual episodes, appears in every case to be remarkably true to the various prototypes. The arrangement of the portraits, on the other hand, is not very different from the full-page compositions on which they were based; but the content of those pages differs fundamentally from the earlier pictures. In each case, the Touronian illuminators added details from various sources to create more complex images in order to extend the meaning of each theme and to connect the image with other subjects depicted in the pandects.

THE ILLUSTRATED PANDECTS

Artists at Tours undertook to illustrate one-volume Bibles at least four different times during the ninth century. Each undertaking was basically independent of the others, although the artists benefited from previous achievements and, each time, turned to some of the same models. As they evolved at Tours, the illustrated pandects became more elaborate and more complex. Ultimately, the tradition culminated in the San Paolo Bible with its twenty-four magnificent and varied pictures.

The question naturally arises: Were the Touronian artists inspired by an earlier, pandect prototype? That question was answered affirmatively by Köhler when he proposed that the Grandval Bible and, to a lesser extent, the Vivian Bible replicate a lost fifth-century Roman Bible.[18] Köhler's hypothesis was based on three fundamental arguments: (1) that the frontispiece images illustrate the *tituli* which presumably were composed during the fifth century; (2) that fifth-century characteristics are evident

---

[18] *Kar. Min.*, I₂, 109ff.

in the Carolingian miniatures; and (3) that the four illustrations of the Grandval Bible comprise a doctrinal program invented by Pope Leo the Great as a weapon in his battle against the Manichaeans.

Köhler's theory had found general acceptance.[19] Recently, however, it has been seriously questioned by A. A. Schmid in his introduction for the facsimile edition of the Grandval Bible.[20] Schmid did not refute Köhler's arguments point by point, but his rejection of the hypothesis that the ninth-century manuscript replicates a fifth-century pandect was based on the same categories of criteria employed by Köhler: philological, iconographic and stylistic, and dogmatic.

It is Schmid's opinion that the *tituli* in the Grandval Bible were invented at Tours during the ninth century.[21] Although the *tituli* are extremely important in Köhler's theory, Köhler had remained uncertain about their origin; and he expressed the hope that the verses would be thoroughly studied: "Es wäre sehr zu wünschen, dass das Problem dieser Tituli, das hier nicht behandelt werden kann, von philologischer Seite nachgeprüft würde."[22] Schmid reviewed in some detail the controversy over the dating of the verses and he concluded that a Touronian origin for the *tituli* is not only possible, it is likely.[23] The dating controversy was generated by L. Traube, who at first had considered the *tituli* to be Alcuinian but afterward had come to favor an Early Christian date.[24] Schmid countered Traube's objection to the ninth-century dating with specific Carolingian analogies and he succeeded in re-establishing the probability that the verses originated during the ninth century. Unhappily, he did not also consider the additional verses found only in the Vivian Bible. Following Strecker, Köhler had separated those *tituli* from the verses common to both pandects.[25] Nordenfalk, however, supposed that the entire set had been taken from the "Leo Bible" and concluded, therefore, that all the verses had been composed during the fifth century.[26] If Schmid is correct about the Grandval *tituli*, then certainly the supplementary verses are also of Carolingian origin. Because the date of the *tituli* remains uncertain, the verses cannot be used to date the prototype.[27]

Schmid's analysis of the iconography and style of the Grandval frontispieces, like Köhler's, led him to conclude that the Touronian artists had had access to good Early Christian models. Schmid, however, was able to adduce a number of parallels in late

[19] Most notably: C. Nordenfalk, "Beiträge zur Geschichte der turonischen Buchmalerei," *Acta Archaeologica*, VII (1936), 281ff.; W. Otto, *Die karolingische Bilderwelt* (Munich, 1957), p. 42; V. Elbern, "Carolingian Period," *Encyclopedia of World Art*, III, cols. 104ff.; J. Beckwith, *Early Medieval Art* (New York, 1964), pp. 52f.; P. Brieger, "Bible Illustration and Gregorian Reform," *Studies in Church History*, II (1965), 154f.; C. R. Dodwell, *Painting in Europe: 800–1200* (Harmondsworth, 1971), p. 36.

[20] *Bibel von Moutier-Grandval*, pp. 149ff.

[21] *Ibid.*, p. 184.

[22] *Kar. Min.*, I₂, 109.

[23] *Op. cit.*, p. 184.

[24] *MGH. Poetae latini*, III, 248; "Palaeographische Anzeigen," *Neues Archiv der Gesellschaft für ältere Deutsche Geschichtskunde*, 1902, pp. 264ff.; *Vorlesungen und Abhandlungen von Ludwig Traube* (Munich, 1920), pp. 244ff.

[25] Köhler, *Kar. Min.*, I₂, 109 and 212.

[26] "Beiträge," pp. 296f.

[27] This investigation has produced no evidence that the Touronian illuminations were actually based on the *tituli*. The verses were used to select and explain the pictures.

fifth- and early sixth-century art that are as striking as the similarities Köhler had noted in earlier monuments. Obviously, if the models of the Grandval Bible post-dated 461, they could not have been created for Pope Leo. Despite the many indications of sixth-century sources, Schmid did not conclude that the Grandval pages were copied from a single sixth-century Bible. The heterogeneity he detected in the *Majestas* composition and his conclusion that the ninth-century artists had freely invented the Apocalypse images from earlier prototypes, persuaded him that the program of illustration was compiled at Tours from various sources.

To replace Köhler's Augustinian-Leonine structure, Schmid suggested that the themes of the four frontispieces were chosen to present aspects of Pauline theology.[28] He cited Paul's acclamation before the court of Areopagus as justification for the selection of Genesis and *Majestas* frontispieces:

> The God who created the world and everything in it, and who is Lord of heaven and earth, does not live in shrines made by men. . . . He created every race of men of one stock to inhabit the whole earth's surface. He fixed the epochs of their history. . . . Now he commands mankind, all men everywhere, to repent, because he has fixed the day on which he will have the world judged, by a man of his choosing; of this he has given assurance to all by raising him from the dead (Acts, xvii, 24–31).

Schmid also referred to other passages from Paul's writings, for example:

> It was through one man that sin entered the world, and through sin death, and thus death pervaded the whole human race, inasmuch as all men have sinned. For sin was already in the world before there was law, though in the absence of law no reckoning is kept of sin. But death held sway from Adam to Moses, even over those who had not sinned as Adam did, by disobeying a direct command—and Adam foreshadows the Man who was to come. But God's act of grace is out of all proportion to Adam's wrong-doing. For if the wrongdoing of that one man brought death upon so many, its effect is vastly exceeded by the grace of God and the gift that came to so many by the grace of the one man, Jesus Christ (Rom., v, 12ff.).

It is from Paul's letter to the Corinthians, moreover, that the best connection between the Exodus and Apocalypse pages can be drawn.[29]

The association of these Pauline passages with the Grandval frontispieces remains speculative as does Schmid's introduction of the interesting ninth-century text by Etherius of Osma. His arguments prove, nonetheless, that one need not limit one's search for a doctrinal basis of the Grandval program to the writings of Augustine and that Köhler's dogmatic structure is not the only program that can be construed in the four Grandval frontispieces.

[28] *Op. cit.*, pp. 184ff.   [29] Cf. Chapter v.

Because he was writing in a publication of the London manuscript, Schmid focused his investigation on the four Grandval frontispieces and introduced the other Touronian illustrations only when they had direct bearing on his prime subject. Consequently, Schmid's conclusions (like those of Köhler which were based on a study of only two of the Bibles) are limited. Any thorough attempt to reconstruct the models known at Tours or to investigate the origin and development of Carolingian Bible illustration must be based on the study of all four ninth-century pandects.

This book is an attempt at such a comprehensive study. The conclusions arrived at in it support Schmid's findings and, in general, contradict Köhler's. They indicate that, not only the Grandval Bible, but the other Touronian Bibles as well, were compiled at ninth-century Tours from diverse sources. In fact, an evolutionary development can be traced in the Carolingian pandects—from the simple two page program of the Bamberg manuscript, to the four Grandval pages, to the elaborate set of eight frontispieces in the Vivian Bible and, finally, to the extended series in the San Paolo Bible.

Whether or not the development of Bible illustrations was motivated by theological considerations is not easy to determine. The *tituli* provide little material for a specific, doctrinal interpretation. No profound explanation is needed, of course, to account for the choice of subjects in the Bamberg Bible. To head the Old Testament, the illustrator chose one of the first and most important themes: the creation and fall of man. To introduce the New Testament, he borrowed a Gospels harmony picture. The Pauline texts cited by Schmid are adequate to explain the choice of these subjects.

The selection of the second pair of frontispieces, the Exodus and Apocalypse pages, is more difficult to understand; and there is considerable evidence that the pair was in fact composed as a theological unit. The essential idea is that the law of Moses is revealed through Christ; the basic image is the unveiling of Moses, a motif invented by St. Paul and elaborated in various exegeses of Revelation.[30]

The expansion of the program to eight frontispieces maintained the overall balance but weakened the theological unity of the pandect programs. The Apocalypse page was displaced from its proper place at the end of the Bible by a dedication portrait; and a translator's portrait was inserted at the beginning. A depiction of David composing the Psalms was introduced as a third Old Testament picture; and illustrations of the conversion of St. Paul form a third New Testament page.

The Psalter miniatures do perpetuate the theme of the unity of the two testaments. Through the caption in the San Paolo Bible and in the Vivian composition itself, David is designated a type of Christ and his co-psalmists are conceived as the Old Testament counterparts of the four evangelists. David "filius Jesse" was recognized in the Gospels as the most important ancestor of Christ; and his relationship to the Savior is both explicit and implicit in the *Origo Psalmorum*. Whereas David's association with Christ was certainly a major motivation for adding a Psalter frontispiece,

[30] Cf. Chapter v.

148

David's importance for the Carolingian monarchs may have been even more significant. The depictions of David were introduced into the Bibles together with the dedication pictures and they share a number of features with the portraits of Charles the Bald. Their inclusion, therefore, may have been determined by concerns more political than theological.

Despite the apparent importance of Pauline theology for the Touronian illuminators, their choice of Paul's conversion as the subject of the third New Testament picture is difficult to explain. Specific connections between David and Paul cannot be established; Paul seldom mentioned David in his writings and there is no obvious parallel between their lives. A clue to the purpose behind the Paul frontispieces may perhaps be identified through their placement within the pandects. The conversion miniatures are placed, not before the Book of Acts where the story is recounted, but before the Epistles. Thus, they serve as frontispieces to Paul's writings and, hence, are really a kind of author portrait. After the evangelists, Paul was the most powerful and most important New Testament writer. The inclusion of a narrative author portrait of him in the expanded Touronian program may, therefore, have had no theological justification.

The Jerome frontispieces resemble the conversion miniatures and also serve as a kind of author portrait. As editor and translator of the Vulgate, after all, Jerome came as close as any mortal to "authoring" the full Bible; and his editorial activities were particularly significant to ninth-century Tours. Portraits of Jerome were popular throughout the Carolingian period, however, and are most common in Psalters. In Psalters, the underlying idea was obvious: David composed the Psalms and Jerome revivified them in his great translations. In the Lothar Psalter (London, British Library, Add. 37768),[31] a portrait of Jerome follows a depiction of David; and in the Psalter of Charles the Bald (Fig. 142) the *titulus* reads:

NOBILIS INTERPRES: HIERONYMUS ATQ: SACERDOS
NOBILITER POLLENS TRANSSCRIPSIT IURA DAVIDIS.[32]

The association of David and Jerome is clearest of all on the covers of the Dagulph Psalter (Figs. 133, 145). There, two scenes represent David composing the Psalms and two others present Jerome's activities as a translator. The indications that the Dagulph ivories and the Psalter of Charles the Bald may reflect the models used also by the Touronian illuminators buttress the theory that the Jerome frontispieces may have been inspired by a Psalter model. Nevertheless, the elaborate biographical sequences in the Vivian and San Paolo Bibles must have been copied from some sort of illustrated prefatory cycle; and in the Touronian context, they refer not just to David's Psalms but to Jerome's contribution to the entire Bible.

Although the three additional portrait frontispieces in the Vivian and San Paolo Bibles may have been related to one another, they form no unified set. The Jerome page

[31] Köhler, *Kar. Min.*, IV, 28.   [32] *MGH. Poetae latini*, III, 243.

could have been inspired by a Psalter model, but no reference to the David picture is evident. David and Paul are not surprising choices for an extension of the earlier, balanced scheme. After Moses, David was the most important Old Testament author; and Paul was the dominant Christian theologian. But the two frontispieces in no way resemble one another. In fact, the David frontispieces are closer to the dedication miniatures; and in the Vivian Bible, the Psalter picture is tied visually to the *Majestas Domini*. Thus, whereas individual miniatures (in particular the *Majestas* and Psalter frontispieces) in the Vivian Bible are theologically more complex, the connections among the pages in the later manuscript are weaker than in the Grandval Bible. A specific doctrinal structure is hard to uncover in the Vivian manuscript; and when the Touronian system was incorporated into the expanded series of frontispieces in the San Paolo Bible, doctrinal programming was totally obscured.

The Touronian pandects do not differ fundamentally from other medieval Bibles in the manner of their construction. The eleventh-century Spanish Bibles, for example, are illustrated with pages compiled from diverse models, as was the tenth-century Regina Bible. The construction of full-page miniatures from more extensive models was, of course, a common medieval practice not limited to Bibles. The great biblical compendia demanded the selection and condensations of various models because Early Christian manuscripts were commonly small units illustrated with rich series of pictures.[33] To produce an illustrated full Bible, illuminators had to copy features selected from more than one model.

At Tours, the heterogeneous sources were adapted to the pandect context only gradually. The two pages in the Bamberg Bible, for example, are not related to each other visually. One retains the character of an Early Christian narrative sequence; the other is a complex, schematic diagram. Even in the later manuscripts, the narrative pictures are unrelated to the portrait pages. In the Grandval Bible, however, the illuminators did coordinate the Exodus and Apocalypse compositions. Although each of those illustrations depends on a specific biblical text, the scenes were chosen and the pages were designed to express the idea of the overall harmony of the two Testaments. Narrative details extraneous to the harmony idea weaken the relationship of the Exodus and Apocalypse images in the Vivian and San Paolo Bibles; but in the later manuscripts other elements contribute to the homogeneity of the program. The Jerome picture serves as a frontispiece to the entire volume; and iconographic and compositional details relate several of the supplementary illustrations to one another. The attempt to coordinate disparate miniatures is particularly clear in the Vivian Bible; and that attempt is one of several indications that the Paris manuscript is the latest of the Touronian pandects, later even than the lost prototype of the San Paolo Bible.[34]

Viewed individually, most of the Touronian pages represent little more than simple adaptations of the pre-existent sources. As full page miniatures compiled from column

[33] Weitzmann, "Septuagint," *passim*.

[34] Gaehde, "Bible Manuscript" and "Turonian Sources."

pictures models, the narrative frontispieces in the Touronian Bibles do not differ fundamentally from similar pages in the Quedlinburg Itala, Paris *Homilies*, or the additional frontispieces of the San Paolo Bible itself. As elaborations of standard author and dedication pictures, the Touronian portrait frontispieces are also part of a long tradition. Even the methods of selection, amalgamation, and adaptation used to construct the ninth-century pages are essentially the same as those employed throughout the Middle Ages to compose full-page frontispieces; nor is the use of *tituli* and biblical prefaces unique to the Touronian pages.

A greater independence toward the models is generally evident in the later Touronian manuscripts. The conflation of episodes is especially evident in the narrative miniatures of the Vivian Bible and the amplification of effigy pages is most successful in the same manuscript. Even in the latest of the Touronian pandects, however, the majority of frontispieces reveals few departures from the basic sources. The illustrations are of greater significance as reflections of Early Christian prototypes than as Carolingian creations.

In several important compositions, the Touronian illuminators did respond creatively to the requirements of the full Bible. They freed themselves from their models and produced original, new compositions. To transform the Apocalypse picture into a harmony page, for example, they departed from the Book of Revelation and developed the image of Moses Unveiled on the basis of exegetic writings. With even greater ingenuity, they extended the references of the *Majestas Domini*. In the Touronian Bibles, the *Majestas* compositions not only express the harmony of the four Gospels, they affirm the unity of the Old and New Testaments. Similarly, the Psalter frontispiece in the Vivian Bible is an original creation formed from various sources. The composition refers pictorially to David's position as an ancestor and type of Christ and as a precursor and model for the contemporary ruler. The inventors of the *Majestas* compositions and of the Vivian Psalter page abandoned the laws of illusionism that had governed their Early Christian models and used effigies, symbols, and schemata to express several ideas simultaneously. In so doing, they passed from a late antique method of pictorial expression to a truly medieval mode. Stimulated by the immediate need to provide suitable illustrations for a pandect, the Touronian illuminators created some of the most complex images of the first millennium.

INDEX

153

154

ILLUSTRATIONS

1. London, British Library, Cod. Add. 10546, fol. 5ᵛ. Genesis frontispiece.

2. Bamberg, Staatsbibliothek, Misc. class. Bibl. 1, fol. 7ᵛ. Genesis frontispiece.

ADAM PRIMVS VTIFIN   CVIVSCOSTASACRAI   XPSEVĀDVITADAS ·   QVAMVOCAT VIRAGINĒ·
GITVR ISTIC·   CARPITVR EVAE   AST EDANT NEPMAVITAE PROIICE IPSECONDITOR·

SVADET NVPERCREATAE ANGVISDOLOT VELLAE   POSTHAEC AMOENALVSTRAN   ADAMVOCAT REDEMPTOR·

VTERQ·ABVMBRIS PELLITVR INDE SACRIS·   ETIAM LABORI RVRA COLVNT HABITI·

3. Paris, Bibliothèque Nationale, Cod. lat. 1, fol. 10ᵛ. Genesis frontispiece.

4. Rome, San Paolo f.l.m., Bible, fol. 8ᵛ. Genesis frontispiece.

5. Hildesheim, Dom. Bronze doors from St. Michael's.
Scenes from Old and New Testaments.

6. Venice, San Marco, atrium mosaics. Forming of Adam.

7. Klagenfurt, Museum Rudolfinum, Cod. vi, 19, fol. 3ᵛ.
Forming of Adam.

8. Vatican, Biblioteca, Cod. Barb. lat. 4406, fol. 24ᵛ.
Forming of Adam.

9. Venice, San Marco, atrium mosaics.
Animation of Adam.

10. Klagenfurt, Museum Rudolfinum, Cod. vi, 19, fol. 6ʳ.
Animation of Adam.

11. Klagenfurt, Museum Rudolfinum, Cod. vi, 19, fol. 8ʳ.
Adam in Paradise.

12. Vatican, Biblioteca, Cod. Barb. lat. 4406, fol. 25ʳ.
Creation of Eve.

14. Klagenfurt, Museum Rudolfinum, Cod. VI, 19, fol. 9ᵛ.
Creation of Eve.

13. Venice, San Marco, atrium mosaics. Drawing of
Adam's rib and Forming of Eve.

15. Venice, San Marco, atrium mosaics. Introduction
of Adam and Eve.

16. London, British Library, Cod. Cotton Otho B. VI.
Introduction of Adam and Eve.

17. Venice, San Marco, atrium mosaics. Temptation of Eve.

18. Venice, San Marco, atrium mosaics. Picking the fruit and Eating the fruit.

19. Klagenfurt, Museum Rudolfinum, Cod. VI, 19, fol. 10ʳ. Temptation of Eve.

20. Venice, San Marco, atrium mosaics. Adam and Eve covering themselves.

21. Venice, San Marco, atrium mosaics. Adam and Eve hiding.

22. Venice, San Marco, atrium mosaics. Reproval of Adam and Eve.

23. Vatican, Biblioteca, Cod. Barb. lat. 4406, fol. 26ʳ.
Fall of Adam and Eve.

24. Klagenfurt, Museum Rudolfinum, Cod. vi, 19, fol. 26ʳ.
Fall of Adam and Eve.

25. Vienna, Nationalbibliothek, Cod. gr. theol. 31,
page 1. Fall, Hiding, and Reproval of Adam and Eve.

26. Klagenfurt, Museum Rudolfinum, Cod. vi, 19,
fol. 12ʳ. Reproval of Adam and Eve.

27. Vatican, Biblioteca, Cod. Barb. lat. 4406, fol. 27ʳ.
Reproval of Adam and Eve.

28. Vatican, Biblioteca, Cod. Barb. lat. 4406, fol. 28ʳ.
Denial of blame.

29. Venice, San Marco, atrium mosaics.
Expulsion and Work.

30. Klagenfurt, Museum Rudolfinum, Cod. VI, 19, fol. 14ᵛ.
Expulsion.

31. Vatican, Biblioteca, Cod. Barb. lat. 4406, fol. 29ʳ.
Expulsion.

32. Klagenfurt, Museum Rudolfinum, Cod. VI, 19,
fol. 16ᵛ. Flaming sword.

33. Vatican, Biblioteca, Cod. Barb. lat. 4406, fol. 30ʳ.
Work.

34. Paris, Bibliothèque Nationale, Cod. nouv. acq.
lat. 2334, fol. 6ʳ.
Adam and Eve repenting, Life of Cain and Abel.

36. Klagenfurt, Museum Rudolfinum, Cod. VI, 19, fol. 9ʳ.
Adam naming the animals.

35. Venice, San Marco, atrium mosaics.
Adam naming the animals.

37. Strasbourg, Bibliothèque de la Ville.
Hortus Deliciarum. fol. 17ʳ. Admonition. (after Walter).

·CR IST? ABEL CERNIT·   N? SVA MVNERA SPERNIT

38. Venice, San Marco, atrium mosaics. Sacrifices of Cain and Abel.

39. Vatican, Biblioteca, Cod. Barb. lat. 4406, fol. 31ʳ.
Sacrifices of Cain and Abel.

40. Klagenfurt, Museum Rudolfinum, Cod. VI, 19,
fol. 19ʳ. Sacrifices of Cain and Abel.

TIN CER SE CTI CVM·:·

41. Venice, San Marco, atrium mosaics. Cain killing Abel.

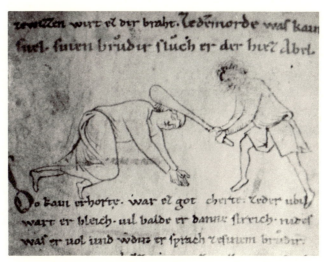

42. Vatican, Biblioteca, Cod. Barb. lat. 4406, fol. 32ʳ.
Cain killing Abel and Cain reproved by God.

43. Klagenfurt, Museum Rudolfinum, Cod. vɪ, 19, fol. 19ᵛ.
Cain killing Abel.

44. London, British Library, Cod. Add. 10546,
fol. 5ᵛ (detail). Cain killing Abel (?).

45. Venice, San Marco, atrium mosaics.
Cain reproved by God.

46. Drawing of an antique pelike in Turin (after Gerhard).
Hercules and the Apples of the Hesperides.

47. Bamberg, Staatsbibliothek, Misc. class. Bibl. 1, fol. 339ᵛ. *Majestas Agni*.

48. London, British Library, Cod. Add. 10546, fol. 352ᵛ. *Majestas Domini.*

49. Paris, Bibliothèque Nationale, Cod. lat. 1, fol. 329ᵛ. *Majestas Domini*.

50. Rome, San Paolo f.l.m., Bible, fol. 259ᵛ. *Majestas Domini*.

52. Berlin, Staatsbibliothek, Cod. Theol. lat. fol.
733, fol. 17ᵛ. *Majestas Domini.*

51. Stuttgart, Württembergische Landesbibliothek, H.B.
II, 40, fol. 1ᵛ. *Majestas Domini.*

53. Autun, Bibliothèque de la Ville, MS. 3, fol. 12ᵛ.
Majestas Domini.

54. Brussels, Bibliothèque Royale, MS. 18723, fol. 16ᵛ.
Majestas Domini.

56. St. Paul in Lavanttal, Stiftsbibliothek, Cod. 1,1,
fol. 72ᵛ. Christ with saints.

55. Trier, Stadtbibliothek, Cod. 31, fol. 15ᵛ.
Christ with Apocalyptic beasts.

57. Mount Sinai, St. Catherine's monastery. Icon.
Christ in Glory.

58. Venice, Biblioteca Nazionale, Cod. Z. 540, fol. 11ᵛ.
Christ in Glory.

59. Jouarre, Abbaye. Agilbert Sarcophagus.
Christ in Glory.

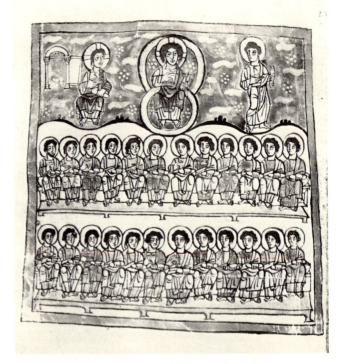

60. Trier, Stadtbibliothek, Cod. 31, fol. 14ᵛ.
Christ and the twenty-four elders.

61. Paris, Bibliothèque Nationale, Cod. lat. 266,
fol. 2ᵛ. *Majestas Domini.*

62. Paris, Bibliothèque Nationale, Cod. lat. 9385,
fol. 179ᵛ. *Majestas Domini.*

63. Paris, Bibliothèque Nationale, Cod. lat. 261,
fol. 18ʳ. *Majestas Domini*.

64. Nancy, Cathédrale, Gospels, fol. 3ᵛ.
Majestas Agni.

65. Trier, Stadtbibliothek, Cod. 31, fol. 17ᵛ.
Lamb of God with four beasts.

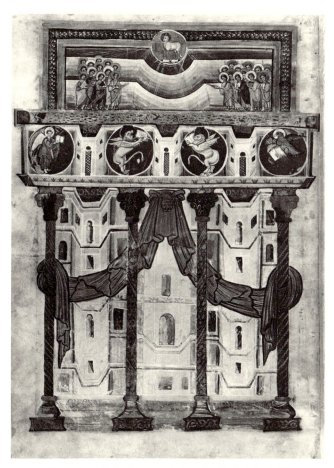

66. Paris, Bibliothèque Nationale, Cod. lat. 8850,
fol. 1ᵛ. Adoration of the Lamb.

68. Vienna, Nationalbibliothek, Cod. 652, fol. 20ᵛ.
Lamb of God with evangelist symbols.

67. Munich, Bayerische Staatsbibliothek, Cod. clm.
14000, fol. 65ᵛ. Luke frontispiece.

69. Montecassino, Biblioteca Abbaziale, Cod. 132, p. 297.
Fountain of Life.

70. Rome, San Paolo f.l.m., Bible, fol. 117ʳ.
Prophets frontispiece.

71. Florence, Biblioteca Medicea-Laurenziana, Cod.
Am. 1, fol. 796ᵛ. *Majestas Domini.*

72. Paris, Bibliothèque Nationale, Cod. Syr. 341,
fol. 180ʳ. Nahum.

73. Nancy, Cathédrale, Gospels, fol. 111ᵛ.
St. Luke.

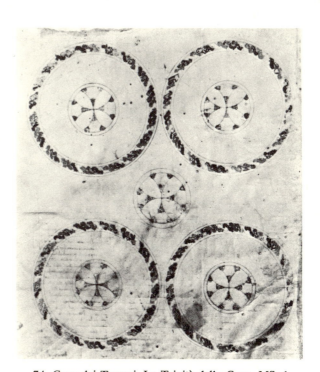

74. Cava dei Terreni, La Trinità della Cava, MS. 1,
fol. 1ᵛ. Frontispiece.

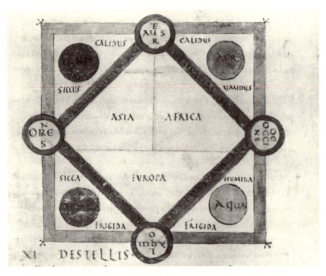

75. Vienna, Nationalbibliothek, Cod. 387, fol. 134ʳ.
Tetragonus mundus.

```
CRVXDECVSESMVNDIIESSVDESANGVINESANC|TA
R EXDEVSEXCRVCEDON AVI TCAELESTETRIBVNA|L
V ICTORTOLLENDOMA LA REG NATVICITETHOSTE|M
X RISTVSNOSTRACR VC I GR ANDISENHOSTIAFIX|A
P ASTOROVESMORI ENSD EXTRA SANANTEREDEMI|T
I NCLYTASANCTA SALVS LIGNI VENERABILISOR|E
A BSOLVENDOTR AHITPR AEDAMC ARNALELIGAMEN
V INCTVSENIM NOSREXS VMMVSSO LVEBATETIPSE
E XTRADENDO CRVCIVIT AMDEMORT ETHRIVMPHAT
R EGIASANC TAPATETMV NDISICHOS TEPEREMPT|O
A MPLIVSHA ECTOTOLAV DANDAVIGOR EPATEBVN|T
S IGNAGE RENDABONISN AMCERNANTOM NIASENS|U
A LTIVS VTVIDEANTQVO TSOLVITPASSI OSANCT|A
L VCTIB VSAETERNISVN VMQVEATEMPORE VICTV|M
V TPRESSOSPLAGISSAN ARETABHOSTISETISTI|C
S ITNVNCNOSTRASALVS EXCELSVSVERVSIOSEP|H
P ASSVSINARCECRVCIS SIGNESEDVCERETERR|O
R AF FICIENSHOMINESTR VDENSQVEEXLVCEFIDE|I
RECTORINORBETVISSANAVITSAECLASIGILLI|S
TE MEAVITASALVSTIBI TANTVMCANTICACONDE|T
ET GENEROSACANETVOX SEMPERCARMINAAPER|T
SI LICEATPLECTROQVI ACLARVSCARMINEDAVI|D
IN SISTENDOPROBATPR ETIOSOSANCTACOTVRN|O
NO BISTESTIFICAREDE CENSESSEINDEPARATV|M
Q VEMPRIMVMINCOEPIT VCHRISTISVMESVPERN|I
V ERASALVSCALAMVMTV LVXPIASANCTAQVEDEI|N
A LMACRVCISVEXILLAC ANVNTGENTILIASAECL|A
T OTATREMENSTELLVSE FFERTVRETVNITENOME|N
T ESTIFICATCRVCISEN ORANSSVBTILIAPANDI|T
V ISCERANVNCVANVSCON FOSSVSINIQVVSAVET|E
O MNIPOTENSFVLGETSIT CORDEBEATAFIDESNE|C
R VRSVSYLIDRVSAGATV ETERIVTPECTORARETR|O
O PTIMVSADREGNVMNOS FIDVSETILLEREDEMTO|R
R EDDIDITETRIGIDVMSIGNO SVPERAVITINIST|O
B ELLIGERVMEVERTENS DEREGNISORTESATANA|N
I NCLYTACRVXMVNDVS DEBETTIBISOLVEREVOT|A
SVSCIPESICTALEMRVBICVNDAMCELSACORONA|M
```

76. Bern, Stadtbibliothek, Cod. 212, fol. 123ʳ.
Carmen Figuratum. (after *MGH*)

77. London, British Museum. Gold glass.
Christ and four evangelists (?).

78. Cambrai, Bibliothèque Municipale, MS. 327, fol. 16ᵛ.
Carolingian king with four virtues.

79. Paris, Bibliothèque Nationale, Cod. lat. 266,
fol. 22ᵛ. St. Matthew.

80. Paris, Bibliothèque Nationale, Cod. lat. 266,
fol. 75ᵛ. St. Mark.

81. Paris, Bibliothèque Nationale, Cod. lat. 266,
fol. 112ᵛ. St. Luke.

82. Paris, Bibliothèque Nationale, Cod. lat. 266,
fol. 171ᵛ. St. John.

83. Berlin, Staatsbibliothek, Cod. theol. lat. fol. 733, fol. 79ᵛ. St. Mark.

84. Ravenna, St. Vitale, mosaic. St. Luke.

85. Munich, Bayerische Staatsbibliothek, Cod. clm. 14000, fol. 6ᵛ. *Majestas Domini.*

86. Paris, Bibliothèque Nationale, Cod. lat. 8850, fol. 6ᵛ. Fountain of Life.

87. London, British Library, Cod. Add. 10546, fol. 25ᵛ.
Exodus frontispiece.

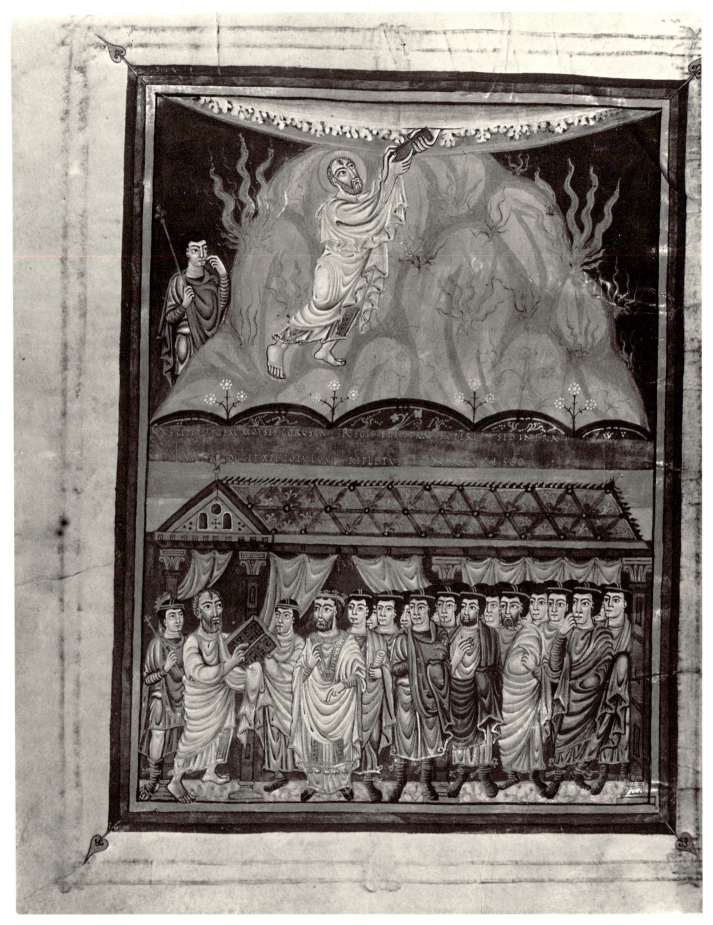

88. Paris, Bibliothèque Nationale, Cod. lat. 1, fol. 27ᵛ. Exodus frontispiece.

89. Rome, San Paolo f.l.m., Bible, fol. 31ᵛ. Leviticus frontispiece.

90. Leon, Catedral, Cod. 2, fol. 46ʳ. Moses receiving the laws.

91. Vatican, Biblioteca, Cod. gr. 747, fol. 114ᵛ.
Moses receiving the laws.

92. Paris, Bibliothèque Nationale, Cod. nouv. acq. lat.
2334, fol. 127ᵛ. Moses addressing Israelites.

93. Stuttgart, Württembergische Landesbibliothek, Bibl.
Fol. 23, fol. 90ʳ. Moses addressing Israelites.

94. London, British Library, Cod. Cotton Claudius. B. IV,
fol. 139ᵛ.
Moses addressing Israelites and Death of Moses.

95. Paris, Bibliothèque Nationale, Cod. nouv. acq. lat.
2334, fol. 76ʳ.
Moses reading the laws to Israelites and Tabernacle.

96. London, British Library, Cod. Cotton Claudius, B. IV,
fol. 105ᵛ. Moses on Sinai and Moses addressing Israelites.

97. Leon, Catedral, Cod. 2, fol. 46ᵛ.
Moses ordering the idolaters slain, the Levites slaying
the idolaters, and Worship in the tabernacle.

98. Leon, Catedral, Cod. 2, fol. 87ʳ.
Moses addressing Israelites.

99. Leon, Catedral, Cod. 2, fol. 87ᵛ.
Moses addressing Israelites.

100. London, British Library, Cod. Cotton Claudius, B.
IV, fol. 136ᵛ. Moses addressing Israelites.

101. London, British Library, Cod. Cotton Claudius, B. IV, fol. 137ʳ. Moses and Joshua in the tabernacle.

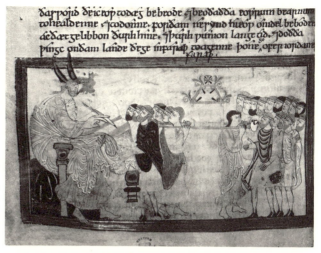

102. London, British Library, Cod. Cotton Claudius, B. IV, fol. 138ᵛ. Moses delivers the laws to Levites.

103. Rome, Sta. Maria Maggiore, nave mosaics. Moses delivers the laws to Levites.

104. Rome, Sta. Maria Maggiore, nave mosaics. Return of the spies from Canaan.

105. London, British Library, Cod. Cotton Claudius, B. IV, fol. 117ʳ. Return of the spies from Canaan.

106. Leon, Catedral, Cod. 2, fol. 86ᵛ. Moses and Joshua in the tabernacle.

107. London, British Library, Cod. Add. 10546, fol. 449ʳ. Apocalypse page.

108. Paris, Bibliothèque Nationale, Cod. lat. 1, fol. 415ᵛ. Apocalypse frontispiece.

109. Rome, San Paolo, f.l.m., Bible, fol. 331ᵛ. Apocalypse frontispiece.

110. Münstereifel, Stiftskirche, fresco on triumphal arch. Opening the sealed book. (after Clemen)

111. Valenciennes, Bibliothèque Municipale, Cod. 99, fol. 12^r. Lamb on the throne.

112. Wolfenbüttel, Herzog August Bibliothek, Cod. Guelf. 1 Gud. 2°, fol. 10^r. Apocalyptic Man.

113. Chicago, University of Chicago Library, MS. 931, fol. 48^v. First seal.

114. Chicago, University of Chicago Library, MS. 931,
fol. 51ʳ. Second seal.

115. Stuttgart, Württembergische Landesbibliothek,
Bibl. Fol. 23, fol. 51ᵛ. Psalm 39.

117. Vatican Grotto. Sarcophagus of Junius Bassus
(detail). *Traditio legis.*

116. Chicago, University of Chicago Library, MS. 931,
fol. 41ᵛ. Apocalyptic Man.

118. Lyon, Musée de la Civilisation Gallo-
Romaine, Gallo-Roman medallion. Caelus.

do q̃ aduersus delicta leue. Sed qm omiu in
uotu bonoꝝ causas. et ratíonabilit et omiu
parens affirmat. et ñ solu hominu. sed etiam deoꝝ.

dmeipsum anima mea conturbatae:
propterea memoꝛ erotui deterra
102 danis & hermonim amonte modico:

119. Madrid, Biblioteca Nacional, Cod. A. 16, fol. 55ʳ.
Zeus.

120. Stuttgart, Württembergische Landesbibliothek,
Bibl. Fol. 23, fol. 54ʳ. Psalm 41.

121. Trier, Stadtbibliothek, Cod. 31, fol. 32ʳ.
John receiving book.

122. Trier, Stadtbibliothek, Cod. 31, fol. 33ᵛ.
Four horsemen.

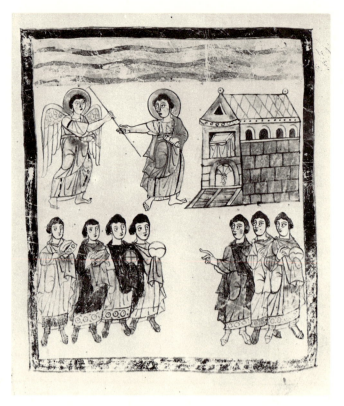

123. Wolfenbüttel, Herzog August Bibliothek, Cod.
Guelf. 1 Gud. 2°, fol. 11ᵛ. Four horsemen.

124. Trier, Stadtbibliothek, Cod. 31, fol. 32ᵛ.
John receiving rod.

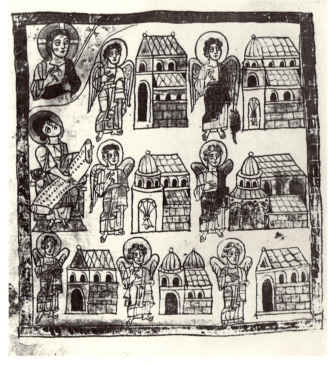

125. Bamberg, Staatsbibliothek, Bibl. 140, fol. 26ᵛ.
John receiving book.

126. Trier, Stadtbibliothek, Cod. 31, fol. 5ᵛ.
Seven churches.

128. Stuttgart, Württembergische Landesbibliothek, Bibl. Fol. 23, fol. 56ʳ. Psalm 43.

127. Wolfenbüttel, Herzog August Bibliothek, Cod. Guelf. 1 Gud. 2°, fol. 9ᵛ. John's vision, the Seven churches.

129. Milan, Castello Sforzesco. Silver plate from Parabiago. Cybele with Attis.

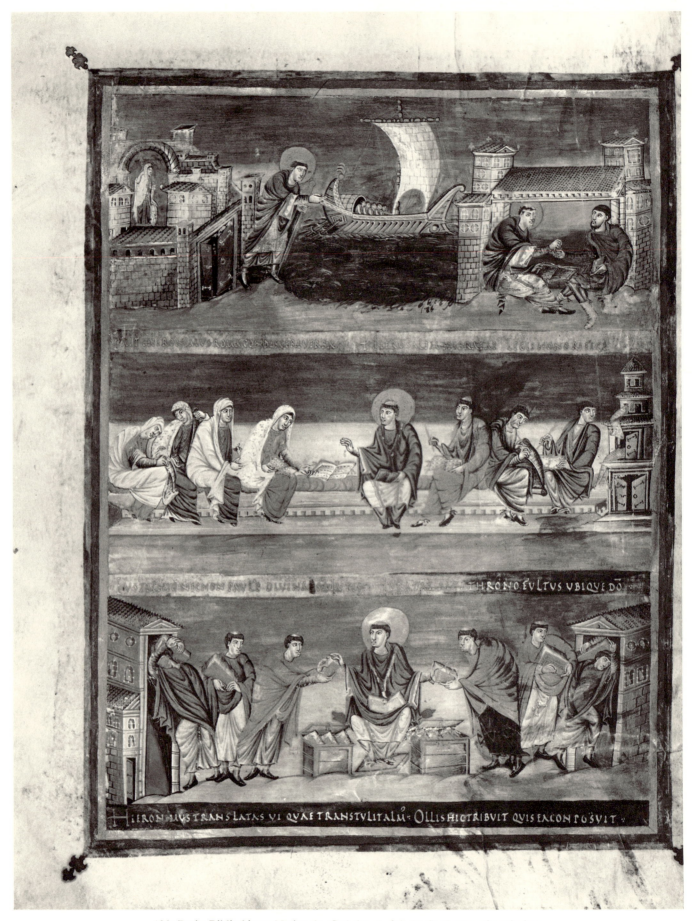

130. Paris, Bibliothèque Nationale, Cod. lat. 1, fol. 3ᵛ. St. Jerome frontispiece.

131. Rome, San Paolo f.l.m., Bible, fol. 3ᵛ. St. Jerome frontispiece.

132. Vienna, Nationalbibliothek, Cod. 652, fol. 2ᵛ.
Hrabanus presenting his book.

133. Paris, Musée du Louvre.
Cover from the Dagulph Psalter.
Jerome receives the letter,
Jerome dictates the Psalms.

134. Paris, Bibliothèque Nationale, Cod. lat. 1152,
fol. 4ʳ. St. Jerome.

135. Autun, Bibliothèque de la Ville, MS.
19bis, fol. 5ᵛ. St. Gregory.

136. Berlin, Staatsbibliothek, Cod. Phill. 1676, fol. 18ᵛ.
St. Augustine.

137. Vatican, Biblioteca, Cod. lat. 3225, pictura 39.
Trojan ship.

138. Vatican, Biblioteca, Cod. lat. 3225, pictura 1.
Georgics frontispiece.

139. Autun, Bibliothèque de la Ville, MS. 19bis,
fol. 1ᵛ. Bishop and other clerics.

140. Paris, Bibliothèque Nationale, Cod. lat. 1, fol. 215ᵛ. David frontispiece.

141. Rome, San Paolo f.l.m., Bible, fol. 170ᵛ. David frontispiece.

142. Paris, Bibliothèque Nationale, Cod. lat. 1152, fol. 1ᵛ. David and his musicians.

143. Munich, Bayerische Staatsbibliothek, Cod. clm. 13067, fol. 18ʳ. David and his musicians.

144. Stuttgart, Württembergische Landesbibliothek, Bibl. Fol. 23, fol. 163ᵛ. David and his musicians.

145. Paris, Musée du Louvre. Cover from the Dagulph Psalter. David and his scribes, David and his musicians.

146. Angers, Bibliothèque Municipale, MS. 18 (14),
fol. 13ᵛ. King David.

147. Angers, Bibliothèque Municipale, MS. 18 (14),
fol. 14ʳ. David's musicians and scribes.

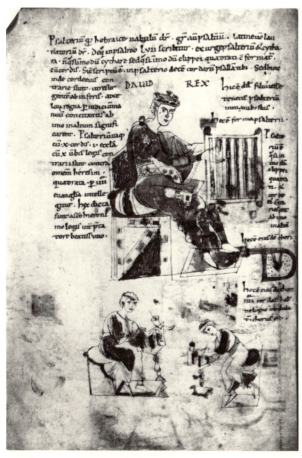

148. Rome, Biblioteca Vallicelliana, MS. E.24, fol. 26ᵛ.
David and his scribes.

149. Rome, Biblioteca Vallicelliana, MS. E.24, fol. 27ᵛ.
David and his musicians.

150. St. Gall, Stiftsbibliothek, Cod. 22, fol. 2^r.
David and his musicians.

151. London, British Library, Cod. Cotton Vespasian A.I.,
fol. 30^v. David and his musicians.

152. Moscow, Historical Museum, Cod. 129, fol. 1^v.
David and his musicians.

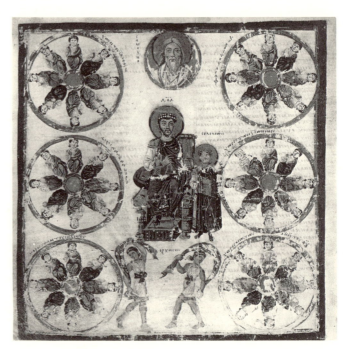

153. Vatican, Biblioteca, Cod. gr. 699, fol. 63^r.
David and the choirs.

154. Vatican, Biblioteca, Cod. Barb. gr. 372, fol. 5ᵛ.
David and his musicians.

155. Vatican, Biblioteca, Cod. gr. 752, fol. 5ʳ.
David and his musicians.

156. Vatican, Biblioteca, Cod. gr. 752, fol. 18ᵛ.
David and his musicians.

157. New York, Public Library, Spencer MS. Greek 1,
fol. 1ᵛ. David and his musicians.

158. Vatican, Biblioteca, Cod. gr. 752, fol. 7ᵛ.
Dance before the ark.

159. Vatican, Biblioteca, Cod. gr. 333, fol. 45ᵛ.
David in prayer, Battle against the Philistines,
David and the ark.

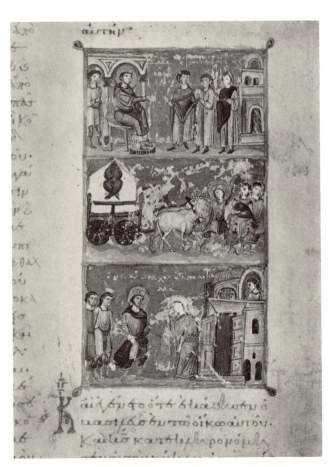

160. Vatican, Biblioteca, Cod. gr. 333, fol. 46ʳ.
David learns that God has blessed Obededom's house,
Dance of David, Michal reproaches David.

161. Paris, Bibliothèque Nationale,
Cod. gr. 923, fol. 369ʳ.
David dancing before the ark.

162. Vatican, Biblioteca, Cod. gr. 752, fol. 8ʳ.
David dancing.

163. Paris, Musée du Louvre. Ivory plaque.
David and his scribes.

164. Florence, Museo Nazionale. Ivory plaque.
King David.

165. Utrecht, Bibliotheek der Rijksuniversiteit, Psalter,
fol. 91ᵛ. Psalm 151.

166. Rome, San Paolo f.l.m., Bible, fol. 185ᵛ.
Solomon frontispiece.

167. Stuttgart, Württembergische Landesbibliothek,
H.B. II, 40, fol. 95ᵛ. St. Luke.

168. Berlin, Staatsbibliothek, Cod. theol. lat. fol.
733, fol. 22ᵛ. St. Matthew.

169. St. Gall, Stiftsbibliothek, MS. 20, p.l.
David's scribes.

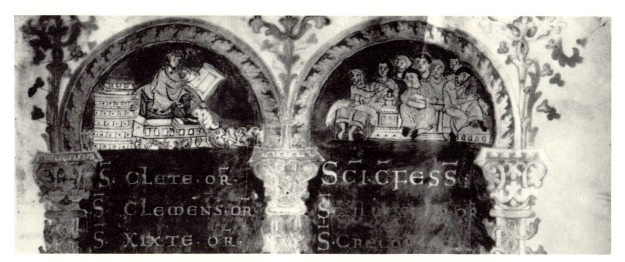

170. St. Gall, Stiftsbibliothek, MS. 23, fol. 9^r. David and his scribes.

171. Vatican, Biblioteca, Cod. 752, fol. 4^r.
Moses writing.

172. Utrecht, Bibliotheek der Rijksuniversiteit, Psalter,
fol. 26^r. Psalm 44 (detail). David and three Virtues.

173. Paris, Bibliothèque Nationale, Cod. lat. 1, fol. 386ᵛ. Epistles frontispiece.

174. Rome, San Paolo f.l.m., Bible, fol. 310ᵛ. Epistles frontispiece.

175. Reconstruction,
Blinding of Saul.

176. Mount Sinai, St. Catherine's monastery, Cod. 1186,
fol. 126ᵛ. Conversion of St. Paul.

177. Vatican, Biblioteca, Cod. gr. 699, fol. 83ʳ.
Conversion of St. Paul.

178. Florence, Biblioteca Medicea-Laurenziana, Cod.
Plut. ix, 28, fol. 171ᵛ.
Conversion of St. Paul.

179. Vatican, Biblioteca, Cod. Barb. lat. 4406, fol. 91ʳ. Conversion of St. Paul.

180. Vatican, Biblioteca, Cod. Barb. lat. 4406, fol. 92ʳ. Paul preaching.

181. Munich, Bayerische Staatsbibliothek, Cod. lat. 14345, fol. 7ʳ. Conversion of St. Paul.

182. Munich, Bayerische Staatsbibliothek, Cod. lat. 14345, fol. 7ᵛ. Paul preaching.

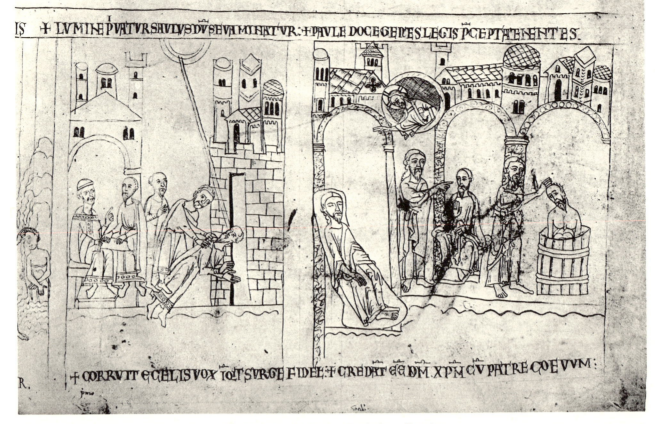

+ CORRVIT E CELIS VOX IOLT SVRGE FIDEL : + CREDAT EG DM. XPM CV PATRE COEVVM :

183. Vercelli, Biblioteca Capitolare, Rotulus.
Conversion of St. Paul.

+ INTER DOCTORES PAVLI SAPIENTIA FLORET   + DV DOLET HOS PAVLVS SO NORVPT ISTE GVTVS :

+ QVOS DOCET ATQ FACIT EREDES DNO NASCI :   + INTENTVS IVSSIS SEDE V MOX VIVE IVSSIT.

184. Vercelli, Biblioteca Capitolare, Rotulus.
Paul preaching.

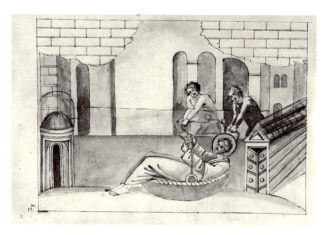

185. Vatican, Biblioteca, Cod. Barb. lat. 4406,
fol. 95^r. Flight from Damascus.

187. Rome, Palazzo Venezia. Ivory casket (detail).
David's Flight.

tempr hoc domos ce fratres ce sorores ce ma
tres ce filios ce agros cum psecutionibus ce
un seculo futuro uitam aeternam.

186. Manchester, John Rylands Library, Cod. 7, fols. 133^v–134^r. Saul led to Damascus and Paul's flight.

188. Palermo, Capella Palatina, mosaic.
Saul receiving letters.

189. Monreale, Duomo, mosaic.
Saul receiving letters (after Gravina).

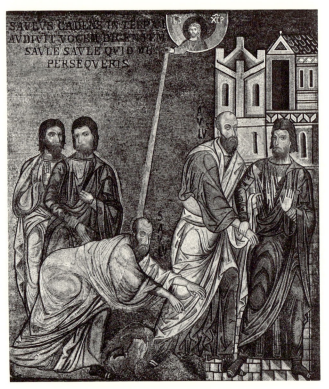

190. Palermo, Capella Palatina, mosaic.
Conversion of St. Paul.

191. Monreale, Duomo, mosaic.
Conversion of St. Paul (after Gravina).

192. Monreale, Duomo, mosaic.
Saul led to Damascus (after Gravina).

193. Monreale, Duomo, mosaic.
Healing of Saul (after Gravina).

194. Monreale, Duomo, mosaic.
Scenes from life of St. Paul.

195. Palermo, Capella Palatina, mosaic.
Paul preaching and Flight from Damascus.

196. Paris, Bibliothèque Nationale, Cod. lat. 1, fol. 423ʳ. Dedication frontispiece.

197. Rome, San Paolo f.l.m., Bible, fol. 334ᵛ. Dedication frontispiece.

198. Paris, Bibliothèque Nationale, Cod. lat. 266,
fol. 1ᵛ. Portrait of Lothar.

199. Paris, Musée du Louvre.
Medallion of Constantine.

200. Munich, Gipsammlung.
Medallion of Constantine.

201. Vienna, Nationalbibliothek, Cod. gr. theol. 31,
p. 35. Joseph before Pharaoh.

202. Florence, Biblioteca Medicea-Laurenziana, Cod.
Plut. I, 56, fol. 1ʳ. Selection of Matthias.

210. Munich, Bayerische Staatsbibliothek, Cod. clm.
14000, fol. 5ᵛ. Charles the Bald.

211. Paris, Bibliothèque Nationale, Cod. lat. 1152,
fol. 3ᵛ. Charles the Bald.

212. Kassel, Landesbibliothek, Cod. Phys. Fol. 10,
fol. 1ᵛ. Constantine.

213. Kassel, Landesbibliothek, Cod. Phys. Fol. 10,
fol. 2ʳ. Apuleius.

203. Vatican, Biblioteca, Cod. Palat. lat. 1564,
fol. 2ʳ. Gathering of authors.

204. Vatican, Biblioteca, Cod. Reg. gr. 1, fol. 206ʳ.
Prophets frontispiece.

205. Dijon, Musée des Beaux Arts. Ivory plaque.
Christ and Apostles.

206. Alba Julia, Batthyaneum Library, Cod. R. II, 1, fol. 14ʳ. Generations.

207. Utrecht, Bibliotheek der Rijksuniversiteit, Psalter, fol. 72ʳ. Psalm 120.

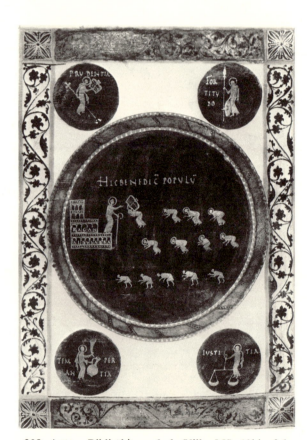

208. Autun, Bibliothèque de la Ville, MS. 19bis, fol. 173ᵛ. Raganaldus.

209. Vatican. Ivory throne of Charles the Bald (detail). Charles the Bald and ministering angels.